MOViE MiSTAKES

Take 2
REVISED &
UPDATED

Jon Sandys

This revised and updated edition first published in
Great Britain in 2003 by
Virgin Books Ltd
Thames Wharf Studios
Rainville Road
London
W6 9HA

First published in 2002 by
Virgin Books Ltd

A catalogue record for this book is available from the
British Library.

ISBN 0 7535 0891 5

Typeset by Phoenix Photosetting, Chatham, Kent
Printed and bound in Great Britain by
Clays Ltd, Bungay, Suffolk

CONTENTS

ACKNOWLEDGEMENTS

Huge thanks to all of my family and friends, for giving me support when I needed it, and considerable mickey-taking when I didn't. A special mention should go to Syrop Jas for maintaining my sense of idiocy.

Enormous thanks must also go to all the visitors to www. moviemistakes.com, and everyone who helped me check out the mistakes – this couldn't have been done without you.

ABOUT THE SITE AND THE AUTHOR

I cannot lie – I haven't spotted all of these myself. After all, I've only got one pair of eyes, and only one lifetime! They've been accumulated over the past five or so years from myself and thousands of other eagle-eyed film fans across the world, and all stored on my website, movie-mistakes.com. However, while the site's a fairly eclectic mix of entries, I thought it would be worthwhile putting together a general collection from the site in paper form because, let's be honest, you can't really take a laptop into the cinema with you.

Back in September 1996, I was 17 years old, a huge film fan, and fairly computer obsessed. I wanted to make a web page but couldn't really think of what to do. I eventually took a few continuity mistakes and film facts, put them into a website along with an e-mail address, and that was about it.

I never really expected many people to look at what was then called 'The big list of movie mistakes' (innovative, I know) but, as part of the learning experience, I submitted the page to search engines, swapped links with people, and spread the word to everyone I knew, just to see how my traffic did. At first I got a few people a day, at most, but those people submitted new entries, which made the site that much bigger.

By 1999, the website had more than 2,000 entries and was getting about 800 hits a day. One day an article about it appeared on the news service Reuters, and the resulting exposure caused a tripling in traffic. Since then traffic has kept going up, submissions have kept rolling in, and the media gets involved every so often to give me a boost (most recently with the release of *X2* in May 2003 – after posting a few mistakes on my site my traffic skyrocketed, peaking at nearly 50,000 hits in one day alone). The total list at the time of writing stands at well over 20,000 entries from more than 2,300 films, with more being added every few days when I can catch up.

We love movies, but we also love to hate them. Some people love spotting mistakes in films to take Hollywood down a peg or two, but most people just view them as fun things to spot in their favourite movies which they'd never noticed after many repeat viewings. Anyway, my experience tells me that spotting movie blunders is one of the most infectious hobbies there is, and if you share your observations with your friends or family, they'll catch themselves doing it too (and maybe even cursing you a little). And perhaps the phenomenon is infectious with any film directors out there, established or wannabe – and production people as well – and perhaps they'll start paying better attention too.

This book is primarily designed to point you in the direction of all those little things in movies that you may not have noticed the first or the second or even the third time around. It is for entertainment and educational purposes only. It should not prevent you from going on with your life as normal. I take no responsibility when you're next watching a film and catch yourself thinking, I'm sure her sleeves were rolled up in the last shot . . . But, if after reading it you no longer can watch movies without picking them apart for the most minute mistakes, I'm afraid there's only one piece of advice I can give you – you'll always find a home with similarly afflicted people at moviemistakes.com.

HOW ARE MISTAKES MADE?

There's no such thing as a simple 'movie mistake'. Films are hugely complicated to make, and all sorts of things can slip through the gaps, such as continuity errors, special effects equipment being a bit *too* obvious, film crew being in shot when they shouldn't be, and factual or historical errors. This book concentrates mainly on the first two, partly because it's rare to find a camera operator in shot (although it does happen), and partly because factual errors aren't nearly so entertaining to read about. This is just a brief guide to how certain types of error get made, in case you're interested.

Continuity mistakes are far and away the most prevalent. Films are never shot in order – even single scenes can be shot out of sequence. As such, objects which feature in scenes can be moved between takes, stains can change shape, and even hairstyles can change. Of course there are continuity supervisors whose job it is to make sure that everything stays the same between takes, but everybody's human, and not everything will be caught. There are cases where they can't be avoided. A good example can be seen in *Mission: Impossible 2*, where the tyres on the motorbikes change in the final chase scene from road tyres to off-road. Given the non-stop nature of the chase, combined with a change of road surface, there really was no way around it. Editing also plays a vital role in mistake creation – if scenes are cut out of a final version showing, for example, a slight change of outfit, then continuity mistakes occur. Even if they're easily explained, they're still movie mistakes.

Crew and equipment being visible can't be so easily justified. Aside from the rare occasions where a camera just has to be in a certain place, such as in *Lethal Weapon 3*, where you can see a cameraman filming a motorbike explosion, it's normally a case of carelessness or accident. The gas canister visible in the back of a chariot in *Gladiator* is a good example of this. Clearly in this case they could only do one take of the crash so, when the covering fell off, whether it was noticed or not at the time, they could only press on regardless. Mistakes like this tend to be more entertaining, but they are also rarer.

Factual errors don't really have much of a place in this book – they're entertaining to those 'in the know' but, by and large, seeing mountains where they don't belong, or pointing out that a historical event took place on a different date, isn't nearly as amusing as other types of errors, and there are definitely enough to go around. However, I know that some things can be so wrong that they're worth including, such as in *Titanic* when Jack says he grew up fishing in a lake which is man-made, and at the time it was still a field!

None of these mistakes are meant to criticise the films they're a part of. Like everything in life, we can love something despite, or even because of, its flaws, and having a few mistakes doesn't diminish a film's quality. I've yet to come across a flawless film and, to be honest, I'd be surprised if one existed. Some visitors to the site seem to think I'm trying to pull Hollywood to pieces, which just isn't the case – no one's perfect!

HOW TO USE THIS BOOK

First off, the mistakes aren't listed in the order they occur during the film – they're in categories and randomly scattered. The reason for this is very simple – it's meant to be a fun read, not a checklist. That's the theory anyway, although no doubt a few people are going to grab a copy and settle into their armchairs to catch 'em all, in a very Pokemon style.

I was torn as to whether use the actors' names or their character names, so in general I've used whichever name I think will be recognised by the most people. It might seem inconsistent on occasion, but the general rule is that I've used the character names for famous characters and minor characters, and for famous people playing less well-known characters I've used the actor's name. Everyone has different film knowledge, so I've tried to accommodate people who know characters but not actors, and also actors but not characters, by choosing the most obvious option in each case.

A slight disclaimer. The material in this book is taken from the moviemistakes.com website, which has been built up by submissions from people around the world since 1996. In a few cases, some people see things differently to others, and some films have different versions available – widescreen videos may show more or less of the screen than 'cropped for TV' versions, and scenes might be added or deleted in the transition from cinema to TV. Quality also plays a part – for some hard-to-spot things, DVD might be clearer than video, but at the same time some mistakes are only visible in video versions. As such, if you can't see or you disagree with any of the mistakes that are listed in this book, please get in touch – while everything in this book makes sense to me, I'm more than happy to be argued with!

I thought I'd get these out of the way first, because otherwise it's a cast-iron certainty that some people will read through and be amazed that they aren't listed with the mistakes. Everyone can think of a few of these. They're the great cinematic debates which have been around for years, and will probably continue to bother people for eternity, despite my best efforts. They're spread because someone hears about it, it sounds juicy, so they tell a few friends without bothering to check it out, because why would they? Their friends pass it on, and on, and on. That stops here. Coming up are a few non-mistakes which some people might swear blind are really true, because they've heard the stories so many times, but ask anyone if they've actually seen it, and you're bound to come up short.

The Wizard of Oz   This one has been around since the film was made, and it still hasn't been put to rest. Apparently in one scene a Munchkin hangs himself in the background. This is wrong, although unfortunately a variation on the story makes it hard to check. The vague movement in the background is actually a large bird, although it has been said that in the original copies it was clearly a hanging body, but they superimposed a bird over it later. Hmm. . .

Three Men and a Baby   Another classic. It's been said that many years ago a small boy shot himself accidentally with a shotgun in the apartment where this was filmed, and his ghost can be seen in the background. This is just plain rubbish. The indistinct shape behind a curtain is a cardboard cut-out of Ted Danson holding a cane (hence the long thin 'shotgun' shape), which was going to feature in another scene but never made it to the final film.

The Little Mermaid   A slightly dodgy one, this. Many, many,

many people say that during the wedding scene at the end, the vicar taking the service gets... er... aroused, and this can be seen under his cloak. Wrong, I'm afraid. He's got very knobbly knees, as is clear to see in other shots of him when his cloak isn't covering them, and so the slight lump isn't anything suspicious at all.

Ben-Hur   There is *no* car visible in the background during the chariot race – it's nowhere to be seen, and various official sources have argued against it too. The closest I can come to any basis in fact is that in an early take of the race there was a car visible (apparently one or two photos exist of it), but it was noticed, moved, and no shot including a car made it to the finished film.

ULTIMATE MISTAKES: THE MOST POPULAR MISTAKES FROM WWW.MOVIEMISTAKES.COM

These are found in their respective sections as well, just for ... ahem ... continuity reasons.

 1. **Gladiator**: In the battle with the Barbarian Horde one of the chariots is turned over. Once the dust settles you can see a gas cylinder in the back of the chariot.

 2. **Star Wars**: When the storm troopers break into the control room where R2-D2 and C-3PO are hiding, look to the right – one of them smacks his head on the door as he comes through.

 3. **Zulu**: Some of the Zulu warriors are wearing the wrist-watches they were paid with – not strictly the right time period!

 4. **Gone with the Wind**: Remember this is set during the American Civil War, with no mains electricity, or even electric light bulbs. In the scene where Ashley is brought back wounded from the raid where Scarlett's husband was killed, Melanie grabs a lamp to follow the man carrying Ashley to the bedroom and you can clearly see an electrical cord hanging down from it – she tries to tuck it behind her arm.

 5. **The Empire Strikes Back**: One of the storm troopers unties Han Solo before he is put into the carbonite, and watch his wardrobe – he has a disappearing/reappearing jacket on, depending on whether it's a long shot or a close-up.

 6. **Pearl Harbor**: In the scene in front of the hotel on the night before Ben Affleck ships out to England, Kate Beckinsale puts a scarf around his neck. There is a camera

shot from his back where there's no scarf in sight, then another one from his front, and he's wearing the scarf again.

7. **Raiders of the Lost Ark**: While Indy and Marion are in the Well of the Souls, and they encounter the snakes, Indy falls to the ground only to get confronted by a cobra rearing its head and hissing. Look carefully and you'll see the reflection of the snake on the safety glass between it and Indy. Briefly, you can also see the torch's reflection while he's waving it around.

8. **The Matrix**: When Neo is going to open the door to enter the oracle's house, you can clearly see a camera on the door-knob. Look more closely and you can see that they've thrown a green sheet over it, and painted a tie on the sheet to line up with Morpheus, who's standing behind it.

9. **Titanic**: In the scene where the ship tilts to a vertical position, you see people falling and hitting objects on the deck. In a close-up of that, you can see that a black metal cylinder has wrinkles in it and bends when someone hits it.

10. **Top Gun**: At the end, a victorious Maverick is hoisted on the shoulders of the guys. As he goes up, he isn't wearing sunglasses, his head goes out of the shot, and when he comes down, he's suddenly wearing a pair.

TAKE 05

MOST MISTAKE-FILLED FILMS:
THE TOP 10

These are judged from the total mistake count on www.moviemistakes.com, not necessarily the number of mistakes listed here. That's mainly because I've only listed major continuity mistakes in this book rather than multiple plot holes or factual inaccuracies, which all add to the overall total.

1. Titanic
2. Spider-Man
3. The Matrix
4. The Lord of the Rings: The Fellowship of the Ring
5. Harry Potter and the Chamber of Secrets
6. Harry Potter and the Philosopher's Stone
7. Terminator 2: Judgment Day
8. Die Another Day
9. Jurassic Park
10. The Fast and the Furious

LETHAL ERRORS: SERIES OF FILMS WITH A SERIES OF MISTAKES

LETHAL WEAPON FILMS

The *Lethal Weapon* films are among my favourites. Most sequels are slowing down by the time they reach their fourth edition but, while the format's changed, and they've had to add characters to keep it fresh, the spirit has never been dampened. However, that doesn't mean they're perfect (unfortunately!). Take a look at these. . .

Lethal Weapon   Near the beginning, Riggs handcuffs himself to the depressed businessman. They jump off the building and, as they jump, you clearly see the handcuffs snap – they grab each other's hands to carry on the pretence. After they land, they're suddenly handcuffed again.

In the scene where the girl jumps to her death from the balcony, it shows her hitting the car towards the right, halfway on to the windshield. Then, in the next scene, it shows her lying right in the middle of the roof of the car.

When Riggs is talking about the special bullet, kept as the suicide special, he describes it as a hollow point – to do the job right. When he shows the bullet you can see it is a full metal jacket.

Lethal Weapon 2   In the famous 'toilet bomb' scene, keep an eye on the bomb-proof jacket that Murtaugh is wearing. While he's getting instructions on how to survive the blast, there's one brief shot that shows him with just a white shirt on – the jacket has disappeared.

In the chase scene at the beginning, the right headlight of Murtaugh's car gets smashed, then later on it's suddenly fine again.

After he's been thrown into the water, Riggs dislocates his left shoulder to escape from the straitjacket, but then slams his right shoulder into the car to put everything back to normal.

At the end of the movie, when Riggs is in the cargo area, a gunman shoots at him, he rolls and starts emptying the clip into him – you see the bullet holes in the gunman. But as Riggs is face to face with the gunman, the holes disappear.

🎥 **Lethal Weapon 3** As the motorbike falls from the highway, just after it explodes there's a very short wide shot of the site, with Murtaugh standing by his car and a couple of guys in hard hats standing around (or running for their life). If you look right behind him you can see two people, one in a white hat, one in a red hat, and one of them's holding a camera – they start moving backwards just before the end of the shot. We then see the bike blowing up, then a close-up shot of Murtaugh, clearly from the camera we've just seen.

As the villains attempt to flee, they and Riggs drive on to a section of freeway that is being newly constructed. However, there are already skid marks on the road surface. These appear to be from previous takes on the scene as they match the truck's path perfectly.

During the chase, an articulated lorry skids. During one of the shots you can see that the trailer part is skidding over skid marks that already exist, obviously from previous takes.

When Riggs is following the villains' pick-up truck, they make a left turn into a highway and a Delta plane is spotted landing. In the next shot, definitely showing the same turn (note the billboard in the background for 'CBS FM' which is in the same place, etc.) the plane changes into an American Airlines plane – note the disappearance of the 'Delta' logo and word at the front, and that the Delta plane has a single thin red line, whereas the AA plane has a blue, white and red stripe along it.

When the suspect is shot in the interrogation room, we can clearly see blood on the wall behind him. But when Riggs walks in and sees him, there's no blood visible.

Lethal Weapon 4   In the scene where Riggs and Murtaugh drive a car through an office you see Riggs floor the car in one shot, but then we see a rear shot of the car, and the brake light has come on!

BACK TO THE FUTURE FILMS

Classic, classic films, but there are a whole raft of mistakes associated with time travel, which I've decided to leave out because you could probably write a book just on those. Examples include, in *Back to the Future Part II*: it's been argued that Marty and Jennifer shouldn't be surprised to see their past selves because, despite being present in different timelines, they're still the same people, so their future selves should remember visiting the future in the past. Get it? Exactly. I'll leave the laws of physics to Stephen Hawking – I'm just a film nut.

Back to the Future   In the scene where Doc is using a remote control to drive the Delorean, they show a close-up of the controller. The controller's power meter (the dial with a needle in the middle) shows no power – it's right over to the left. How's he driving with no battery?

In the scene where Marty is being chased by the Libyans, a few times they cut away to show the instrumentation in the car. The first and second time are the same, but a few seconds later we see it as he turns the corner, and not only has the odometer gone *down* from 33,061 to 32,994, but also the trip counter has gone from 86 to 19.

When Marty is in 1955, he is in shock and walking on the pavement when a car comes by. On the first shot, when it comes towards him it has two speakers; on the second shot, when it's moving away, it only has one.

When Marty is standing over his father's bed in 1955, persuading him to date Lorraine, there is a hairdryer in Marty's belt that appears and reappears between different frames.

While George McFly is pegging out the laundry, Marty is explaining his plan as to how he can make Lorraine fall in love with him. At the start of the scene one of Marty's breast pocket flaps is tucked in. When the camera returns to him, *both* flaps are now out. When the camera returns to him a third time, one of the flaps has again magically tucked itself back in.

Back to the Future Part II   Doc says, 'This is our exit' when they are exiting the futuristic freeway. He turns the steering wheel counter-clockwise, but in the next shot, the car is exiting to the right of the freeway.

When Biff is unconscious, Marty kneels next to him, unzips Biff's jacket, and is seen reaching in for the almanac. In the next shot Biff's jacket is zipped again and Marty's knees are above Biff's chest.

Back to the Future Part III   When Marty finally gets back to 1985, he runs home. He surprises Biff in the garage, and gets into his truck. Take a close look behind his head – there's no driver's headrest there. However, after he goes to pick up Jennifer, he pulls up at some traffic lights, and we can clearly see a headrest.

While at the dance, Marty is showing off at the shooting gallery. After shooting all the targets he twirls the gun and hands it back to the booth operator with the barrel in his right hand. Very clearly the next frame shows the gun in his left hand.

When Doc is getting Marty ready for going back to 1885, take a look at the shadows. When Doc is over by the Delorean we can see a shadow of a building stretching part-way into the shot. Doc then mentions 'that floating device', and the shot changes to Marty bringing the hoverboard over – look at the shadow. It's suddenly covering both of them.

When Clara realises who the men sitting behind her on the train are talking about, she stops the train by pulling on the emergency cable. Take a look at the right side of the train as it stops – the steam, which should be pouring out of the side, is actually being sucked back into the train, showing that the train screeching to a halt is actually just reversed film.

ALIEN FILMS

Although they eventually lapsed into by-the-numbers fare, the first two remain classic films – both very different, but equally effective, and Ripley became one of the most memorable heroines of all time.

Alien When Ash and Dallas first attempt to remove the face hugger from Kane's face by trying to make an incision in the knuckle with the laser, it is obvious that the ensuing 'acid blood' comes from the laser device rather than the incision.

In the scene where Ripley reconnects the dismembered Ash droid, the switch from dummy to actor is blatantly visible. A few minutes later the android is incinerated, at which point the dummy head has reappeared and the android's left arm has disappeared.

When Ripley is talking to 'mother' by typing, it types 'can not compute', then a question: 'overide?' Now, isn't override spelled with two Rs?

In the scene where the crew is chiding Parker for Brett saying nothing but 'Right' all the time, Brett's cigarette is first short, then long, then short again.

Near the end of the movie Ripley gets into a pressure suit to hide from the alien. During the scene they cut to a close-up of Ripley's face several times. In some shots you can see the glass of the helmet she's wearing; in other shots her face is uncovered.

When Ripley goes down to check out how Brett and Parker are doing with the repairs, she says, 'Don't worry, Parker. (pause) You'll get whatever's coming to you.' In the short pause between these two sentences you can hear Ripley say, 'You have'. It seems to be a wrong line which has been deleted, but not properly.

In the scene where Parker is burning Ash with the flame-thrower, you can see that motion-tracking device in the background of Ash (it's very clear on DVD). In the very next moment, Lambert has it in her hand. It would not seem likely that Lambert picked it up while everything near it was burning.

After the alien leaves Kane's face and the rest of the crew are looking for it in the infirmary, there is one shot that bears re-watching. When Ripley is looking upwards over the prone Kane, you begin to see the dangling tentacles of the alien in the background. At the same time, the collar on her outfit begins to pull downward, unnaturally, until the alien drops on to her shoulder. It looks like there was some sort of string or rope fed from below, through her clothing, that was attached to the alien and was pulled to have the creature drop on to her.

After Ripley fails to cancel the self-destruct mechanism, we see a shot of the countdown clock showing about 4 minutes 50 seconds left to destruction. Then there's a shot of Ripley being frustrated, and then another quick shot of the countdown clock, now showing 10 minutes 39 seconds left to destruction.

🎬 Aliens   Pulse rifles use 10mm caseless ammo, but if you look closely at them when they're being fired, you can still see cases coming out of them.

Towards the end of the film, where Ripley and Bishop are in the drop-ship flying towards the atmosphere processors, Ripley begins to build a composite weapon from a flame-thrower and a pulse rifle. She pulls a flame-thrower from a rack on the wall, but lays a pulse rifle on the deck of the ship, and then she pulls a pulse rifle from the rack and lays a flame-thrower on top of the pulse rifle.

In the scene where Newt is sliding across the grated floor, Bishop reaches out to save her and you can clearly see his waist – after he was cut in half.

During the inquest on what happened to the *Nostromo* and its crew, Van Leuwen refers to Ripley's company ID number as NOC14472, while the data screen in the background displays NOC14672.

When the Marines and Ripley are inside the armoured personnel carrier that they use on the planet, they are able to stand up quite comfortably. In that case, how are they taller than it when standing next to it on the outside?

When Ripley and the mother Alien are fighting above the floodgate, we can clearly see that the light on the top of Ripley's robot is broken, but in the next scene this light is absolutely fine.

In the part of the film where Ripley and Gorman are inside the RV tank, and Ripley is trying to get the Marines to get out of the bowels of the atmosphere processor before any more get killed, she has the headset on, then in the next shot of her she doesn't, then she does, and then it gets ripped off by Gorman.

In the reactor room scene, where the Marines first encounter the aliens, there's a part where Dietrich is grabbed from behind and accidentally ignites Frost with her flame-thrower, causing him to fall down the stairwell. As he's falling, if you look closely, you can see part of a leg and a cable belonging to one of the technicians on the set.

In the scene where the Marines first enter the reactor room, the 'Mission Time' readout on the shoulder-mounted cameras jumps backwards and forwards in time with every cut.

When Ripley is giving Newt the cup of hot chocolate, the handle is on Newt's right. When it shows the close-up shots, the handle is on Newt's left.

When Bishop is doing his knife trick on Hudson it's obviously fast forwarded as you can clearly see the head of Apone in the background move way too fast for real life.

When Gorman and Burke come to see Ripley to persuade her to come to LV-426, Burke hands her a plastic card so she can call him if she changes her mind. At this point Ripley lights a cigarette. The scene then cuts to a view of the whole room, and Ripley can be seen lighting the cigarette again.

Alien³ Just after the doctor started the post-mortem on that little girl, the front of his gown is covered with blood. Yet, a few seconds later, after the two other guys appeared, his gown looks better, with less blood. And during the whole post-mortem scene, the blood spot actually changes its size a few times.

Alien: Resurrection Ripley kills the alien in the corridor after it has killed the first member of the *Betty* crew, but there is no melting of decks or bulkheads from the creature's acidic blood. Also, the *Betty* crew seem unaffected by all the acid.

When the whole crew of the *Betty* are being arrested in the mess hall, Christie puts his hands behind his back to get the guns on his arms. But in the next shot, when Christie is behind Wren, his hands are by his sides. There's no way he could put his hands by his sides without the guns showing.

STAR WARS FILMS

I could write a book just on these movies alone — not just the errors, I hasten to add. They've got quite a few, but not *that* many! They fought their way into cinematic history over twenty years ago and, with Episodes I, II and III being made, they're working their magic on a new generation as well. *The Phantom Menace* makes an appearance but, just for the record, 'Jar-Jar' does *not* count as a mistake, I'm afraid. Love him or hate him, he's meant to be there.

Episode I – The Phantom Menace   Qui-Gon's comlink is a Woman's Gillette Sensor Excel Razor — we see a very brief close-up, and it's clearly a grey razor without the blade, with one or two little bits stuck on it. Good for a laugh.

When Queen Amidala is being escorted by some droids after she has been captured, there is a shot of Obi-Wan and Qui-Gon watching the queen from a balcony. The shot shows the queen passing by them. Qui-Gon then takes a few steps and is somehow very far ahead of the queen and the droids. In exactly the same clip, the shadows change completely. When we first see everyone walking past, their shadows stretch ahead of them, but when we see them walking towards Obi-Wan and Qui-Gon, the shadows are really elongated and at an angle. It can't be due to changing direction, partly because we've seen the way they're walking, and also because the shadows would only have changed direction, not stretched as much.

When the flags are first brought out on to the course, we see C-3PO carrying Anakin's flag (a blue cross) three back from the front. Then, in a close-up of him, he's suddenly between two different flag carriers. Worse still, in a wide shot of the flag carriers leaving the course before the race, he and the flag have disappeared completely.

When Anakin attaches C-3PO's right eye, one shot has the eye in his left hand, then the angle changes and the eye is being applied with the right hand.

After R2-D2 has saved the ship, Padme is cleaning him up while talking to Jar-Jar. In the last shot of this scene, look closely, because the film has been reversed. Easiest way to spot this is that when we're looking at R2-D2, normally his lens is to the right of a blue/red light, but in the final shot the lens is now to the left of that light.

When Darth Maul is harassing Obi-Wan as he dangles in the pit, the first swing of Darth Maul's saber is out of sync with the resultant sparks (very evident in slo-mo).

In the final fight between Obi-Wan and Darth Maul, Obi-Wan leaps up out of the vent/pit, calling Qui-Gon's lightsaber to his hand using the force. As he leaps, Darth Maul's lightsaber is in his right hand. However, when he goes over Darth Maul's head, the lightsaber has switched to Darth Maul's left hand.

Episode II – Attack of the Clones In the arena scene, Anakin's pillar already has a chain hanging from the top before he is led to it. However, when he is led there, the chain is no longer there and a new one is hoisted to the top by the flying Geonosian guard.

Padmé's hands are chained to the pillar and pulled up above her head in the arena scene. The chain is taut. Subsequently the chain becomes sufficiently slack for Padmé to bring the cuffs to her mouth and unpick it.

During the sequence where Obi-Wan goes to meet Yoda regarding the absence of Kamino from the Jedi Archives, look closely at the collection of children Yoda is training. While most are human, there is one that is alien with a reptilian face of dark skin. He moves extremely fast because, at first, he is at the back of the group of trainees in the centre, in the next shot he is at the front of the group of trainees and, by the end of the scene, he is on the far left, yet neither he, nor any of the other children, are seen to move.

The twin-engine speeder that Anakin is using to pursue Zam is equipped with four antennas, two of them between the headrests. In the shot when Anakin is trying to catch the falling Obi-Wan, the two antennas in the middle are missing.

When Padmé gets her back scratched she seems to bleed. Even though she is wearing all white and the scratches seem to be deep, her white top remains squeaky clean during the rest of the movie and does not get dirty from her wound.

How is it that one slash on Padmé's back ripped off the entire midriff of her shirt and a sleeve?

The aliens that populate the planet of Geonosis have an extremely peculiar method of speech – consisting of clicks and weird ringing sounds. However, despite the fact that they make up 99.9 per cent of the crowd in the arena, the sound of the crowd cheering is human.

When Padmé and Anakin are eating, he cuts her a piece of the fruit and 'floats' it back to her. The bite appears in the fruit a split second before she actually eats it.

In the scene where Anakin and Padmé are about to eat, Anakin uses the force to levitate her pear-like fruit to his plate. He then proceeds to cut it pretty much in half. However, the piece he sends over to her is much smaller than half and the remainder of the pear on his plate is substantially larger than it was in the shot before.

On Tatooine, Padmé presses a button to retransmit the message from Obi-Wan. A moment later, she presses the same button to bring up the map showing Obi-Wan's location and the distances between Tatooine and Coruscant. Not only does this same button do double duty but, with one press, it knows she wants to show the location of the three planets.

After the fight scene between Obi-Wan and Jango Fett at Kamino, as Jango runs up the walkway into his ship, the door closes from above and knocks Jango in the head as he enters. That shot is almost certainly computer generated, so it must have been deliberate – a little nod to the storm trooper in *Star Wars*, perhaps?

During the scene when Obi-Wan attempts to capture Jango Fett as he departs Kamino, Fett and his son Boba can be seen about to load crates on to his ship. As soon as Boba warns Jango about Obi-Wan's presence, Jango tells Boba to get into the ship. The scene switches view, the fight between Jango and Obi-Wan starts and where did the crates go?

When Anakin is getting ready to ride off after his mother, a small pile of boxes is right next to his shadow that is being cast on the side of the Lars' house. Padmé comes out and their shadows, and the boxes, have gone. Then, when Anakin gets on the hoverbike and rides off, the boxes return.

When Anakin and Padmé are standing outside the Lars' house, we see their shadows projected on to the side of the house (with Anakin's shadow looking worryingly like Darth Vader's). However, in the next shot, their shadows have moved about four feet to the left.

While chasing Dooku over the desert, Padmé and some of the clone troopers get blown out of the ship. Not long afterwards, Padmé regains consciousness and one of the troopers approaches Padmé and asks about making their way back to the front lines, but Padmé says they should go to the hangar to help Obi-Wan and Anakin. How did she know about the hangar, having left the ship quite some time before it arrived at the final destination?

Right after Zam's speeder crashes near the bar and Anakin is chasing her through a crowd, there is a shot of him running really fast through the crowd. Then it cuts to her and, when it cuts back to Anakin, it is exactly the same shot as the previous one (you can tell because he passes a bright yellow light and then he puts his left hand on someone's shoulder as he passes them; all this repeats on the second shot).

When Palpatine is speaking to the Jedi near the beginning, the ships in the suspended invisible freeways on the background are always going on the same pattern. Notice that there is an elongated ship with a large rear tip, and then two smaller ships always seem to catch it at the same time. This goes on for about three minutes.

Episode IV – Star Wars After Darth Vader kills Obi-Wan, there's a shot from the docking bay towards the scene of the fight. The special effects crew forgot to colour in Darth Vader's lightsaber.

When the storm troopers break into the control room, watch very carefully and you will be able to see a storm trooper nearly render himself unconscious by smacking his head on a door frame.

In the special edition, in the scene where Luke Skywalker and Princess Leia swing across the missing bridge, a number of the shots fired by Leia are 'bangs' instead of the laser 'zap' sound. The bang is probably from the prop gun used (it shot blanks) and was never dubbed over.

When Luke and Obi-Wan walk into the bar in Mos Eisley, there is an alien without a brain. As the scenes jump around, showing different creatures, you see a small creature, squealing to the bartender for a drink. For a few seconds, you can look into his left eye and see out of his right eye.

At one point, Han Solo yells from inside the *Millennium Falcon* for some help to two storm troopers guarding the entrance to the ship. You can hear five laser blasts, indicating that Han has shot and killed the storm troopers. But why is it that when Luke and Han wear the uniforms that the storm troopers were wearing, there are no signs of blast marks anywhere on the entire uniform?

Towards the end of the film, the Death Star rounds the planet towards the moon in order to destroy it. The movie continually reverts back to the Death Star, where a commander informs us of the time until the Death star is in range of the rebel base. It will then show the panel with the Death star's co-ordinates and how long until contact. However, it does not count down in minutes, it counts down in seconds; e.g. the commander will say, 'forty minutes till contact', yet the screen will start at 40 seconds and count down, 39, 38, 37. Regardless of whether or not they use the same time system as us, the time would have run out far too quickly.

In the final award scene, there is a long shot of Luke, Han and Chewie walking through rows and rows of Rebel troopers. If you look quickly, the troopers on both ends of the screen are cardboard cut-outs. They are cropped off in the pan-and-scan version, and digitised in the special edition, so its got to be the right copy to see this mistake.

The microphone on Red Leader's helmet switches from one side of his face to the other, then back again as he pulls out of the Death Star trench (just before he crashes).

When everyone is getting in fighters for the final battle, they all have white helmets with blue insignias. However, they aren't wearing them when they're flying.

When Luke and R2-D2 are doing the trench run, a TIE fighter shoots at Luke and blows the top of R2's head off. But in the next scene R2's top is on again.

When Luke and his uncle buy C-3PO and a white-and-red R5-D4 robot from the Jawas, the R5 unit blows up after travelling a few feet. There's a quick shot of R2-D2 back at the Jawa's transporter, and behind it you can see the same white-and-red R5-D4 unit being set up by the Jawas.

Luke dives into the hole and then Han dives in right after him. Later, after Han fires his laser and it ricochets all over the place, Luke says, 'I already tried it – it's magnetically sealed.' There wasn't nearly enough time for Luke to have landed and made the decision to fire his laser. Even if he did, Han would have no doubt been hit by the laser when he came down.

When Leia shoots a hole in the detention area wall for their escape, the hole is not big enough to jump through, but when they all jump in, the hole is much bigger.

On the Jawa's transporter, when R2 looks around in one of the shots, you can very clearly see Kenny Baker inside R2 through his little eye hole.

Just after the scene where R2-D2 is riding shotgun on Luke's X-wing fighter and is hit by a shot from Darth Vader, there's a shot of C-3PO standing beside Leia in the rebel HQ, and the dent on C-3PO's head is on the right side (it's on the left side throughout the rest of the movie).

When Luke is eating with his uncle and aunt, the cup he's drinking from keeps switching hands.

When Obi-Wan and Luke are watching the hologram of Princess Leia projected on to a small table, the objects on the table change position and number in each shot.

When Darth Vader and Ben are fighting, Darth's chestplate is on backwards.

The first time that Luke plays Leia's message from R2-D2, he jumps back (which looks fine), but C-3PO flinches and slips off the little four- or five-inch ledge between him and R2.

After the droids land in the desert, C-3PO has a streak of oil running down his left shoulder. A couple of scenes later, when he is walking after he splits up from R2-D2, there is a long shot of him and he still has the streak on his left shoulder. There is an immediate close-up and the streak switches to the right shoulder.

During the Battle of Yavin at the end, Jed Porkins is X-wing Red 6. Red 6 gets destroyed. Later, during the battle, over the communicators someone asks, 'Red 6, can you see Red 5?' Red 5 is of course Luke; Red 6 is gone, but somehow he answers.

Episode V – The Empire Strikes Back   One of the storm troopers unties Han Solo before he is put into the carbonite, and watch his wardrobe – he has a disappearing/reappearing jacket on.

After Luke Skywalker frees himself from the cave in the beginning, he stumbles out. You can hear his lightsaber go off, but you don't see it go off. The next scene, he's walking out of the cave and his lightsaber is not on.

Near the end of the film, when the *Millennium Falcon* is trying to get away from Vader, there's the scene in which Vader asks the admiral if he disabled the hyperdrive on the *Falcon*. This scene is backwards, as you can tell by the insignia on the admiral's chest. Normally it should be on the left side of the chest, but in this scene, it is on the right side of his chest.

Chewbacca enters the 'junk' room to collect the remains of C-3PO, and in the close-up scene of C-3PO's head on the conveyor belt, you can see a reflection of the camera and several of the crew.

Right after Luke and Darth fight for the first time, Darth gets kicked off the carbonite freezer. Then Luke jumps down to fight him again. After he jumps, you hear the sound of a trampoline. Then in the lower-right screen you can see his head jump back up.

Episode VI – The Return of the Jedi   When Lando is hanging over the pit, he has gloves on, then he has no gloves, then they're back and so on.

In the scene where Lando says, 'Go on, you pirate', his sash goes from one shoulder to the opposite hip. In the next scene it goes from the other shoulder to the other hip. Then it flashes back again. His rank insignia move too.

When Princess Leia offers the Ewok food, she holds it out in her left hand, but from a different angle it's in her right.

When Luke Skywalker is prodded out to 'walk the plank', into the Sarlaac pit, he jumps off the board and springs himself back up. If you watch this in slo-mo, you can clearly see that only one hand catches the board and that just by the fingertips, but in the next shot both hands are springing him upwards.

In the space battle, when Lando says, 'fighters coming in!' the millions of TIEs come in. Watch in slo-mo – a TIE can be seen going through the *Millennium Falcon*.

As they take Han Solo away, watch Lando. Just before he tilts his mask down so we can see who he is, he knocks his head on the doorway.

As Boba Fett nods to Boushh his costume is reversed due to the negative being flipped. The easiest part of his costume to see this on is his antenna, which is on the left-hand side of his head, whereas normally it would be on his right.

Luke tells C-3PO to tell the Ewoks that if our heroes are not set free, he will use his magic. If you look on the right of the screen, R2-D2 is standing untied, even though at that point in the movie he had not been untied yet.

On the forest moon of Endor, when Princess Leia first meets the Ewok, she takes her helmet off and is holding it in her hand (which frightens the Ewok); in the very next shot she is removing it again to show it to him.

The big procession of ships that accompany the Emperor's arrival at the Death Star have a group of three, right near the bottom left-hand corner of the screen, which vanish.

An Imperial in black appears from the right of the screen in front of the ledge with the railing. Han throws the container in his hands at the Imperial. If you notice, the Imperial actually begins to jump over the railing before the box even hits him.

This is only noticeable in the widescreen version, but during the scene where Luke levitates C-3PO there is a wide shot of the droid in midair, about to start its descent. If you look closely to the far left you can see Chewbacca's head emerge from behind an Ewok hut. Not bad, considering we've already seen him hanging from a log alongside Han and Luke.

In a scene on Endor, Han attempts to sneak up on a trooper, when he accidentally steps on a stick and breaks it, giving away his presence. The trooper turns and punches Han. If you look closely (or are good with a pause button), you'll notice Han acts as if he were being punched without the trooper's fist coming into contact with his body.

In the fight scenes on the skiffs with Jabba the Hutt's men, the skiff that Han and Chewie are on is hit with a laser blast and Han falls over the edge feet first, yet in the following scene he is hanging upside down with Chewie holding his feet.

In the scene where Han Solo is running from the explosion of the shield generator on the Ewok planet, you can see his reflection in the plexiglass that is used to protect him from the explosion.

As we follow Fett's flight after being hit by Han, we cut to a scene showing the front half of a skiff. Luke then kicks one of Jabba's henchman. He very clearly misses the man by a few inches, yet the man tumbles to his doom nonetheless.

INDIANA JONES FILMS
The best-known and least-dodgy whip user in modern culture, Indiana Jones is one of cinema's true heroes, with universally recognised trademarks: the hat, the whip, the music... and the mistakes.

Raiders of the Lost Ark   As Indy and Marion are being shut into the Well of Souls, take a close look at Marion's mouth – she counts down the cue to her scream. It's easiest to see her mouth the final 'one', then she screams.

While Indy and Marion are in the Well of Souls, and they encounter the snakes, Indy falls to the ground only to get confronted by a cobra rearing its head and hissing. Look carefully and you'll see the reflection of the snake on the safety glass between it and Indy. Briefly, you can also see the torch's reflection while he's waving it around.

After Marion goes in the basket, there is a chase and a truck tips over, if you look amidst the dust, you can see the ram used to put the vehicle on its side.

Once Indy and Sallah have descended into the Well of Souls, they slowly begin to approach the concrete structure that houses the Ark. As they approach, the camera pulls back to reveal the huge scale of the Well of Souls, and across the top of the screen, in perfect silhouette, is the lighting rig – you can clearly see three lights.

When Indy and Sallah visit the gentleman who translates the staff headpiece for them we hear the staff should be 'six cadams high.' Indy replies, 'That's about 72 inches.' Then, turning the headpiece over, 'Wait – take back one cadam to honour the God of Israel.' So, about five feet now, right? But, when Indy goes to the map room the staff is much taller than him. If the staff is about five feet high, Indy would be around three feet tall.

At the very beginning, keep an eye on the back of Indiana Jones's jacket. The spiders on it appear and disappear.

Indiana Jones and the Temple of Doom   At the end, the elephant that the kid is riding sprays Indiana and Willie with water. If you watch very carefully or in slo-mo, Indy winces in anticipation right before the water hits them.

Indiana Jones and the Last Crusade   When they're trying to burn through the ropes, Henry Jones drops the lighter. In the first shots the top of the lighter is to the right then, after he blows a bit, it's suddenly facing left.

The sky colour/condition changes between the shots of Indy and his father in line to get on board the Zeppelin and the scene just before. In one, it is cloudy, and in the other it is a clear blue.

STAR TREK FILMS

I've always been loath to get involved with commenting on the *Star Trek* films, for a reason which is quite obvious if you visit my site. Sure, they've got normal mistakes in them, but in the process I open the doors to huge numbers of people who know all about the *Star Trek* universe and can spot an inconsistency from a hundred light years away. Needless to say, most of those have been excluded because the average viewer won't get the reference. I'm not going to embark on a geek-bashing mission because I'd certainly be first on the list. Look at what I do, after all!

🎥 **Star Trek: The Motion Picture** In the final scene on the bridge, Spock and McCoy are wearing coloured arm bands, which identify their departments: Spock's is orange (for science) and McCoy's is green (for medical). In the very last shot, Spock is wearing the green band and McCoy is wearing the orange one.

This is only in the 'extended version' of the video, as far as I know. Spock leaves the ship and flies around in a spacesuit. He exits and re-enters the ship in a white spacesuit with a round helmet, but is shown flying around in an orange suit with a conical helmet.

🎥 **Star Trek II: The Wrath of Khan** When Khan's number one officer is dying in the arms of Khan, they exchange a word or two before the first officer dies quite dramatically with his eyes open. Khan then fully embraces the corpse and looks up to the viewer screen and vows to get even with Kirk. However, the 'corpse', whose eyes are open, closes them upon Khan's embrace.

The blood stain on Kirk's jacket keeps moving around.

When Spock is dying within the glass confines of the ship's nuclear power source room with Admiral Kirk on the opposite side of the glass, in one scene, speaking to Spock, Admiral Kirk's red Federation uniform jacket lapel is unbuttoned at the top. In the very next scene the uniform jacket is buttoned.

🎥 **Star Trek III: The Search for Spock** Early in the film, when a life form was detected in Mr Spock's quarters, you see a blip on the screen inside the old *Enterprise*, not the new *Enterprise*. Notice the outline of the ship – different engines.

🎥 **Star Trek IV: The Voyage Home** In the second-last scene, when the *Bird of Prey* crash-lands under the Golden Gate bridge, Kirk orders Spock to blow the hatch so the crew can escape. The camera is pointing up inside the ship to the outside of the ship and you can see the top of an industrial shed.

Notice the candle on the table in the Italian restaurant scene during Capt. Kirk and Dr Gillian's dialogue. It changes height depending on who is talking.

Star Trek V: The Final Frontier   Spock lifts his crewmates with the rocket boots. He passes deck numbers 35 through 78 from bottom to top. First off, deck numbers go from top to bottom. The bridge is on deck 1. Second, the *Enterprise* of that class only had 23 decks anyway. Aside from that, the deck numbers in the background as they rise upwards go as follows: 35, 52, 64, back to 52, 77, 78, and then 78 again.

Star Trek VI: The Undiscovered Country   At the beginning, when the USS *Excelsior* is caught in the shockwave, one of the bridge officers is delivering a report to Captain Sulu when the shockwave hits. When the camera cuts away the same officer is leaning against one of the consoles for support. When the camera cuts back he's running towards the console.

When the USS *Excelsior* first encounters the shockwave, Sulu has a cup of coffee in front of him that begins to vibrate. It eventually falls off the edge of the table and hits the deck, smashing. When the shockwave scene is near completion, there is an overhead shot of the bridge and the smashed cup of coffee, along with the spilt contents, can be seen quite some distance from the table it was on.

Star Trek: Generations   The footage of the *Bird of Prey* exploding is the exact same footage of the *Bird of Prey* exploding from *Star Trek VI*.

Near the end of the film when the Klingons are attacking the *Enterprise-D* and the *Enterprise* crew is discussing how they can defeat the Klingon ship, Riker orders Worf to prepare a full spread of torpedoes. Yet, when Riker gives the order to fire, only one torpedo is launched.

When Capt. Picard is talking about a prisoner transfer, he says he will beam over to the Klingon ship, then they can beam him down to the planet. So, he beams off the ship, and in the next scene he is on the planet, but his transporter pattern, which should be red (as that is the Klingon transporter pattern colour) is blue, the Starfleet pattern colour.

Soran needs to get to the *Nexus*. There is a planet that the *Nexus* will miss unless the sun is destroyed, in which case the *Nexus* will fly right through the planet. So Soran camps out on that planet and tries to destroy the sun. Before he blows up the sun, the *Nexus* is seen flying through the sky below the clouds! This is just not possible. On the enterprise, Picard and Data study holographic charts that clearly show how huge the *Nexus* is, and how far away from any clouds the *Nexus* will miss the planet by.

When Picard is fighting Soran at the end, he is wearing a jumpsuit, with red at the top and black going down. When he is sifting through the wreckage of the *Enterprise*, he is wearing the other kind, as used in the TV series, with black at the top and waist, and red across the front.

🎥 **Star Trek: First Contact** When Picard is explaining the *Enterprise* to Lili he states that it comprises 24 decks. Later one of the officers explains to Picard that the Borg have taken over decks 13 through 26.

🎥 **Star Trek: Insurrection** In the beginning scene on the Bak'u planet, the stone bridge bends under the weight of the child.

When they reach the holoship they look up to the door when Data opens it. However, as they are seen entering the ship from the inside they just step up to that same door. Later, when Anij is thrown out, she falls down about two or three metres, also visible when Data and Picard jump after her.

📽️ **Star Trek: Nemesis** The *Enterprise-E* only has 24 decks (stated in *First Contact*), so the Remans can't be on Deck 29.

When the viewscreen of the *Enterprise* is blown away, leaving just a hole in the hull for the crew to look through, all that can be seen is space. The bridge of the *Enterprise* is underneath the saucer section; half of the saucer section would have been visible from that hole.

When the Viceroy jumps into a Jeffries tube Riker yells for Worf to cover him so he can follow the Viceroy. Worf jumps forward and to the ground and starts shooting and Riker runs right in front of him while Worf is firing his Phaser rifle. Riker's legs should have been blown off.

When the Scimitar disables the second Romulan vessel with pinpoint disrupter fire, the warbird loses all power and comes to a stop. The laws of physics state that an object in motion remains in motion and in the vacuum of space, the Romulan vessel should just keep on moving.

THINGS THAT MOVE BETWEEN TAKES

I've tried to split the mistakes up as much as possible, but loads of mistakes do just fall into this general category featuring 'bad continuity'. Things disappearing, colours changing, legs crossing and uncrossing – little bits and pieces which you might never have noticed . . .

Air Force One   In the beginning, it goes from five guys with white parachutes to four guys with black parachutes, back to five guys with white parachutes.

Three parajumpers (PJs) get aboard *Air Force One*, but four leave. This is confirmed by a voice-over saying that PJ number 3 is aboard and that they are switching to receive mode (or something like that).

At the beginning, when *Air Force One* is landed and the two pilots and navigator get shot, a Russian guy takes over. The plane is then driven around the airport. The Russian guy controlling the aircraft speeds up to take off again. When he does take off he barely misses a plane that was on the ground. The next shot is from the back of *Air Force One*, and the plane that was on the ground has disappeared.

When the President is fighting one of the terrorist guys, they go into a room with two chairs. Harrison Ford spins a chair to knock down the guy, and they keep fighting. As they go at it we see a knocked over stool with a black seat. Instantly, in the next scene, the stool is standing up and in a perfect position for Ford to knock the guy out with.

Aladdin   In the part of the movie where Aladdin and Jasmine are singing 'A Whole New World' you see them pass in front of a full moon on the magic carpet, and then you see them pass over water, and the reflection is of a crescent moon.

When Jafar is taking the half-bug piece from the peasant, it looks like the piece he needs. Later, though, it is the piece he already has.

In the scene where Jasmine is in her room, the number of flowers in the vase on the table changes from shot to shot.

The Sultan is not wearing the 'sacred blue diamond' when Jafar cons him out of it. Suddenly, the diamond appears on the Sultan's hand.

When the thief is first going to go into the Cave of Wonders, the lion has bottom teeth all the way across. When it shows him stepping into the cave, the bottom teeth are gone.

Almost Famous   Towards the end, where Russell comes to talk to the kid at his house, he turns the chair around to sit on it backwards, but throws the shirt down on to the ground. When he sits down the shirt is back on the chair.

In the scene where Russell and Jeff are arguing about the band's T-shirt, when Jeff says that Russell 'allowed Dick to manage us', Dick is sitting on the couch. Then, shortly afterwards, he suddenly appears between them. He can't have stood up to be in shot, because in the wide shot we see behind him is the ironing board, not the sofa (that's over to the right, not that it matters – had he walked from right to left we would have seen him).

American Beauty   After Kevin Spacey throws the pillow, it bounces off the couch and lands in the chair. In the next shot it's gone, but reappears in the following shot.

When Annette Bening is driving home, before she notices the new car in the driveway she starts turning the wheel, when in the background she's going straight.

When Ricky Fitts comes home and starts to watch TV with his parents, on close-up shots of the TV there are pictures and a vase on top of it, but when they show shots of Ricky and his parents, they mysteriously vanish.

American History X   When Edward Furlong gets shot at the end of the film, his paper flies out of his hand. But the very next shot of him shows that the paper is still in his hand, being held over his head while he falls backwards. In one of the following shots the paper is back on the floor, but it's on the opposite side it should have been when it flew out of his hand. It's all in slow motion and it's very obvious.

American Pie   When Nadia is going through Jim's drawer in his bedroom, a tub of Vaseline magically disappears from one shot to the next.

When the boys are sitting in the living room talking about how they have to 'do it' before graduation, one of the boys sitting on the couch has his legs crossed, then they uncross, cross, and uncross. They keep changing positions.

The American President   When the President and Sydney are entertaining the French President and his wife in the ballroom, they show Sydney speaking French to their guests and her hands are in front of her. The next scene shows Sydney from behind, while she is still talking, and she is fiddling with her ring. The third scene is back showing her from the front and her hands are not fiddling with her ring.

Animal House   In the scene where Otter and Boon are hitting golf balls near the ROTC drills, Otter puts down the golf bag he is carrying and draws a club. The camera moves to the ROTC trainees, and when it comes back to the golfers, the bag is back on Otter's shoulder and there is no club out of the bag.

Apocalypse Now   In the *Playboy* Bunny scene, the helicopter's main rotor keeps starting and stopping.

The day after the USO *Playboy* Bunny show, the patrol boat canopy is set afire by some pranksters from a passing boat. Yet, that night, in the scene at the Do Lung Bridge, the canopy is intact. It goes through some amazing transformations during the remainder of the picture.

Armageddon   In the scene on the asteroid, where they are discussing the plan to jump the Armadillo, Ben Affleck's left ear goes from having a clear earpiece over it in profile, to having a yellow earplug in from the front.

On the oil rig, the golf ball changes between shots – first the pits are separate, then interconnecting. The logo also changes from 'Srixon' to '3 Srixon'. The final shot (split second before it's hit) shows that it's also rotated on the tee.

A dog is seen chewing on a miniature Godzilla toy. In the next shot, he is chewing on a much bigger, balloon-type Godzilla. But throughout, a guy has been trying to remove the toy from the dog's mouth – we see him pulling on it constantly, so there's no way the dog could have put it down and picked up another one.

When Bruce Willis is going to Ben Affleck's room, he bangs on the door with a golf club. You can see the white fan fall to the ground. Then, when Harry walks in, the fan is back on the ledge.

Austin Powers: International Man of Mystery   When Austin is unfrozen he's got crocodile clips on his ears. In one shot we see some scientists remove them, but they reappear in a later shot.

After Austin and Vanessa's night on the town, she falls asleep on him, holding a champagne glass. When the laptop computer starts beeping, the camera angle changes as we see Austin push her off him, and the champagne glass has suddenly disappeared.

Austin Powers: The Spy Who Shagged Me In the famous 'fight scene' with Austin and Mini-Me, we see Mini-Me picking Powers up in a gorilla press and turning him round. Well, when the camera is closing up on Mini-Me, he is standing still, twisting him round. However, when the camera isn't closed-up on him, Mini-Me is turning round.

Bad Boys Martin Lawrence is walking upstairs to tell his wife why he is late coming home. She starts to yell at him and say he isn't wearing his wedding ring. But in the first shot he has it on – it's only after she points it out that he isn't wearing the ring.

Batman & Robin The first confrontation with Mr Freeze and his henchmen involves them skating around a large ice-covered area. The henchmen are not using ice skates, but rollerblades. In the same scene we see ice skating blades pop out of Batman and Robin's boots, but when we actually see them skating, they are on rollerblades as well.

Being John Malkovich The comforter changes patterns in the first scene as the camera switches back and forth to John Cusack in bed.

Ben-Hur In the famous chariot race, keep an eye on the number of chariots. Nine are announced at the very beginning then, over the course of the race, one crashes, then a second, then a third, two crash at the same time, then one more crashes out, making six crashes in total. However, at the end of the race we see four chariots crossing the finish line – where did the spare one come from?

In the climactic moment of the chariot race, just after Ben-Hur delivers an ass-whipping to Marcellus, the wheel of the beaked chariot is pulled off and clearly disintegrates. Lo and behold, a split second later, when the same chariot is vaulted into the air, two intact wheels are clearly seen.

When Ben-Hur walks in to see the dying man, he puts his laurel wreath on a small table to the right of the door. When he walks out a bit later on, it's disappeared.

🎥 **Beverly Hills Cop**   When the police arrive at Victor's house the guards in the security room decide to run. At this time they are wearing guns in shoulder holsters. When you next see them, running out the door, they are unarmed. You see them again in the van, again with guns and shoulder holsters.

When Rosewood is lifting his sergeant over the wall at Victor Maitland's house, you see it is a solid wall all the way to the top. When the sergeant finally makes it over the wall and lands on the other side, we clearly see that the wall – from the other side – has columns and holes in it. We see it more than twice from each angle, and it's definitely not the same wall.

🎥 **Beverly Hills Cop II**   In the scene where Rosewood steals the cement truck and picks up Axel, you can plainly see Axel's firearm fall from his waistband on to the road underneath the truck. When Axel sits down inside a split second later, he's reloading the lost firearm.

The guy in the armoured car's passenger seat disappears and reappears during the chase.

🎥 **Bicentennial Man**   The caption 'Twelve years later' comes up on screen and there's a shot of the Charney family on the beach. It's late afternoon and the long shadows of two people playing ball fall towards the family. In the next shot, which is a close-up of 10-year-old Lloyd and his sister, it's the middle of the day, with short shadows falling in a different direction.

Big Billy makes a mess of scoring at basketball and the kids on the side pelt him with balls. As the players run up and down the pitch you can see where the spectators are sitting, and there are only a few kids. But when the boys start throwing the basketballs at Billy, there are suddenly many more boys.

Blade II After Blade emerges from the blood fountain, he fights a lot of henchmen in hand-to-hand combat before taking on Reinhardt with his sword. After Blade kills Reinhardt, and Whistler shoots the incubator, where are the bodies of the henchmen Blade fought hand to hand? None of them was a vampire, so they wouldn't have disappeared.

In the scene where Blade and the Bloodpack go to the club to find Reapers, there is a clip where Lighthammer and the girl go into an area by themselves. When it shows the two of them, the girl has a blue light filter on her gun, but when it cuts back to her, there isn't any filter on it.

The Blues Brothers When we see the Nazis falling in their car, one shot shows the car from above falling into an area without any buildings around the docks. When the car lands, however, it is in a built-up area of the city.

The Bourne Identity This is the scene where Jason Bourne is on the fire escape platform in the embassy in Zurich: before he goes down below, the platform is seen to be cleared of all snow. Then, moments later, when the security guard opens the door and Jason is under the platform, the top of the platform is fully covered with snow again.

When Bourne gets the box from his numbered bank account, the bank clerk carries it by holding its handle. Then he puts it on the table tipping it over to the side, so Bourne can open it. Thus the ingredients (especially the heavy weapon) should all be lying on the right side, which has become the bottom of the box. But, when Bourne opens it, everything is nicely arranged.

When Bourne approaches Marie about a ride, they talk across the top of her Mini. First, there is lots of snow on the car's roof. Then, there isn't.

In the scene where Bourne steals a grey Ford Sierra, when Marie walks from the phone booth to the car (Jason is taping the window) she passes a red car and there is a grey estate car two spaces along from it. The car they are stealing is out of shot. When they drive off their car is suddenly on the spot where the grey estate car was.

When Bourne is escaping the embassy, he has to scale down a wall below a broken fire escape. As he is inching his way to his right, towards the corner, the shot changes to one from below and he is suddenly about six feet lower than he was the moment before (there is a curved pipe jutting out of the wall that allows easy judgement of his actual position).

Braveheart In one of the major battles, William Wallace is charging down a hill with a large sword in his hand, then nothing, then a large axe.

When Wallace tries to escape from the English with his wife, not knowing that she has been captured and executed, he is seen running through the woods. To start with he's got no sword visible, then when he stops to take off the stolen uniform, a sword has appeared out of nowhere in his hand, which he sticks in the ground.

When the English spy tries to kill Wallace, and you realise the crazy Irishman is a good guy, you see the spy drop his sword as soon as he is hit by the Irishman's weapon, but as soon as he hits the ground, dead, the sword is back in his hand.

🎥 **The Breakfast Club**   There is a scene where the janitor catches the principal looking through the confidential files. The label on the front of the file drawer is first aligned correctly, then it is angled and sticking out of its holder, and then it is properly aligned again.

🎥 **Bridget Jones's Diary**   There are two types of string used in the blue soup scene – the plasticky type that florists sometimes use for the blue stuff, then ordinary string for when the dye has come out.

When Mark finds her diary at the end, he moves a newspaper off most of it, so it's just resting on the left-hand side. When we see a close-up, it's disappeared.

Towards the end, when Mark Darcy finds her diary, you clearly see the number 29 as he pulls it from under the magazines, then, when you see the diary, it's open on pages 10 and 11.

🎥 **Broken Arrow**   In the scene where Christian Slater and Samantha Mathis are radioing for help in the ranger's truck, the enemy helicopter comes from behind a ridge and shoots at them. They get out of the way, and the bullet fire continues and hits the truck on the driver-side door, the roof above, and then the ground after that. In the next scene, you can clearly see bullet holes on the hood, going from front to back, but the fire was from right to left.

🎥 **Can't Hardly Wait**   When Seth Green is getting teased by the girl, as she is calling him 'Chester Cheetah', the foreign guy is at first standing there growling at him. Seth then turns and walks away, and the foreign guy has completely disappeared.

🎥 **Casino**   When Remo Gaggi is talking to Andy Stone about Ace cussing out the Board, there's a pack of cigarettes beside Gaggi in his car. The camera angle changes to show Stone's face, who is outside the car, and when it flips back to Gaggi, there is a Zippo lighter in place of the cigarettes. The camera goes back to Stone, and when it comes back again, the Zippo is gone and the cigarettes are back.

When Arnie Piscano is complaining to his brother-in-law about Las Vegas, he backs into about ten bottles. They all fall except for two, and then the scene cuts to his brother-in-law and when the scene cuts back to Piscano, all the bottles are back up.

When Robert De Niro is having a meeting with Kevin Pollack about him firing the cowboy, Robert De Niro stubs out his cigarette. In the next shot, from behind, he is still smoking, but when in the front he has no cigarette.

Cast Away   When Tom Hanks first drifts on to the island and is asleep, his head is facing out to sea. In the next scene when he gets out of the raft, his head is in line with the rest of the beach.

After becoming stranded, Tom Hanks discovers the first package to wash ashore. While he is walking towards it you can clearly see some of the stretch of beach behind him (as well as some in front of him). This shot is somewhat of a tight one. When the camera 'seamlessly' cuts back to a shot of him bending over to pick up the package, you can clearly see that the beach is now covered with dozens of jagged rocks. The rocks would have been seen in the shot before this. But in this case, the shoreline was cleared of them in the first shot.

When Tom Hanks is looking through the wallet of the dead pilot you can see the corner of a dollar bill, then the shot breaks away and, when he takes the photo out, the dollar's disappeared.

Cats & Dogs   In the scene in the flocking factory, when Jeff Goldblum is being confronted by the cat leader (Mr Tinkles), another cat (Calico) is on Goldblum's shoulder. When the shot changes to an angle behind him, Calico disappears only to immediately reappear when the shot changes back to the angle facing Goldblum.

Charlie's Angels   In the scene where the Angel throws Lucy's 'homemade' muffin: the first muffin actually breaks through the door and you can see the depth and the cracks around the point of entry. When Bill Murray comes through the same door, you can see the door no longer has a hole in it, just a fake muffin with adhesive attached to the door.

They print out a photo of the 'creepy thin man' – we see a close-up of him (Crispin Glover) looking shiftily over his left shoulder. But in the next shot Cameron Diaz is holding the photo, and we can clearly see it's changed.

The shards in the broken window, from which Drew hangs with her sheet, look different after the repetition. In the original take it's made up of many more fragments than after the slow-motion.

When the Agency building is blown up, you see Cameron Diaz and Lucy Liu fly to the left of the screen and Drew fly to the right, but when they show them hit the car windshield, they are right next to each other, perfectly spaced out.

Chasing Amy   Ben Affleck is talking in the diner. He is smoking, but the cigarette ash appears then disappears, then appears again.

When Silent Bob is telling the Amy story in the diner, his cigarette is constantly changing length with every cut.

Chicago   During the 'Razzle Dazzle' number, a girl on a swing drops a gun. Billy catches the gun in his right hand and moves stage left. In the next shot Billy, moving stage left, has no gun in his right hand. He looks up and a gun drops in his hand.

In the scene where Velma offers Roxie some chocolates, Velma puts the box down on her left. In the next shot it is at the corner of the table, on Velma's right and with the long side facing Roxie. In the next shot the short side is facing Roxie, then the long side again.

🎥 **Clear and Present Danger**   In the scene where Jack Ryan is printing out the evidence before it is deleted, the printer indicates 'out of paper'. Ryan rips open the drawer, sees that there is no paper, turns round, grabs some, then shoves it into the printer ... that now has paper in it.

🎥 **Clerks**   The 'No Shoplifting' sign is gone when Randall sells cigarettes to the girl.

When Veronica enters the store and starts spraying everyone with a fire extinguisher the Chewley's Gum Rep tries to make a run for it. As he heads to the door you can clearly see the fire extinguisher still hanging on the wall near the door Veronica just entered.

In the scene where the angry customers hurl cigarettes at Dante, Veronica sprays a fire extinguisher at the unruly crowd, dispersing them in a cloud of white retardant. When the camera cuts to Veronica, she is holding the hose to a water-based fire extinguisher, not the type that expels fire retardant.

🎥 **Close Encounters of the Third Kind**   Richard Dreyfus, having seen flying saucers, is haunted by this vision of a rock (Devil's Tower in north-eastern Wyoming). Then he sees it on TV and has to go there – he jumps into the family station wagon, roars out of the driveway, and we get a close-up of the Indiana licence plate. Next we see him in Wyoming, south of Devil's Tower, supposedly having driven straight through, yet he seems to have stopped off long enough to pick up Wyoming licence plates.

When Richard Dreyfus has his first UFO encounter at the railway crossing, all the gauges in his truck go wild and stuff goes flying everywhere. After the encounter finishes, and the vehicle's power comes back, Dreyfus starts the engine and drives off. Miraculously, the interior of the truck has tidied itself and everything is back in its proper place.

Clueless When Cher is taking her driving test she smashes into a car and knocks the side mirror off the jeep. In the next shot, a second later, it is back on.

When Cher is walking down the stairs in her white dress to meet Christian, and Josh gets dazzled by her beauty, you see Christian talking to Josh and Cher's dad, and there is no way (from that angle) that Josh could have seen Cher until she reached the bottom of the stairs, but it shows him staring before she even gets to the landing.

Cocktail When Tom Cruise takes a picture of his friend Doug on the boat, the picture shows Doug with his legs crossed. After the photo's been taken, he puts one foot up on the sofa. However, when Brian looks at the photo later, Doug has his foot up.

Coming to America When Akeem and Semi get their apartment, the owner says that the room has only one window facing a brick wall. But when Hakeem is out on the fire escape, he yells out to a street, not a wall. And there are two windows.

In the scene towards the end of the movie you can see the dog sitting by the piano. At that time the keys are revealed. A few seconds later the lid is closed.

Commando After chasing down Sully, the yellow Porsche is totally wrecked on the left side, until Arnie drives it away, and it's fine.

When Arnie is riding on the plane's landing gear, there is one quick shot where you see the plane lifting off the ground with Arnie nowhere in sight. Right after that, when he lets go of the landing gear, you see a quick shot of him falling and the plane lifting away with the landing gear already up.

The truck that Arnie pushes down the hill won't run because the bad guys have trashed the engine, but after freewheeling down the hill, when it finally crashes, the exhaust is smoking away.

Con Air   When Johnny tries to rape the female guard, Nicolas Cage comes to the rescue and knocks him out. Cage then handcuffs him to an overhead rail with both hands in the cuffs over the rail. Yet after the crash, while the police are doing clean-up, they drag away Johnny, leaving one arm hanging off, as if Cage put only one of his hands in the cuffs and one cuff on the overhead rail. Even with one arm severed, they couldn't naturally have got out of that position without the severed arm going over the rail, in which case it would be lying on the floor with the rest of him.

Cool Runnings   When the bobsled team are getting their act together in Calgary, there's a scene of them pushing off with an unpainted bobsled. In the shots of the feet of the guys pushing at the back of the sled, you can see that the lower back of the sled is painted black with green stripes, the colours that they paint the sled in a scene a few minutes later.

Coyote Ugly   When the guy at the bar orders eight shots and Cammy (the blonde) tosses up eight shot glasses in a fancy manner, as you can see, she throws them up into two rows of four. But then in the next shot they're all just in one long row of eight. It would be impossible for her to arrange them that quickly – there is only about a second between the two shots.

On Violet's first night at Coyote Ugly, the girls are on the bar dancing to 'The Devil Went Down To Georgia.' Lil and Violet are behind the bar. Violet says to Lil, 'I can't do that dance.' The scene then goes back to the girls on the bar and Lil is the only one behind the bar dancing. In the very next scene, Lil gives Violet her coat and some money. The scene went from Violet and Lil standing together, to Lil being the only one behind the bar, back to Violet and Lil standing together in three seconds.

In the last scene when Violet says to Kevin, 'So what do you do when you realise all your dreams have come true?' Violet moves in to kiss Kevin and she gets really close. Then the camera cuts away to a different view and it shows Violet taking a step towards Kevin from 2–3 feet away.

Crimson Tide   When it shows the outside of the sub in some underwater scenes, the propeller slowly rotates clockwise. But in another scene the propeller is rotating the other way.

The Crow   In the scene at the bar with Gideon, when the black guy pours Gideon a drink it is only about a third full. When Gideon drinks it in the next shot it is almost full.

When Lee takes T-Bird in his car and the chase with the police begins, the camera flashes to look at the chase through the eyes of the crow, and the police car's emergency lights are strobes, but when the camera reverts back to the chase scene they are the old-style rotating flashers.

Cruel Intentions   In the final scene where Reese Witherspoon is driving the Jaguar and having flashbacks, watch as she drives past lovely rolling hills and pastures. Cut to a helicopter shot, and she's suddenly driving the car along a New York freeway.

At the end of the film Sebastian gets hit by a taxi. Take a close look at the licence plate – it changes during the scene.

Dances with Wolves   In one scene, the US Army kill the wolf friend of Kevin Costner, and in the following scene the camera shows the wolf body while the army moves away. If you stop the scene, you can see that the 'wild' wolf has a strap around his neck.

Dante's Peak   When they are crossing the river in the boat, the acidic water is eating through the blades of the motor, so Pierce Brosnan wraps his shirt around his hand to help them paddle manually, and nothing happens to his hand. Yet when Grandma, in her final heroic effort, leaps into the water to pull the boat ashore, she receives third-degree burns all over her legs.

Daredevil   In the funeral scene, Elektra is exposed to the rain for a few moments so that Matt can 'see' her face. Then she is under an umbrella. When she gets in her car, her hair and face are completely dry.

When Elektra's father dies, Daredevil's baton/cane was obviously the only weapon he had to hand, because he gets a bit panicked when he realises he's facing Bullseye without it. So where does the grappling hook come from that he uses to escape? He didn't have any other equipment.

In the scene following the death of Elektra's father, Matt hits all of his weapons and helmets to the ground. As he is knocking down all his 'numchucks' notice that one in the centre stays on the hook. He puts his back to the wall and begins to slide down, but look to the left of the screen where the last weapon has disappeared.

When Matt Murdock's father is killed in the alley, Matt is wearing his father's robe and hood. As he runs towards his father's body, the robe falls off and lands behind him. Matt kneels down, without turning, to hold his father but, when the camera pulls back, the robe and hood have somehow moved several yards in front of them.

Dave   At the beginning, when the president lands in the helicopter, the shots go back and forth between the rotors spinning and the rotors stopped.

Days of Thunder   In one scene Tom Cruise gets knocked into Brett Bodine's car, number 26, which then spins. When Cruise explains the incident to his crew chief he says he was knocked into Gant. When the shot switches back to the wide shot, the spinning car is Gant's number 33 car.

Deep Blue Sea The sharks can break through metal, but not the glass in the oven where one of the characters is 'hiding'. Must be some strong glass.

At one point LL Cool J throws a rope down a shaft to save a few of the characters from the fast-rising water. The shot shows them pull back the rope and shut the door. A few scenes later, the rope is hanging down the shaft again.

Diamonds Are Forever When James Bond drives into the alleyway during the car chase, the car gets tipped up on two wheels. However, when it emerges from the other side, it's on the other two wheels. The explanation is that the exit was re-shot after onlookers were visible in the original take, and no one checked which way round it was in the original shoot. Some versions have a bit of footage inserted whereby the car seems to drop back down on all four wheels, then rolls on to the other two wheels, but aside from it being a bad effect, this is a mistake in itself, as the alleyway's not wide enough for that to happen, hence why the car was on two wheels in the first place!

Die Another Day When Jinx and Bond sneak on to Graves's plane, Jinx can be seen with a nickel-plated pistol (this is also evident throughout the entire film). Yet, when Jinx is in the cockpit and Frost tells her to hand over the gun, it's now no longer nickel plated but standard gun-metal black.

During the car chase on the ice, Bond's Aston Martin flips over; you can see the right wing mirror break off as this happens. All through the rest of the chase, both wing mirrors are fine.

Bond opens up the necklace that Zao had and there are four diamonds inside. Later when he shows them to someone else it changes to five. Where did that extra diamond come from? It can't be that Graves gave him another one after their bet – that was settled by cheque.

At the beginning of the film, James Bond steals a suitcase full of diamonds. He takes the compartment with the diamonds out and sets a bomb under it. When he puts the C4 in it, the explosive is very nearly as high as the edge of the case, but the diamond compartment still fits back inside perfectly.

When they are all on the plane near the end of the film, Graves is able to watch Icarus blasting the land mines through the glass at the front of the plane. However, in a much earlier shot, there is no glass at the front of the plane, just a normal nose.

Die Hard   When Bruce Willis is trying to find his wife on the computer, he can't find her under 'McClane' so looks for 'Gennaro', clearly her maiden name. When he touches the screen, the spelling suddenly changes to 'Gennero' – obviously a dodgy computer effect they didn't check properly.

When Bruce Willis breaks through the window (as the roof is blown), he lands on his back, head pointing towards the window. However, the next moment we see him catching his breath, lying on his stomach and feet aimed at the window as the firehose hanger falls past the window.

After being shot at by the terrorists through the window, Al puts the car in reverse and swerves around for safety. There is one shot where it shows the car backing through a wooden fence, but the next shot is of the car crashing into a steel gate.

Die Hard: With a Vengeance   When they drive through the park and jump off the rock they land on a pile of leaves, which covers the bonnet. Some of those leaves fall off but not all of them – in the next shot the bonnet is completely clean.

At Yankee Stadium, the pipe in the picture behind Samuel L Jackson changes size and position, depending on the view of the camera.

Dirty Harry   During the scene on the football pitch, where Harry Callahan is torturing Scorpio to force him to say where the kidnapped girl is, there are several shots as if from Callahan's viewpoint. As the camera switches between the two characters, the white painted lines on the pitch mysteriously move or even vanish underneath Scorpio.

Dogma   When Matt Damon and Ben Affleck are in the board meeting, Damon is carving the voodoo doll out of the onion. At one point he is cutting close to the neck, and the doll's head falls off. In the next shot, where Damon is placing the doll on the table, the doll is completely unscathed. He still has his head!

When Linda Fiorentino is being attacked by the 'hockey players' she is knocked down and her keys fall across a puddle. When the kid lines up his slapshot, there is no puddle. When the camera angle changes the puddle has returned.

In the scene where Jay tries to have sex with Linda Fiorentino, the condom goes from being red and rolled up to white and unrolled as Jay talks about John Doe Jersey.

When Matt Damon and Ben Affleck are at the airport and Matt Damon is done talking to the nun, he jumps over the seat to sit next to Ben Affleck, but watch where he starts to where he ends. On the away shot of him, he is coming across from two seats away from him, then in the near shot, he is moving into the seat right next to him.

In the scene where Chris Rock falls out of the sky, it shows his body lying down. When Jay makes the comment about 'Con Air', Rock rises up while saying, 'Con Air'? Con shit!' Yet in the next (non-close-up) scene his body is still flat on the ground.

In the scene where Linda Fiorentino is approached in her bedroom by Alan Rickman, her sheets are plaid, with a plaid quilt. After their trip to the restaurant, and she's just waking up again, her quilt is still plaid, but her sheets are solid green.

In the scene where Alan Rickman enters the bedroom, the phone in the background seems to be jumping around because every time the camera switches from the girl to the angel and back, the phone moves! Watch it closely and it's a laugh.

Dumb and Dumber   In the scene where Nicholas Andre shoots Jeff Daniels twice in the chest, the gun is empty after the two shots. The camera then moves to Daniels getting up and shooting back. When the camera returns to Nicholas, the gun is not empty.

Empire Records   In the scene where Liv Tyler and Renée Zellweger are having lunch, Liv takes off her bra and puts it on the table. After that, the bra moves around constantly, all over the table, and eventually ends up on the floor somehow, with nobody ever touching it.

End of Days   After the priest writes down 666 on a piece of paper, he holds it upside down to reveal that it is 999, but we also notice it's in someone else's handwriting.

At the end of the movie, in the church scene, the 'wind of evil' blows down all the benches like dominoes. In the next second they're all back in an upright position again.

When Arnie goes to the church for the first time, the priest dismisses him and exits through a door. When the door is open you see an ornate banner on the other side in a well-lit room. When Arnie walks through the door it is into a small dark room at the top of some steps with no banner.

🎥 **Entrapment** In the scene where Catherine Zeta-Jones knocks out the crook with a vase and jumps into the car with Sean Connery, one of the bad guys jumps on to the car and sticks a knife through the roof, tearing it open. Yet when they park the car outside the hotel a few moments later the roof is in pristine condition.

🎥 **Eraser** Arnie dives to save the girl under the lid of a fridge. Knives are thrown at him, with his hand above the fridge door. The knives are all thrown and none hit his hand. But the next angle shows he's got one in his hand. Even worse – in the next scene he's driving a van with both hands, and when he swipes the credit card the wound appears and disappears.

🎥 **Erin Brockovich** When Erin Brockovich and Ed Masry are talking to the PG&E representative, Erin puts the paper in front of the PG&E guy. It is about in the middle of the table. It is there for most of the shots, but then the angle changes, and changes back again, and the paper is all the way over on the PG&E guy's side, practically falling off the edge.

🎥 **E.T. The Extra Terrestrial** When Elliot is sitting in the garden waiting for ages for ET to come out of the shed, the position of the moon in the night sky doesn't move during that time.

🎥 **Evil Dead 2** In one scene, Ash finds some pages from the *Necronomicon* lying in a mud puddle. He picks up the pages, and they're suddenly dry.

🎥 **Evolution** When everyone is looking at the hidden cameras, someone says that the aliens 'destroyed video 4'. When we see a close-up of the screen, it's clearly video 2 that's showing static.

Exit Wounds   In an early scene, Steven Seagal handcuffs TK to the grille of his Dodge truck. Upon his return, he finds that TK and the truck's grille have gone. Later in the film, the truck miraculously has its grille back. A few scenes later, when Seagal confronts TK, he says, 'Your grille is downstairs.'

When Steven Seagal is held captive in the speeding black van, one of the captors is pushed out the side door by Seagal and is crushed when the passenger side of the van hits a row of parked cars and one of the side doors gets knocked off – we see a few shots of the van with the left side missing a door, but while the van's hitting all the cars there's a very obvious shot of the van with both doors intact again.

Eyes Wide Shut   In the scene where Tom Cruise calls the woman whose father has died and the boyfriend answers, a rubber band appears on the desk next to the pen after he hangs up, which was not there before he made the call.

Just after being followed on the curiously empty streets of Manhattan, Tom Cruise makes his way to a coffee shop. The last shot from the street before he turns to enter the shop shows not a person on the sidewalk, but the next shot of him from inside the cafe, of Cruise opening the door, shows about three people passing in the background.

When Nicole Kidman is doing some maths with her daughter, keep an eye on the bottles in the background. A blue bottle suddenly appears out of nowhere.

Face/Off   When Nicolas Cage and that big guy are making their escape, the big guy falls over the rail and Cage catches his gun and tries to save him. In the last scene before he falls, Cage is holding on to the very last tip of the gun, but it shows a wide shot and he is holding a lot more of the barrel.

In the boat scene, when the white boat crashes through the police boat you can see the front of the white boat shatter, there's even an explosion, and then it's OK again, with no fire visible.

Fatal Attraction One scene, shot from profile, has Glenn Close in bed, and the sheet is down, exposing her breasts. The film cuts to a frontal shot and the sheet is up around her neck. When it cuts back to profile, the sheet is down again.

When Michael Douglas puts on Glenn Close's tape in the rental car, the radio is set at 97.1. When he removes the tape, it's at 107.9.

Ferris Bueller's Day Off When Jeanie is racing home, the rear view mirror disappears.

Jeanie doesn't undo her seatbelt before she jumps out of the station wagon. And, additionally, in one shot of the car parked, the seatbelt is slammed in the door of the car and hanging out, but when they cut back to the car seconds later, the seatbelt is gone.

A Few Good Men In the first scene with Tom Cruise and Demi Moore, in her office, one button on his shirt is buttoned, unbuttoned, and buttoned again. This is a bad scene for mistakes because there's also a stain on his shirt which disappears, let alone the fact that the apple he's eating gets bigger while he's eating it.

Fight Club Close to the end when Edward Norton runs up to the front of the empty building and Brad Pitt appears, he tries to break the glass door by pushing a bench into it, but it doesn't work. He doesn't move the bench and he then shoots at the glass and breaks it. When it shows him walking through the broken door, the bench has disappeared.

Final Destination At the memorial service the principal says that it's been 39 days since 39 loved ones had died. But there were 40

THINGS THAT MOVE BETWEEN TAKES

students on the plane and 4 chaperones, making the total 44. Now 7 people got off the plane which means 37 people actually died, not 39.

From Dusk Till Dawn In the opening scene, the pages change in the magazine the convenience store clerk is reading, depending on the shot.

The Fugitive After the bus has crashed they show a shot of a dead convict with his feet against a broken window, looking out at the train. Two or three shots go by and his feet are in a different position each time.

When Deputy Marshal Samuel Gerard has found out that Richard Kimble is in 'the presidential suite' he turns the car and goes to the hotel. If you look at the way he is turning the wheel compared to what direction the car actually moves, you will see that it doesn't fit – the car turns around to the left but the wheel is turned to the right.

Full Metal Jacket In the scene where DI Hartman dumps the contents of Private Pyle's footlocker on the floor, in the next few shots the layout of the clutter on the floor changes.

Galaxy Quest In the ending scene, where the crew is bowing to the fans, Sigourney Weaver is shown moving her right leg back a small bit. However, when they show them standing up from the bow, her right leg is fully crossed behind her.

When the four 'nerds' first approach the captain to talk about their supposed problem, the girl is standing in a different place than when they cut back. In a later scene the girl is in this position – they probably reshot the earlier scene while they were doing the later scene.

Gangs of New York When Leonardo DiCaprio arrives in New York and is talking to his new friend, the bag he is holding keeps switching from being held under his arm (camera shot from the front) to being carried on his back (camera shot from the back).

🎥 **Gladiator** During the final scenes, when Maximus has been killed and his corpse is lying on the sand, we can see both the slaves and the praetorian guards forming a semicircle around Maximus. When someone asks for help to carry his corpse, during the second it takes to raise it up (shot change), the slaves have moved and the praetorian guards are forming a perfect honour corridor through which Maximus's corpse is about to go by.

During Maximus's death scene you can clearly see the entrance that Commodus and Maximus entered the arena through in the floor of the arena. After Maximus's gladiator friend is done burying the figures of Maximus's son and wife, you cannot see the entrance anymore when he is walking away.

In the scene where the Emperor is standing over his nephew, touching his face while he sleeps, his sister enters the room and you hear only her footsteps, but he is then standing at the end of the bed out of reach of the boy. He does not have time to make that move.

When Maximus falls to the ground at the end, there's flat sand under his head. Then when the angle changes, he suddenly has a pillow of sand under his head to support his neck with the bulky armour.

🎥 **The Godfather** When Michael Corleone and Kay are eating lasagne during the wedding, Kay is holding a cigarette in her left hand, which disappears in one shot.

🎥 **Godzilla** Godzilla noticeably changes size throughout the movie. For example, he is shown in a subway tunnel, but he cannot fit into the Hyde Park tunnel (taxicab scene), which is significantly larger than a subway tunnel. Also, compare the size of Godzilla's eye next to

Matthew Broderick during the fish scene and Godzilla's death scene. The eye is way bigger in the latter.

GoldenEye When James Bond and Natalya eject from the helicopter, you can clearly see two white parachutes (white inside and out), but when the capsule lands, as the parachutes collapse around it, we can see there are very large red bits on them.

Gone in 60 Seconds During the scene where Nicolas Cage is driving the lovely Shelby GT500 Mustang and he knocks off the mirror, the car stalls, as if it is reacting to the damage. He then leans down and tries to start the car by simply turning the ignition like he has a key, but when he gets in the car and first starts it he uses two thin pieces of metal, and he had to use both hands.

When Nicolas Cage is driving Eleanor he backs up and hits the right rear-view mirror. He stops, leans out of the window and sees that it is dangling. The very next shot it is back to normal and it stays that way for most of the rest of the movie.

During the first chat between Nicolas Cage and Angelina Jolie (she's under the car) there are a number of wrenches or tools that can be clearly seen near her on the ground. Every time the camera cuts from Jolie to Cage, then back on to Jolie, the tools are in a different position or place than they were a second ago. First, they are together, then they are far apart, then they are in a different direction and so on.

When 'Gilligan' steals the 83 El Dorado, Donny finds a package of heroin in the trunk and spills some on the floor. When Castlebeck shows up, Nicolas Cage tells Donny to cover it up with his foot. In this part, it looks like only a small amount of heroin. Later, when Castlebeck walks over to the driver's side of the caddy, it shows Donny's foot again, and it appears to be a larger amount of heroin, at least twice as much.

When Donnie and Fred are stealing the Jaguar from a parking garage, the window is over halfway rolled down on the way out. When the other guy comes and puts the gun in Donnie's face, the window is all the way down.

🎥 **Gone with the Wind**   Scarlett is attacked on a bridge in the woods while on her way to the lumber mill. At first, the buggy very nearly goes off the bridge backwards. Then Scarlett faints, but when the camera returns to the full shot of the buggy, suddenly it is squarely in the middle of the bridge and in no danger at all of falling over the edge.

When Scarlett is attacked in the woods, Big Sam drives her carriage out of danger. When the scene cuts to a far shot of the carriage driving through the woods, Big Sam is no longer with her. She is driving it by herself.

🎥 **Good Will Hunting**   In the beginning, take a look at the black-boards during the lecture. They're movable boards, and they're raised in some shots and lowered in others.

🎥 **GoodFellas**   In the scene where Pauly talks to Ray Liotta and the restaurant owner about Liotta's possible involvement in the restaurant biz, Pauly is talking with the cigar clearly in his hand, and it cuts away to him saying 'No?' with the cigar jammed directly in his mouth.

When Karen is sitting on top of Ray Liotta in the bed, with a gun pointed to his face, the gun keeps changing colours. One second it's silver, the next it's black.

Ray Liotta is wearing the Star of David around his neck in a shower scene, then the camera cuts away and then back again – and he is wearing a cross.

🎥 **The Green Mile**   'Roll on one' means to crank up the generator all the way. On top of the machine are light bulbs that all light up when the generator is turned up. However, when they are executing Del and Percy is asking him if he has any last words, they have a sideshot of Percy and you can see the lightbulbs all lit up, but he didn't say 'Roll on one' yet.

Grosse Pointe Blank   In the scene where John Cusack gives Minnie Driver an aeroplane ride on his feet, he takes off his cap to lie on the bed. When he gets up to leave, the cap appears in his hand without his ever retrieving it from the bedpost where he hung it.

In the scene where John Cusack and Dan Ackroyd meet each other in a diner, there are some pills on the table. The pills keep moving around the table for every cut.

Halloween   When Jamie Lee Curtis is walking home the pavement instantly goes from dry to wet.

Halloween: Resurrection   When at his house, the first crew member Michael kills has a camera. Michael puts that camera on the ground, tripod closed and lying down. When the people first walk into the house the camera view switches to one that's up the stairs and the camera that was lying on the floor is now propped up against the wall.

Hannibal   When Clarice opens the letter we see that it's just sealed with wax, not glued down. However, when we see the flashback of Hannibal writing the letter, he licks it. Obviously he could have put the wax on off-screen, as it were, but that doesn't explain why the letter wasn't glued down when she received it.

When we see Hannibal signing the letter to Clarice, you can see he writes 'M.D.' quite small, but when Clarice gets it, the writing is much larger. Other variations include a line across the top of 'Lecter', which has expanded across his whole name on receipt. A hyphen also appears between his name and the M.D., which he never wrote.

The search returns one page, showing the text as starting 'in 1992 ...' He follows the link and we see a close-up of Hannibal, with the text 'in 1992' just visible at the top right of the screen (we only see half of it, but it's clearly a 2). Then we see a wider shot, and it's suddenly become 'in 1990'.

Inspector Pazzi's cellphone is switched off in the library, when Lecter takes it and talks to Clarice. Although it is on vibrate mode, the LCD display is blank.

Harry Potter and the Chamber of Secrets When Lockhart falls down the hole into the Chamber of Secrets, the sound of him hitting the ground comes a second or two later. When Ron and Harry jump down, not only do they take longer to get down, they also slide down the pipe, rather than fall straight down.

When Harry arrives at the Weasley's, on the clock that shows where everyone is, the picture for the twins and Ron is moving to show they're home, but no one else's picture is in the same place. Shortly afterwards it's clear that everyone else is already home, except Mr Weasley.

When Myrtle is flooding the girls' bathroom, the tap that later doesn't work (the entrance to the chamber) is happily churning out water – it's on the side nearest the door, so it's clear both times.

When Harry is stabbing the diary, he stabs the cover and the tooth doesn't go very far through. Later, in Dumbledore's office, though, he holds up the book and we see both sides, with a clear stab mark going right through.

In Moaning Myrtle's bathroom, the mirrors don't reflect at all as they're very dirty. But, when Harry changes into Crabbe, his face is reflected in one of the mirrors.

When the basilisk bites Harry, he pulls out a straight fang. When he carries it across the room, it is a curved tooth, but there were no curved teeth in the mouth of the basilisk, let alone Harry's arm.

When Dobby visits Harry in the hospital he bashes himself on the head with the bottle of Skele-Gro; he puts the bottle down on the table at the foot of the bed. After he disappears and the shot changes, the bottle is back in its original place on the side table at the head of the bed; the table at the foot of the bed is empty.

Heat When Robert De Niro confronts Ashley Judd in her motel room, he knocks all but a few hangers off the metal coat rack. While the camera goes back and forth as they argue, the remaining hangers disappear and reappear several times.

In the shoot-out scene when they drive away in the car, Robert De Niro is seen in slow motion as he realises there are cops in front of them as well as behind. He raises his weapon and fires, knocking the rear-view mirror off. In the shot directly after he is seen still firing his weapon, and the mirror falls off again.

Highlander In the Madison Square Garden fight scene between Connor MacLeod and Fasil, Fasil's mirrored shades fall off and we see Fasil run off in the reflection of his mirrored shades. In the very next scene Fasil jumps into shot and whacks a junction box, and he is wearing his mirrored shades.

In the climactic fight scene on the rooftop, the amount of water which pours from the overturned water tower is not nearly enough to flood the roof to the depth shown. The water level also alternates in depth, going from waist deep to knee deep and then back to waist deep again. At one point it's deep enough for both actors to fully submerge themselves and the next it's only up to their knees.

Hollow Man In the beginning of the film, when the invisible gorilla has escaped, as Kevin Bacon is getting the tranquilliser guns from the cabinet, he bets Matt that he can get the gorilla first. He does shoot the gorilla first, with the aid of infrared goggles. The problem is, we blatantly see him close the goggle/tranquilliser gun cabinet before he ever gets a pair of goggles. In fact, as he runs down the hall we see both of his hands, and all he is carrying is a tranquilliser gun.

When the gorilla is lying on the bed you can't see any marks on the mattress, but when they make Kevin Bacon invisible you can see his shape marked on it.

The doctors never cut nostril holes in the mask for Kevin Bacon to breathe. Later on when he puts the mask back on, it does have nostril holes.

Home Alone   In the scene where Harry and Marv are in Kevin's neighbour's house, when Kevin's dad calls, Harry picks up the phone to listen to the message, and the phone is on the hook. It shows him listening, then he calls out to Marv, and the camera looks at Marv, then when it returns to Harry, the phone is off the hook.

Independence Day   When the president's assistant is waiting for him on the first morning, she is reading *USA Today*. On the back there is a weather map and it is blue and green, the colours for cold in *USA Today*. It was a hot July day!

When Will Smith goes out to get the paper, the paper has a string around it to keep it closed, yet he opens it up as if it was only folded.

When Jeff Goldblum is in the Oval Office waiting to talk to the president he stands up and closes his laptop and sets it on the desk with the opening side facing the front of the desk. When he tells the president, 'And the clock is ticking,' he turns the already opened laptop around towards the front of the desk.

In the scene where Jeff Goldblum is getting the alcohol out of the fridge, he opens the fridge door and it is full of food. When his ex-wife puts the bottle back in the fridge, it's virtually empty. It's still empty when Jeff reaches back in to get the bottle back.

It's a Wonderful Life As George and Mary prepare to drive Martini's family to their new home, Mary (in a close-up) is holding the goat's horn/antler. The scene cuts to an extreme long shot in which her hand is nowhere near the goat – she's got both arms round the child in her lap.

In the first scene where George finds his brother Harry's grave, the year of death (1919) is clearly visible. The next time we see it, it is obscured by snow and George has to dig it out to find the year his brother died.

Jaws At the scene just after the fake shark scare, the real shark shows up at the pond area of the beach. As the lifeguard in a small boat reacts to everyone's panic, the shark tips over the boat and then appears underneath him to tear his leg off. We watch as it sinks slowly to the bottom. You can plainly see that the lifeguard is barefoot in the boat. The severed leg has a tennis shoe on.

After the orca breaks down for good, Hooper goes into the shark cage to try to kill the shark. The shark proceeds to completely trash the bars on one of the sides. After Hooper escapes to the bottom, the camera shows the shark attacking the top of the cage and the bars are now intact.

When the shark is harpooned to some rope, Brody and Hooper tie the rope to the stern cleats, causing the boat to be dragged backwards. Quint gets a machete to cut the rope to limit the boat's damage. At this point the sea is somewhat choppy. He throws the machete, making it stick into the edge of the boat. The sea in the background is now completely calm.

Jerry Maguire When Jerry is at Cushman's house to make sure he's staying with him, the car he leaves in isn't the one he arrives in.

Simplest way to tell is that the one he arrives in has a red plastic bit across the boot, whereas the one we see him driving home while singing has a painted bit there.

In the play before the final touchdown play, the announcer says it's now second and whatever, but the down marker in the background is set to first down.

When Jerry comes out of his office with all his stuff, he has a leather bag over his shoulder and he is carrying a box. He puts the box down, makes his speech and takes the fish and then leaves with Dorothy but he never gets the box back from where he set it down.

Jurassic Park   The satchel of money Dennis Nedry receives as a down payment for getting the embryos off the island vanishes from his arms as he looks at the false container of shaving cream. It vanishes mid-sentence; he had no time to put it down.

In the scene where the baby dinosaur is born, one minute the robotic hand is there behind the egg as it's hatching, then in the reverse angle the hand's suddenly disappeared.

In the scene when Lex and Tim are in the car and the T-Rex is attacking them, at one point the T-Rex smashes through the roof of the car and the clear roof falls through on top of Lex and Tim. Well, at one point it's whole, then the T-Rex breaks it with his teeth, but in the next moment it's whole again.

When the Raptor is chasing Alan, Ellie, Tim and Lex through the computer lab, and they get into the ceiling, the Raptor jumps up on a table and pokes its head through the ceiling. When Grant kicks it in the eye, and it falls, the table is gone.

In the scene right before we meet the T-Rex, outside the cage, the jeeps are wet before it starts to rain.

Jurassic Park III   At the very end of the movie, when the group is cornered by the Raptors, Tea Leoni gives them the eggs. When the first Raptor picks up the first egg it is safe in its mouth, but in the next shot it is barely in its mouth, then in the final shot when the Raptor runs away, if you look closely at the Raptor's mouth, the egg is well into the mouth.

Keeping the Faith   In the first scene where Edward Norton is telling his sad story to the bartender at the bar, he pulls out a picture of him, Ben Stiller and Jenna Elfman. Then the movie progresses to a sequence of their childhood, and then focuses back in on the picture. The two photos are different. One is a close-up of the three kids' heads; the other is taken from much further away.

Kingpin   Randy Quaid clearly has a tattoo of a four-leaf clover on his chest when he is rescued from the strip club, well before they even make it to Reno, where he allegedly gets the tattoo.

Woody Harrelson puts down his sun visor in the car, but it is up again in the next camera view.

A League of their Own   In the scene where Tom Hanks is about to say a team prayer before the final game, his unfolded towel mysteriously becomes folded when he throws it to the ground to kneel on it.

Legally Blonde   When Elle is called to the lawyer's office, she holds some files and no bag. After he tries to pick her up, she leaves with empty hands. A few seconds later in the corridor, she's walking with her bag.

Legends of the Fall   When Brad Pitt and his brother hug in the trenches in the war, at first Brad's chin is on top of Samuel's hat, but when it cuts to the other angle, their heads are level, side by side.

🎥 The Living Daylights   The wheel that is shot off James Bond's car during the frozen lake chase scene is back on the car seconds later as Bond is jumping over the Russian/Czech soldiers.

🎥 The Lord of the Rings: The Fellowship of the Ring   When the fellowship are sailing down the river (through the two statues) the foot of the left statue looks as if it's at the same level as the water. Then in the next scene (camera angle from above) the foot is not at water level. It appears to be on a high rock.

When Gandalf and Saruman are talking in Orthanc, we can see a black strap around Gandalf's fingers on the hand holding his staff. In some shots it's around different fingers; in others it's disappeared completely.

Near the end, when Frodo has tears running down his face, in the first shot the tear on his right side is short and the left-side tear is down to his chin. in the next shot they are reversed. Some people have said it's just that one tear lengthened and a new one started, but look at the right-hand one (the longer one in the first shot). If there was a new tear, we'd still see the damp path of the first one, but it's rolling down a dry cheek.

At the end of the movie, when Frodo takes the boat to continue on his own, Sam runs into the water to follow Frodo, as he promised Gandalf. When Sam is about halfway to the boat, he goes under water because he cannot swim. He almost reaches the bottom of the flood, and does not swim up at any time. Suddenly, Frodo takes his hand and pulls him into the boat, but Frodo has not moved an inch and Sam did not swim to the surface.

At the beginning, when Gandalf is guiding the cart with Frodo, Gandalf's pipe keeps mysteriously vanishing from each scene.

When they are all walking up the snowy mountain the camera starts off with a larger view and then goes to a closer view of the people. In the larger view there are no footprints but in the closer view there are.

When Sam tells Frodo that if he takes another step, he will be further away from home than ever before, he stands next to a scarecrow. In the next scene, we see both Sam and Frodo, and Sam has passed the scarecrow by several metres. Another zoom at Sam, and he stands by the scarecrow again.

The Lord of the Rings: The Two Towers Merry and Pippin were bound when taken by the Uruk-Hai and their bonds weren't cut until after they managed to escape during the fight. Yet, when the horse almost crashes down on Pippin during the night, he has his arms spread out up near his face, not bound.

In the scene when Gandalf and company first visit Theoden's hall, keep an eye on Gandalf's staff – it's in very different positions depending on the shot.

Very near the start, when Frodo and Sam are talking, keep an eye on Sam's backpack. The blanket rolled up at the top of it moves up and down his back, without him adjusting it.

When Gimli is talking to Eowyn about dwarf women and his horse throws him, the axe in his hand goes flying. In the wide shot, the axe is shown going a fair distance from the horse, about four or five metres. In the shot of Gimli on the ground, however, the axe lands right next to him, only about a metre from where it flew out of his hand.

The Lost World: Jurassic Park When they're on the island and the INGen helicopters are flying in, Jeff Goldblum takes the binoculars and looks through the wrong end, but when we see what he's looking at, the image is magnified as if he's using them properly.

Mallrats In the scene where Shannen Doherty dumps Jason Lee, she pushes the dresser against the wall to go through the window. She then opens the window and sticks the window to the roof. The camera flips to Jason Lee, and when it goes back to Shannen Doherty the window is not stuck to the ceiling, it is suspended inches below the roof.

When Jeremy London and Jason Lee come back from the Dirt Mall, they park with a green saloon to their right. Then when they get out of the car, the saloon has been replaced by a black truck.

Man on the Moon   When Jim Carrey is preparing to do his Elvis imitation he puts a guitar on as if he's getting ready to play it, then we cut to another shot and the guitar has mysteriously vanished.

The Man with the Golden Gun   When James Bond is flying over China and landing on the sea by Scaramanga's island, you can see that his plane has two floats – one on either wing. But in the shot where he is heading for the beach it is clearly seen that the left float has gone.

Mars Attacks!   When Sarah Jessica Parker is talking to Pierce Brosnan on her show, her dog suddenly ends up in her lap. While she is talking, her dog is beside her, sleeping; the camera cuts to another angle and the dog is wide awake and sitting on her lap.

When the president shouts at the major, the clipboard is under his arm. After the president has shouted, the major picks the clipboard up off the table.

Mary Poppins   The father tears the children's advert for a nanny up into eight pieces, but when it comes out of the chimney it's in far more bits.

The Mask   When Jim Carrey is in jail, he puts toilet paper on the toilet seat. But a few seconds later the toilet paper is not on the toilet.

The Mask of Zorro   When Antonio Banderas is in the *cantina*, he has a little scuffle with Anthony Hopkins. When Hopkins knocks him over to the wall, he knocks what looks like stalks of corn rolled up in a bundle into the doorway. In the next shot, when Banderas moves into the doorway, the bundle of corn is gone.

The Matrix   In the scene where Agent Smith is interrogating Neo, and after Smith has sealed Neo's mouth shut and he is backed into the corner, when the camera cuts back to Smith you can clearly see a reflection in his glasses of Neo calmly sitting down in the chair.

In the beginning of the movie, when Neo gets the FedEx envelope, he is shown at his desk opening the envelope and then pouring it out. As he is pouring the phone out, with the green packing label on the top, the shot cuts 'seamlessly' to a close-up of the phone being poured out the rest of the way. However, the envelope is now flipped over. The FedEx logo is now on top (the packing label is facing down).

When Neo first meets Morpheus, Morpheus extends his right hand with his other hand behind his back, the next shot shows him with his left hand at his side, and when he withdraws his hand, it is back behind his back . . . talk about fast hands!

In the scene where Morpheus is being interrogated by the agent alone, the camera switches from behind Morpheus to just forward of him and back a few times. If you look at the agent's hand on Morpheus's head, you can see that his fingers switch from behind his ear to both sides of his ears as the camera changes.

When Neo tells Tank that they need 'Guns, lots of guns' he cocks the MP5 that he picks from the rack. It is matt black, but when the camera focuses in, it is shiny and reflective.

When Trinity is making a getaway from the agents she is not carrying a weapon, neither is there a sign of one. But after she jumps over to the next building she magically pulls two big handguns out of her leather suit.

After the lobby scene in the government building, Neo and Trinity enter the elevator and the pillars are shown falling to pieces. Where are the dead/unconscious guards?

When Neo walks through the metal detector, you can see quite clearly that he is wearing a tight black shirt under his trenchcoat, but no guns are visible. The metal detector beeps (of course) and he is stopped by the guard. In the next frame he opens up his coat, revealing a ludicrous amount of guns which were not there before.

In the scene with Morpheus fighting the agent in the bathroom of the building they were trapped in, the agent punches through a brick wall, yet next time we see the wall, there is no damage.

When Neo is running to room 303, before he enters the building he steals a phone. For a moment, he has no phone in his hand, then it's back again.

Maverick   When Mel Gibson walks into his room at the beginning of the movie after playing poker, he doesn't shut his door, but it is mysteriously shut when Jodie Foster knocks on it a couple of seconds later.

During the scene when the trio are attempting to rescue the mission women's money, Mel Gibson goes on a rant about how he is outmatched in bullets when set up against the thieves. He complains that he has only six, so he takes Jodie Foster's gun as well, yet when the shooting finally begins, he fires about fourteen shots from his six-shooter before pulling out his second gun.

Me, Myself & Irene   When Jim Carrey is taking Renée Zellweger back to New York on his motorcycle, they come across a supposed dead cow in the middle of the road. Carrey pulls out his gun and shoots the cow a few times, then throws his gun off to his right, way off the screen. Next screen shot, the gun is right next to him.

Meet the Parents   In the scene where Pam and Greg are arriving at Pam's house, she throws the cigarettes to the roof and they land with the top part of the box facing down. But later, when Greg is on the roof looking for Jinx and finds the cigarette box, the box is the other way up.

Just before the lie-detector test, watch the lava lamp in Robert De Niro's little back room. It's cold a couple of times, then the lava's flowing freely, then cold again.

Memento   There are scenes in which Guy Pierce is looking at the back of Teddy's polaroid. If you look at the serial number of the polaroid when he is writing 'Don't believe his lies', it is a different number than when he looks at it during the beginning of the film.

In one of the final scenes, Teddy's licence plate is the focus of Guy Pierce's new tattoo note. We see a close-up of the plate that reads 'SG13 7IU', with a space in the centre. However, earlier, in a scene where Guy Pierce, Teddy and Dodd are leaving the motel, Teddy's car backs into frame and we see the plate read 'SG137IU' straight across, with no spacing at all.

When Dodd's truck drives behind Guy Pierce's Jag, in the long shot that features one car behind the other, it is clear that the driver's-side window is down. When Dodd pulls up beside the car, the window is up.

Men in Black   In the scene where Zed sends Will Smith and Tommy Lee Jones out on Will Smith's first mission – Reggie's unauthorised departure from Manhattan – Tommy Lee Jones's legs cross and uncross from shot to shot.

🎥 **Men in Black II** When J is in the fight scene with Jarra and his clones, J jumps over two clones to get to Big Jarra, but when the camera angle changes, the Jarra clone he jumped on is gone.

At the beginning of the movie when Serleena first lands on Earth, her ship crashes into the ground and creates a mound of dirt. When the dog, Harvey, comes over to check it out, the mound is gone.

When Serleena is holding K up with her tentacles, you can see the tentacles coming out of her fingers; when they show her up close, there's at most just the one tentacle coming out of them.

When MIB agents exit the lift to get into the main hall of the MIB Office, the lift opens halfway up the wall and they need to go down a little platform. But when K and J return during the lockdown and face the rubbish bin with guns, the lift opens at floor level – so it can be conveniently peppered with bullets.

🎥 **The Mexican** Throughout the film there is a statue on the dashboard of Brad Pitt's rental car, along with a string of rosary beads hanging from the rear-view mirror; both these items disappear a lot. This is most noticeable when Brad Pitt, Julia Roberts and James Gandolfini are driving together.

At the end of the movie, when Julia Roberts is boarding the plane to leave Mexico, she is the last one to enter the plane and the stewardess begins to close the door behind her. The next shot is of a moping Brad Pitt, but in the reflection of the glass he is standing behind, you can see an open door with people still boarding the same plane.

🎥 **Minority Report** When Tom Cruise is in his car and Pre-Crime finds him, the car gets locked down. So he simply kicks out a window against the direction of travel and climbs out of the car and on to the roof. The car then starts going vertically (without swivelling round), so in order to stand upright he stands on the window . . . which he kicked out just before.

Miss Congeniality   When one of the entrants finishes the flaming-baton twirling, the ends of the batons are (unsurprisingly) charred black. However, after hugging Sandra Bullock, they're unburned again.

Mission: Impossible   After retrieving the NOC list from Langley and escaping to London, Franz Krieger pulls the disc from his pocket and attempts to blackmail Ethan Hunt. Ethan responds by making another disc vanish in a feat of magic. Krieger, angry, storms from the room and chucks the disc he had into the wastepaper basket. It clearly breaks into several pieces. You can even see a chunk fly out of the basket, yet when Ethan pulls it once again from the basket, it's perfectly intact.

Mission: Impossible 2   The tyres on the motorcycles they're riding at the end keep changing from knobbly tires to road slicks, back and forth depending on what terrain they are on. Easiest to see when Ethan skids on the road to avoid the white van – clear shot of slick tyres – then about 30 seconds later they're on the dirt, he skids into the old car and you can easily see that he's got off-road tyres front and back.

During the chase at the end the registration plate on Ethan Hunt's bike changes between 'NI 89' and 'ND 69'.

Near the start of the car chase at the end, a white car loses a hub cap in extreme close-up, but when it wipes out completely and flips over a few seconds later all its hub caps are still on.

Ethan is chasing Nyah in his car in an early scene. He tries to fasten his seatbelt, and finally manages it. But later, sometimes he has his seatbelt on, and sometimes he doesn't.

In the shots after Ethan made the white smoke-like stuff, it shows the accident in the background shot of Ethan, but the next time, it's miraculously cleaned up.

When Nyah and Ethan are in the tub at the mansion, one shot shows Nyah with the heels of her feet up, then it switches to where they're facing the bottom of the tub.

Monsters, Inc. In the opening scene there is a toy train set on the rug on the floor. When the monster falls on to the jacks on the floor the train set has gone.

The Mummy When Evelyn is putting the book in its right place, near the beginning, and she drops the book as the ladder goes vertical, the book would clearly be on the floor. But when they show the whole view of the ladder and her, the book has disappeared.

Rick places Evie's clothes in her suitcase. Evie grabs them out and puts them on the bench in the background. Just after she slams the suitcase on Rick's hand she walks right in front of the bench, and the clothes are gone.

The Mummy Returns When Rick jumps over the fire to save Evie in the museum, her arms are tied together. The instant he hits the board and the camera is at another angle, her arms are free (it's about a five-frame shot, but very clear on slo-mo/freeze frame). Then, when she falls over his shoulder, they are bound again.

When Rick is trapped in the bathroom, he finds Jonathan underwater in a bathtub full of suds. As Jonathan climbs out of the tub, his body is, of course, covered in suds. However, when he and Rick jump out the window and start running away, his body is completely suds-free. We never see any bubbles flying off him or anything.

My Best Friend's Wedding Dermot Mulroney opens the door while Julia Roberts is leaning against it, and while she has a cigarette in her left hand. With no solid object to lean against she falls on to the floor of the room, and the cigarette is in her right hand.

When Julia Roberts goes into the office to type the e-mail, she grabs the copy of the letter from her pocket. She types it up but is distracted by the cleaner. She leans back and falls off the chair. When she gets up the ring box is now sitting on top of the letter she was typing up. In fact, she moves the ring so she can continue typing it up. At no time before she falls did the ring box ever appear on the piece of paper.

Mystery Men When the squad is making new costumes with the sphinx, and the Shoveller is talking to someone, the tape measure keeps changing places. First it's outside his collar, then it's inside it . . .

Never Been Kissed During the sex talk, when the kids are putting the condoms on the bananas, watch the curves of the bananas. They switch throughout the different scenes.

Ocean's Eleven According to Andy Garcia at the end of the movie, the word Belagio on the vault floor was made a few days before. Now, go back and look at the images when Mr Wash was showing the old man his briefcase through the monitor – at that time the word wasn't even there at all. Even when Qin was placing the explosive devices on the door and his team-mates were watching him through the monitor, the word wasn't written on the floor.

The car dealer has two pens in his coat pocket, then one, then two and then back to one.

When Rusty is teaching the actors to play poker early in the film, there's a scene when Rusty says, 'Shane, you've got three pairs . . . you can't have three pairs. You can't have six cards in a five-card game.' Look at Tofer's (the guy who wanted to pay Rusty by cheque) cards during this scene. He goes from having nothing in his hands and playing with his rings, to holding his cards up stiffly in front of him, to having the cards down flat on the table, to flipping the cards over from what appears to be an elevated position (not flat on the table).

Panic Room In the scene where Forest Whitaker finally drills the lock on the safe, he slides the magnetic drill press out of the way with the magnet still on – the camera even zooms in on the orange light that indicates that the magnet is on.

The Patriot During the battle of Cowpens, the French-general points out to Mel Gibson that the line is faltering. Gibson runs to stop the retreat. As he runs towards the camera, he holds his pistol by the barrel, to act as a hammer or a club; however, when he runs away from the camera, he holds it by the grip, as if to fire it. Watch how the gun is held in each different angle.

Mel Gibson's son, Heath Ledger, dies with his head facing straight up. The shot cuts to Mel Gibson and when Ledger is shown again, he is facing his father. If you look at the way his head is lying on the ground, you can see that he is looking straight up. Gibson touches him, but doesn't move him, so there's no reason for him to change position.

Payback In the scene where the Asian gang is ramming Mel Gibson with their car, when they hit him the windshield gets smashed. When they all get back in their car and drive off, the windshield is fine.

Pearl Harbor When Ben Affleck and Kate Beckinsale go to the *Queen Mary* and they are rising on the platform and kissing, one camera shot shows them rising but when they stop the camera does a close-up and you can see they are still at the red-painted waterline indicator. The next shot shows them above it again.

After Ben Affleck hits himself on the nose with the cork, Kate Beckinsale puts snow on it. She is then seen removing it, but when the camera angle changes, the snow is back on his nose.

Pretty Woman In the scene with Julia Roberts taking a bath, she is singing that song and the walkman is lying on the right side of the tub with the wires resting along the edge of the tub. When it flashes from Richard Gere back to Julia the walkman is in a different place and the wire from the headphones is in the water.

When Julia Roberts is standing at the elevator at the hotel after the polo match, trying to leave because she is mad at Richard Gere, the clothes she's holding change position depending on the shot.

Pulp Fiction   At the beginning of the film, when Brett is initially shot by both Jules and Vincent after Jules's Ezekiel speech, we see Jules's gun become empty on firing the last shot. However, on returning to the same scene at the end of the film, when Jules and Vincent shoot Brett the gun does not empty; in fact, Jules is able to repeatedly shoot the guy who comes out of the bathroom afterwards and the gun still isn't empty.

Early in the film, Vincent tells Jules, 'I don't watch television'. Later in the film, in order to explain the 'miracle of the misguided bullets', Jules mentions he was watching *Cops* on TV the other night.

Red Dragon   In the final shoot-out, Graham's gun appears to be a revolver. When he tells his wife to shoot Dolarhyde, the gun she picks up from beside her husband appears to be an automatic.

When the janitor goes back to mopping after returning the letter written to Hannibal to his cell, he stuffs the rubber glove into his back pocket. When it is first shown, there is one finger sticking out but, when Hannibal notices it, there are two.

In the scene near the end where Graham and his son are trapped in the bedroom, the Red Dragon attempts to break down the door. After many forceful attempts, parts of the doorjamb and moulding break away and stick out from the wall. However, when Mrs Graham enters the room after the shoot-out, the doorjamb and moulding are in perfect condition.

📽 **Reservoir Dogs**   During the opening scene, Mr Blue's cigar goes from long to short and lit to unlit.

In the scene where Mr Blonde is pouring gasoline over the cop, the cop's legs are flying around trying to kick him. Later, we see that the cop's legs are still taped to the chair.

When Mr Pink is running away from the cops, he gets hit by a car, gets up, pulls the woman out from the car, opens the door and leaves the diamonds on the floor to shoot the cops. He then runs out of bullets, gets in the car and drives away. He never picks up the diamonds and puts them in the car, but he has them later.

📽 **Road Trip**   When we first see the padded envelope, Josh has put three stamps on it, spaced out. Then, when he finally retrieves it, there are eight stamps. Admittedly his friend might have replaced them with the correct postage, unlikely though it is, but unforgivably, the address is completely different – most noticeable is the middle line. The first time it's '5893 Tyler' and the second time it's '695 University Dr.' The sender's address also changes from 'Columbus St.' to '549 Campus Drive'.

Two obvious times the bus has a front number plate (clearly visible on the front bumper), then soon afterwards it disappears.

📽 **Robin Hood: Prince of Thieves**   When Robin is challenged by John Little after attempting to cross the river, watch John's staff. The scene cuts between shots from in front of and behind John. All shots from in front show him leaning closely on the staff; all shots from behind show him holding it to the side and not leaning on it.

At the start, Azeem is tied up in the prison and at one point, when he asks the Christian to free him, his hands are tied at the wrists, then they are apart and tied to the wall, and then back to his wrist – all in three quick takes.

When Robin and Azeem are about to be launched in the catapult, look at Azeem's sword. When he first gets in, the blade is facing down. It then cuts to Will, then back to Azeem, whose sword is now facing blade up. Then they are launched and Azeem lands with the sword blade down again.

RoboCop   When Murphy and Lewis are chasing the villains in the beginning, one of the bad guys shoots the windshield of the cop car, leaving a hole and messing up the glass. Not even a second later, the windshield is fine.

When everyone's at the shooting range, and Lewis notices RoboCop for the first time, look at RoboCop's hand. We see a long shot of him firing his gun, but the second time he pulls the trigger the gun doesn't fire. The third time it works again.

When all the bad guys turn up at the steel mill to find RoboCop, they're walking along when RoboCop appears behind them on a higher level. He's already holding something reflective in his right hand, but when we cut to a close-up his hands are empty, and *then* he bends down to pick up a shiny bit of metal, which he throws to create a distraction.

The Rock   Nicolas Cage is chasing Sean Connery in the yellow Ferrari. The windshield breaks at least twice, but is perfect in the next shot.

During the Hummer chase scene, after the Hummer smashes into the truck with all the water jugs, you can see from a shot inside the Hummer that the windshield is cracked. For the rest of the chase, it isn't.

In the car chase scene, Connery is driving the stolen Hummer and he hits a meter maid truck, sending it flying into a telephone pole and blowing it up. They slow down the film a little here and show us this hit from several different angles including from above. When they slow down the film you can see that the Hummer is turned sideways in the impact, but in the next frame it drives off as if it had just tapped the meter truck and not slammed into it as shown.

When Nicolas Cage steals the motorcycle and is talking on the cell-phone, the camera shows a close-up. For a split second it shows the front tyre of the bike and, if you look closely, the tyre is not turning.

As the planes are flying towards Alcatraz, we see four of them bank towards the bridge, but five fly under it.

The Rocky Horror Picture Show   Near the beginning of the movie, in the 'wedding scene', when we first see the little cameraman his camera has an old-fashioned flash (a round metal dish with a flash-bulb inside). When he takes the wedding photo, the camera has a modern electronic flash on it.

When Brad draws the heart on the door, it's a different shape than in the close-up.

As Brad and Janet enter the ballroom at the beginning of 'The Time Warp', a red carpet runs from the throne at the opposite end of the room, down the steps and clear across the floor to the ballroom entrance. After the second verse, as Riff-Raff and Magenta dance across the floor, the carpet stops short at the bottom of the steps. The full-length carpet reappears and disappears several times during this number.

During the song 'Dammit Janet', as Brad presents the ring to Janet, her purse is behind her at the top of the church steps. A few seconds later, the purse has moved to the left of her feet.

During the sequence where Frank is waiting for the 'colour machine' to be lowered, watch his reflection in the monitor on the console where Riff-Raff is turning the crank. The reflection does not match Frank's gestures. For example, when the machine has been lowered and Frank has opened the spigots, the reflection shows him with his hands up in the air, waiting for the 'colour machine' to be lowered – which, of course, it already has been.

Saving Private Ryan Towards the end of the movie, Private Ryan tells the soldiers who came to save him that the last time he and his brothers were together was before they went off to boot camp. But in the pan shot of the interior of the farmhouse, you see a picture of all four brothers in their uniforms.

When Captain Miller is collecting Corporal Upham from the group of translators and map readers, Upham is so confused and clumsy that he knocks everything off the table on to the floor, e.g. typewriter and helmets. Told by Miller to leave everything except his helmet, he picks up a German one by mistake. When sent back to the table to get his own, everything has miraculously jumped off the floor back on to the table.

When they go to find Private Ryan there are eight of them. Then they go to a French town and the guy picks up the little girl and he gets killed. Then there are seven, right? Wrong. A few scenes later they show all eight of them marching on to the next town, only in a far away camera shot, so it's hard to see.

At the first battle scene, when the camera is up in the pill boxes looking down at the soldiers, there are hardly any wounded or dead or even live soldiers, but when the camera comes back down to ground level, there are clearly more soldiers. This happens a number of times.

When Daniel Jackson has been given the dog tags to search through he looks for a place to sit. In this scene you see a black box with two yellow boxes at either side in the background. In the next scene the yellow box on the left has magically jumped up on to the black box in order for Jackson to kick it off and sit on it.

Scary Movie In the scene where they hit the fisherman, they spin the car. Notice the yellow line; they are somewhat over it in one scene, then in the next the line is to the right of the car, not under it.

Scooby-Doo During the skateboard scene at the beginning of the movie, when Shaggy and Scooby are riding along the conveyor belt, Scooby grabs a hook and they both jump off the skateboard. The skateboard can be seen falling off the conveyor belt, but in the next scene it is on the conveyor belt and being crushed.

When the monsters all come out in the hotel at Spooky Island, Scooby hides under the table and Fred is standing in front of him. The camera angle then changes to a long shot, in which Scooby-Doo is not under the table, but when the camera cuts back, Scooby-Doo is still there as though he hadn't moved.

Scorpion King When The Rock is stabbed with the poison arrow it goes into the side of his thigh but, when he removes his bandage after the sorceress has healed him, he checks the front of his thigh just above his kneecap for the injury. A subsequent bandage is too far down as well.

Scream 3 When Sidney is talking to the killer in the police station, her phone has a Nokia sticker on the bottom of it. Later in the scene, it's gone.

Se7en Brad Pitt gets out of a bed with only a quilted mattress cover on it. He puts on his shirt and tie and walks back to the bed, which now has a sheet on it.

When they are in the car and it's raining heavily, you can see the pedestrians are *not* using umbrellas or wearing raincoats. It's also raining far harder on the left of the car than the right. In addition, Morgan

Freeman is turning the wheel to the right, and yet they're driving in a straight line.

Shanghai Noon   At the last part of the hanging scene when Roy falls into his casket, you can see that his hands aren't tied together when he falls in. But in the next shot, he's on his back with his hands still tied.

When Jackie Chan is fighting the bad guy at the top of the bell tower, the bad guy bends his sword very badly. When they fall to the bottom and the bad guy retrieves his sword, it is perfectly straight again.

The Shawshank Redemption   When Morgan Freeman is talking to Tim Robbins while throwing a ball, Freeman catches the ball twice without throwing it back.

The Shining   When Wendy goes to talk to Jack Nicholson for the first time, while he is working on his 'book', he rips the paper out of the typewriter upon her entrance. He then proceeds to yell at her and rips the paper into pieces. When she leaves, another piece of paper has magically appeared in the typewriter and is halfway through the page. He never replaced the paper while yelling at her.

When Jack Nicholson is breaking down the bathroom door he is cutting one panel but then, when he sticks his head through and says, 'Here's Johnny,' the other panel next to him is perfectly cut out, even though he didn't touch it.

In the scene at the beginning of the film, when Doc and Mr Halloran are eating ice cream, pay attention to Danny's hands – they move from folded in front of the ice cream bowl, to the back, and so on. They move about five times, each movement different.

Shrek In the scene where Donkey and Shrek are crossing the bridge to rescue the princess, Donkey trips and breaks a board. When we see him looking through the gap, there's a little bit of wood still attached. Then when he jumps round it's disappeared, but it reappears when he steps over the gap.

After one of Robin Hood's Merry Men shoots and misses Shrek with his bow and arrow (and then gets the snot knocked out of him by the princess), Shrek turns to join the princess. There is clearly nothing stuck in his ogre-backside. Yet, seconds later, she blurts out, 'There's an arrow in your butt!'

Smokey and the Bandit Sheriff Buford T Justice gets out of his car and leaves the door open. A few moments later we see a different shot of the car, with the door closed. Then a truck drives by and tears the car door off, which is open again.

Snatch In the scene where Boris goes to Vinnie and Sol's shop to get the briefcase, Boris puts in earplugs and then shoots Frankie. Then either Vinnie or Sol starts to talk to him and you see Boris remove his left earplug. They cut to Sol and Vinnie. When the camera cuts back to Boris, the earplug is still in his ear.

The Sound of Music In the scene where Maria is singing her way up to the front door of the Von Trapp home, the house has several large windows in front by the door. However, once inside in the grand hall, there are no windows by the door.

South Park: Bigger, Longer, & Uncut In the scene where Mr Mackey is conducting the class on not swearing, we never see Kenny in the scene. Then all of the sudden we see him in the musical number. Where was he before?

🎥 **Speed**   When Keanu Reeves and Jeff Bridges are pulling people out of the elevator there are two men offering to help the stubborn lady get out. Two seconds later there is only one man jumping to get out.

When Keanu Reeves tries to get on the bus on the highway, he hits the door window and breaks it with his elbow. Later, when he catches up with the bus and gets on from the moving car, the door window is intact. Several times later it is visible – no break. Then, when the bus is on the freeway, the glass is shown broken again, but in a different pattern.

When at the airport, the crooked zebra-patterned sign on the side of the bus disappears then reappears.

🎥 **Spider-Man**   In the final cemetery sequence, Peter and MJ square off for a little heart to heart; MJ touches his face tenderly with her black leather gloves. The camera intercuts between frontal views of both: in hers, her fingers are touching his ear lobe, in his, they are an inch below his ear lobe. In one quick cut of hers, the hand has disappeared completely then, in mid-sentence, as it cuts back to Peter, it's there again.

At the end when Spider-Man dumps the brick wall on the Green Goblin, the wall is seen to be neat (when it fell) but, when the Green Goblin sticks out his hand, the wall is completely destroyed.

In the scene just before the final fight between the Goblin and Spider-Man, Spider-Man gets knocked through a wall and smashes into another wall but, when he stands up and the bomb explodes in his face, there is no wall at his back.

When Osborn is on the table with the wires attached to his chest, they go from lying up on his chest to lying down on his chest. They continue to go back and forth throughout the rest of the scene.

🎥 **Spy Kids**   Lifejackets appear magically on the two kids when they emerge from the inside of the weird bubble ship. When they re-enter, they magically disappear. Likely, they simply didn't want the actors to be on a boat without lifejackets, but there could've been a more graceful way to do it.

Steel Magnolias After Shelby dies, her mother (Sally Field) goes to pick up Jack Jr. While he is running to her, in one scene he has a toy in his hand, the next he doesn't and when Sally Field picks him up, he has it again.

Superman When Superman is spinning the world backwards, the earth is spinning in the opposite direction to Superman's flying.

Superman II When Clark Kent reveals who he really is to Lois Lane, the lava in the lamp beside him goes from barely warmed up (hardly any bubbles) to flowing freely, with lots of bubbles, in the two seconds the camera's on Lois.

Swingers When Mike talks on the phone for the first time, there is an answering machine next to it. Then, when we see the phone system again, the answering machine is gone. Then Mike walks into the next room and when he walks back the whole phone system is gone.

When Mike is gambling and Trent is telling him to double-down, the camera focuses on his cards. His initial bet is $100 and to double-down will mean a $200 bet. Before he has decided to do this, the camera shows two chips, representing a $200 bet.

Swordfish In a chase scene with Hugh Jackman and Don Cheadle, they catch up with Jackman and slam him up against a black car. The car dents and gets dusty from the dirt on him. The camera cuts to Don Cheadle and then back to Jackman and, hey presto! the car behind him is undented and cleaned. Funny how repairs can happen within seconds.

Where Hugh Jackman drops his 'daughter' off at her mother's home, the headrest behind her is down. After she leaves, the cop jumps into the passenger seat and the headrest is up.

Hugh Jackman is thrown a package which apparently contains $100,000. However, when we see a quick shot of the bundle he was thrown, there are four lots of notes, each clearly labelled '$10,000'.

10 Things I Hate About You When Bianca takes Cameron to Kat's room, she opens the third drawer down. But when the camera angle changes, it's suddenly the second drawer that's open.

When she's talking to the guidance counsellor, in the close-ups we can see some stadium lighting outside the window over the counsellor's shoulder. In the wide shots it disappears, and is replaced by the sea. It's definitely the same window – the ornaments on the window sill are the same, the plant to the right is the same and there's a mark at the bottom left of the pane that stays constant. Obviously they put the light up for the stadium scene and forgot it would be in shot on some days and not on others.

The Terminator When the Terminator's stolen police car is shown up close in the parking structure, the motto on the left side of it reads 'To care and to protect'. After the car crashes, you can see the motto on the left side again, but this time it reads 'Dedicated to serve'.

The Terminator looks up Sarah Connor's address in the telephone book. The telephone book address has four digits, but he goes to a house that has five digits on it.

Kyle loads a shell into his shotgun then falls asleep and dreams of his past in the future. When he wakes up he pumps the shotgun, so the first shell should come out, but doesn't.

When the Terminator says 'I'll be back' and leaves the police station, he throws both the doors open. One of them falls back into place but the other one stays open, but when he drives his car through the window both doors are closed.

After Kyle saves Sarah Connor from the dance club and has her in the car she tries to get out. Kyle stops her by grabbing her. In one scene he's holding her by the back of her hair, and when it cuts back to him his hand is across her chest. It goes back and forth like that.

Early on in the film Kyle cuts the wooden handle of the shotgun with a saw, but then later on, when they are in the car park hiding from the cops, you can clearly see that the handle is back to its original size.

In the scene where the Terminator enters the police department and he bends over to say 'I'll be back', you can see through his shades and he has both of his eyes, despite cutting one out in an earlier scene.

In the second 'future flash-back' scene where Kyle battles the huge ground HK tank, he tries to disable it by throwing a grenade at it. We see the grenade go under the HK's right wheel tread yet, strangely, in the next shot the left wheel tread explodes before the right one does.

Terminator 2: Judgment Day When Arnie is riding the Harley, chasing young John Connor, John is down in the reservoir and Arnie is up on the ledge. As he approaches the end of the wall we can clearly see that it tapers to a point. In the very next scene, as he makes the jump, the point has all of a sudden become a squared-off edge. Obviously the jump would have been a disaster if the end of the wall was pointed.

When the truck lands after the jump, both windscreens fall out completely, very clearly. Then in all the subsequent shots we see the T-1000 driving with a damaged windscreen in front of him.

When Arnie arrives between the tractor-trailers, you can see a yellow sticker (i.e. 'Vehicle makes wide turns') on the back of the right-hand trailer when the sparking begins. When Arnie arrives in the bubble the screen flashes for a second, and the sticker is no longer there. Obviously they built two model trailers – one complete and one with the corner gone, and they forgot to recreate the sticker.

After Arnie exits the bar at the beginning, and takes the gun from the 'bar owner', he moves his arm down from the barrel. Next scene, his arm is back in the original position on the barrel.

The T-1000 punches his body through the window of a helicopter to get inside. An instant later, the hole in the windshield is gone.

In the scene where Sarah Connor shoots Dyson in his house, it pans back and forth from him to her. In each shot of Dyson in his living room, the magazines on the coffee table are scattered, then stacked, then scattered again.

If you watch carefully when the T-1000 has driven off the bridge in the truck, you can see the suspension and steering gear collapse and shift (severely) to the driver's left. A moment later, the alignment is perfect.

At the end of the film, when the T-1000 is trying to get Sarah to call to John, Arnie hits him from behind with the big metal pole. At this point the T-1000 turns round and gives Arnie a kick. The camera turns back to Arnie and he clearly loses his grip of the pole and it flies off screen. Back to the T-1000 and he still has the pole stuck in him; he pulls it out and beats Arnie with it.

In the scene where Arnie and John are at the pay phone and John takes the gun away from Arnie, when Arnie has the gun it is cocked, and when John takes it, it isn't. It goes back and forth a few times like that, scene to scene.

When the T-1000 drives his bike through the glass of the Cyberdyne Systems building to get on to the helicopter, the windshield falls off. When you see it drop to the ground, it's still attached to the bike.

When the T-1000 is chasing John, Sarah and Arnie out of the hospital, the licence plate on the cop car changes several times.

When John Connor and Arnie are at the payphone calling his step-mom, Arnie punches the phone and puts a massive dent in it and change comes out. If you look at the bottom of the phone before he punches it there is already a dent there (pan-and-scan version only).

Titanic   When Jack hands Rose the note at the dinner table, the paper is yellow. Later, when the note is read, the paper is white.

When Jack is handcuffed below deck you can see the waterline on the porthole. Then we're taken to where Kate's at for her dialogue. Then we get a cut to the outside of the ship with a water level view. The camera then dips into the water down to Jack's porthole, clearly underwater now by five to eight feet. Yet in various scenes after this point there appears a waterline on the porthole, sometimes there and then sometimes not.

Tomb Raider   After the fight, Lara Croft kneels down to get the pocket watch and we can clearly see that she doesn't have her pistols in her thigh holsters, having taken them out before the fight. The building then starts collapsing and she starts running for the exit. She doesn't stop to pick up her guns, but they magically appear back in their holsters.

In the scene when Lara is getting into her car, she has a headset-type microphone going down the side of her face. Yet when she gets into the car, the microphone is gone.

Tomorrow Never Dies   In the scene where the ship is being confronted by the Chinese MiGs and is attacked by the stealth boat, an alarm sounds on the ship and all the sailors in the mess hall leave and go to their battle stations. A few shots later, when the drill hits the ship and water rushes in, it shows three or four sailors in the mess hall getting hit by the rushing water.

In the scene where there is a car chase with the very nicely equipped BMW, you can clearly see before the chase that the car is equipped with five-star rims, but during the scene it shows the back left tyres having hubcaps instead of the five-star rims.

In the BMW chase scene the back window is clearly blown out; however, as the camera goes back on Bond it is intact, but is then handily missing as the rocket goes cleanly through moments later to blow up the bad guys' car.

When James Bond goes to the hotel to find Carver's wife, he parks quickly and runs off. The tyres are at an angle, but they are straight when the bad guys try to break in shortly afterwards.

Top Gun   When Maverick goes to land while Cougar is in fuel trouble, the tailhook is down. He decides Cougar needs help and launches back off the carrier – the tailhook is up. In the next view, as he flies away from the carrier, the tailhook is once again down.

In the bathroom, Charlie has a tube of lipstick, next cut it's gone.

Toy Story   In the beginning of the movie when Andy takes his baby sister out of the crib, he lowers the crib side to get her out. He does not put the side back up, but in the next shot the crib side is up.

Twister   During the scene when a cow blows by the truck, the truck is driving down an empty dirt road with water on both sides. During the shots of the occupants, the road behind the truck is paved, and in one of these rear shots a truck drives by in the opposite direction.

In the scene where the telephone pole falls on the truck, you see Dorothy get thrown off the bed and the tailgate gets broken off. A couple of scenes later, the tailgate is back and hanging there like it was untouched.

During a scene in the middle they drive the red Dodge solo into the hills to face a twister. As they bail out they find that they can't free the 'Dorothy' from the back of the truck, so they have to run for it. As they look back they watch power poles start blowing up. Finally, the one next to the truck goes and falls across the bed of the truck, smashing Dorothy on to the roadway and spilling the sensors. As they come back to the truck, because the twister has disappeared, they realise the twister is 'jumping' and pile into the truck for their escape. The power pole is no longer resting across the truck and there is no damage to the bed.

During the big falling debris scene, Bill Paxton and Helen Hunt are in the red truck. The truck hits a tractor. The impact damages the windshield and it is clearly broken, but a second later the windshield is perfect and untouched.

When Helen Hunt, Bill Paxton and Melissa are in his car, they see Jonas wave from *his* car. Just before this had happened, Jonas looked in his rear-view mirror. He only saw a red car with a background of a paved street. Where is the rest of the crew?

In the scene where Helen Hunt's truck is lifted by the first tornado they encounter, it is dropped on the road in front of the red Dodge driven by Bill Paxton's fiancée. When we see the truck drop, the driver's window is closed. As the Dodge swerves to avoid hitting the other truck, the window is now open. And finally, in the last shot where everyone is running to her aid, the window is closed again.

🎥 **Unbreakable**   In the final scene of Samuel L. Jackson's office when we see Jackson wheel himself down the last ramp towards his desk, three computer towers sit below the desk – two off to the left side and one off to the right, with space between to wheel his chair up underneath. After the scene cuts to Bruce Willis and then back to Jackson, the two towers on the left have been moved closer to the one on the right.

Vertical Limit   The boiling nitroglycerine in the shed, on the floor and around the boot is bubbling in different places depending on the shot.

When Kareem is praying halfway up the mountain, we can see that his prayer mat is covered in snow from the shot on the left. It then cuts back to the right side, when the Australian is trying to talk, and all the snow has somehow disappeared.

Wayne's World   During the first *Wayne's World* show in the movie they bring out a guy with a haircutting machine. The man sits down next to Garth, with the hose in front of Garth. The camera angle changes and the hose is now behind Garth.

What Women Want   When Helen Hunt first gives Mel Gibson a tour of her new apartment, she shows him the bedroom, where you can clearly see brown paper taped on the floor where the head of her bed would be. While they are dancing, there is no paper there.

Bette Midler lights up a joint and then goes to sit next to Mel Gibson. She has the joint when she sits down, but in the next shot she's gesturing with her hands and the joint is gone.

When Harry Met Sally   During the first car ride scene Harry is spitting the seeds out the window. One of the shots shown of the car from the outside shows the window still up after he has rolled it down.

Also on the trip, there's a conversation scene in the car in which the camera flips back and forth from Harry to Sally as they chat/argue/flirt. Although the action/dialogue (and therefore the movement of the car) is continuous, the lock button on the driver's-side door alternates between up and down with almost every camera cut.

William Shakespeare's Romeo + Juliet Juliet's position changes when she is lying down after taking the poison – her arm goes from over to under the cover.

The Wizard of Oz When Dorothy first meets the Scarecrow, sometimes the top of his head is above the pole he's attached to, other times it's below it.

During the scene where the Tin Man begins chopping down the door to save Dorothy there are no handles, but when he continues chopping the handles appear.

X-Men When Wolverine stops his truck to check out the funny noise, there are no tracks in the snow behind his car, but when he begins to leave after ditching Rogue, the tracks are back.

In the beach scene when Senator Kelly is watching the news at the hot dog stand, we can see a big chain behind it; the next shot shows Kelly taking some clothes that were hanging on the chain; those clothes were not there in the previous shot.

In the scene where Wolverine gets thrown on to the hood of the truck by Sabretooth, one scene shows him lying on the hood, the next shot shows him halfway in the windshield and then he is back on the hood again.

When Sabretooth kills the harbour patrol guard he throws the guard down right next to him and looks at him for a few seconds. You then get a shot of Sabretooth taken from the water and this gives you a large area around Sabretooth to see. Sabretooth begins to walk off and the dead guard is no longer there, even though no attempts to move the guard out of sight were made. Where did the guard go?

During the final scene with Xavier and Magneto playing chess, there is a pawn missing from the board after Xavier leaves and Magneto pushes over his king.

The chain that Mystique wraps around Wolverine's wrists during their fight scene near the end of the movie mysteriously disappears shortly after that moment.

xXx When Xander steals the Corvette, he breaks one of the side view mirrors – on the following shot it can quickly be seen that, though one mirror is broken, the other is not. When Xander starts talking, however, both mirrors are broken.

You Only Live Twice While James Bond prepares 'Little Nellie' for flight, a Japanese technician removes the red rotor tether from the front of the autogyro. In the next shot, while Bond is putting his flying helmet on, the tether is still attached to the rotor.

You've Got Mail When Tom Hanks is at the street fair with Annabelle and Matt, the colour of the ring he gives Annabelle to throw is different from the colour of the one that lands on the pole.

When Meg Ryan is waiting at Lalo, she puts the rose inside her book to stop it falling off the table. She then sees Tom Hanks come in, and when the camera cuts back to her, the rose has jumped on top of the book again.

NOW THAT WAS JUST PLAIN BAD

To refer to bad acting might be slightly harsh, but... no, actually it's entirely fair – this section is indeed about bad acting. Actors and actresses don't always stay true to the spirit of the scene, or do exactly what they should. Fortunately there aren't too many examples of these, demonstrating the normally outstanding quality of acting in multi-million-dollar films.

Austin Powers: International Man of Mystery   In the scene near the beginning when Austin is walking around naked and Vanessa is holding a magnifying glass, she is concentrating very hard on watching the monitor off the screen.

Big   Josh as a boy types in MEET WIZARD in his computer game. He does not hit the enter key, which is needed for the instruction to be accepted. He then replies to the question WHAT DO YOU WANT TO MEET HIM WITH ? You can see him typing, but watch his right hand, he just hits the same keyboard key over and over again.

Entrapment   When Catherine Zeta-Jones practises with the bells and strings maze, she is careful to lift her left leg over one of the first strings, then brings her body through, and then brings her right leg over the string. Too bad when she does the heist of the mask for real – she lifts her left leg over the unseen laser beam but keeps her arms dangling as she brings her right leg over. This would have set off the alarm because she forgot to lift her arms over the laser beam!

Me, Myself & Irene   After Jim Carrey gets his thumb shot off by Dickey near the end, in most of the shots you can easily see that he is bending his thumb behind the rest of his hand instead of computer graphics removing it.

Mission: Impossible When Ethan Hunt is hanging in the room, trying to get the NOC list, the guy that is supposed to be working in there comes back and sits down, and just before he pukes his brains out his eyes look straight up towards Ethan.

North by Northwest In the shooting scene in the Mount Rushmore cafe, a boy in the background puts his fingers in his ears, because he knows the gun is about to be shot.

The Patriot After ambushing the British to save his son, Mel Gibson surveys the carnage, and the scene ends with a silhouette of Mel walking off and the scene of dead men and a wagon with a dead soldier on it. As the scene fades, the 'dead' soldier lifts his head up.

10 Things I Hate About You In the scene where the kids are firing arrows and the coach gets hit by one, they send a girl to call 911. If you look closely and follow her in the background, after she runs a few yards she slows down and stops, turning back to look at what's going on (obviously thinking she's out of shot).

WE CAN SEE YOU

Let's face it, there's always a lot happening on a film set, with people scurrying around, using the equipment and making the effects go bang at appropriate moments. Unfortunately, every so often someone pops up on screen when they really shouldn't, and it's not always behind-the-scenes crew – even cast members can be seen when they shouldn't.

Animal House   When John Belushi is putting food on his tray, look at the very top of the reflective counter – you can see the cameraman's feet as he moves along the line.

Austin Powers: The Spy Who Shagged Me   When Mini-Me is first introduced and is sitting with Dr Evil, stroking Mini Mr Bigglesworth, you can clearly see he hands it to someone barely below the table line instead of all the way to the ground.

Batman   When the Batmobile is driving itself to Batman and Vicki Vale, you can clearly see a hand turning the steering wheel.

Blade Runner   As Deckard stalks Batty in the building at the end, you see him walk through a room and, briefly, the shadow of two crew members (one is the director Ridley Scott) skims across the wall.

Chasing Amy   The cameraman is visible in the reflection of the window while Ben Affleck is walking back to his car in the rain.

Dazed and Confused   During the grab-and-go stop, Pickford, Don, Pink and Mitch are in the GTO. Pickford is the first to climb out of the car. If you look closely you can see the crew in the reflection of the door. This happens not once but twice, the second time when Don and Mitch return with the beer.

Dirty Dancing   After Patrick Swayze leaves, they show Jennifer Grey standing on the porch of her family's cabin. If you look in the background you see two people waiting for their cue before they start walking.

Fatal Attraction   In the library, right after Michael Douglas breaks into Glenn Close's apartment, a cameraman's reflection is visible in a window as a librarian pushes a cart past it.

Full Metal Jacket   When Cowboy, Joker, Rafterman and the other soldiers are running across the buildings to get to Animal in the final sniper scene, watch the foreground. If you freeze the movie just as they reach Animal, you can see they run by a boom mike and a crew member. A bicycle is also there (just to help you out).

Gladiator   The morning after the battle with the Germans, Maximus is walking in the army camp and he feeds a horse a piece of apple. If you look closely between Maximus and the horse, there is a crewman wearing a pair of blue jeans.

During the scene where Maximus throws the sword into the crowd and yells 'Are you not entertained?' the camera pans round and in the crowd, for a split second, you can see a cameraman in jeans and a shirt standing next to a camera. This is visible on the big screen but hard to see on video, unless you see it on DVD and can zoom in.

Hannibal   As Pazzi arrives at the library in order to visit Hannibal and pick up some suitcases, watch the right of the screen. There's a group of monks there who are clearly waiting for their cue to start walking down some steps — as they appear in the shot they start moving.

Harry Potter and the Chamber of Secrets   When Harry is writing to Tom Riddle through the diary there is a close-up of Harry's face and, in the reflection of his glasses, you can see the cameraman and a woman standing next to him and they are moving around.

🎥 **Jurassic Park**   Watch carefully the scene where the Raptors enter the kitchen (that angle where you can see almost the whole kitchen while Raptors are coming in from the far away door). As the first Raptor enters the kitchen, you can see someone grabbing its tail to hold the puppet-thing steady.

🎥 **The Lost World: Jurassic Park**   When Jeff Goldblum is talking to Richard Attenborough in the bedroom you can see a mirror. After Attenborough tells him about the project, the camera moves to the bed and there is a reflection of blue jeans, probably the cameraman's.

🎥 **The Man with the Golden Gun**   When James Bond is in the bathroom with Andrea Anders, there are some circular mirrors on the wall. When Andrea tells Bond to hand her a towel and he walks towards her, you can see one of the crew's head in one of the mirrors.

🎥 **The Matrix**   In the scene where Neo is at the office, while in his cubicle he gets an express delivery. As he signs for it you can see another arm lying on the desk behind him. In the next scene he hands back the clipboard and you see it is only him and the delivery man. (This one's only visible on the non-widescreen video).

🎥 **Mission: Impossible 2**   When Ethan Hunt is receiving his mission, you can clearly see the cameraman in Ethan's sunglasses.

🎥 **The Mummy**   When Rick, Jonathan, Winston and the Americans are sitting at the bar in Fort Brydon (after Winston's introduction), you can see the hand of a crew member looking at his watch on the very left side of the screen. It's very quick, so look closely.

The Mummy Returns   When Ardeth, Rick and Evie arrive at the first city where Imhotep took their son, Evie is walking through the hall where she had the vision of fighting with Anck Su Namun in her previous life. As she's walking past/behind a column, you can see someone's head and shoulder poking out from the right side of the column.

A Nightmare on Elm Street   Near the beginning, during Tina's first dream, Tina gets cornered in front of one of the furnaces. She steps forward and Freddy jumps out from behind her and scares her. When she steps forward, Freddy (who is trying to lean down out of the shot) is seen stepping sideways to position himself to scare Tina.

North by Northwest   When Cary Grant and his film-mother enter the elevator at the Plaza this is filmed through a glass door, and you can see the reflection of a crew member in a white shirt who is crouching below or next to the camera.

Ocean's Eleven   In the scene where the Chinese acrobat is actually climbing out of the movable money safe in the casino vault, you can actually see someone behind the movable safe helping the acrobat out. As the camera angle changes, at the left side, behind the safes, you can see the person's foot or back – it's black in colour.

Reservoir Dogs   The camera crew can be seen reflected in the store windows as Mr Pink is running from the cops.

Road Trip   In the scene when Josh and Tiffany go into her dorm after the mail room scene, Josh goes to close the door and a mysterious hand catches the door from the outside and closes it for him.

Scream 2   When Sarah Michelle Gellar is thrown off the balcony you see the stunt co-ordinator (I would imagine that's who it is) pop his head up at the very bottom right-hand corner of the screen.

Speed   When Jack and Harry are bursting on to the roof, you can see another trooper behind Harry. Harry and Jack should be the only ones up there as everyone else had a job to do and only they went to the roof. After this, the third guy is never seen again.

Superman   When Clark Kent and Lois Lane are leaving the *Daily Planet*, Clark gets stuck in the revolving door. Look closely at the door – you can see a member of the crew reflected in it.

The Terminator   In the scene where Sarah and Kyle run into the factory, the Terminator is breaking through the armour-plated door. As the Terminator comes through you can clearly see the two operator guys crouching behind the model.

In the scene where the 'naked' Terminator rises from the ashes of the tanker truck, you can see a stagehand in the background reach up and pull down a hydraulic lever that makes the robot stand up.

Terminator 2: Judgment Day   When Arnie is trying to save John Connor from the T-1000 in the truck, he makes the jump. Look at his face and hair while he's airborne, you can clearly see it's a stunt double.

Where the car is driving fast in reverse to escape from the mental hospital, the stunt driver's head is clearly visible sticking up from inside the trunk – he's driving the car from the back.

Titanic   In the scene where Jack enters the first-class door for the first time in his tux, if you look closely in the glass door you can see a cameraman behind him.

xXx   When Xander and Yelena are in the restaurant and they are shown through the window from outside you can see the reflection of a film crew member in the window.

THE AMAZING CHANGING WARDROBE

This is no doubt the major bane of film-makers everywhere. Multiple takes and lots of movement mean that clothes, and hairstyles in particular, can change at any time. Now of course not every little thing really matters, but when jackets disappear and hair's flying all over the place, someone's going to notice . . .

Aladdin   The tiger bites the seat off the suitor's trousers, allowing the viewer to see his polka-heart boxers. When we see the tiger in the courtyard, he has a part of the same boxer shorts in his mouth. So if he bit off the seat of the trousers, shouldn't he have purple cloth in his mouth?

American Beauty   Near the end of the film, Kevin Spacey has removed Angela's trousers; in the next scene, they mysteriously reappear just below her knees.

American History X   In the first basketball game in Venice Beach, Edward Furlong leans on a fence and his school bag's strap slips off his shoulder. In the next shot, the strap is back up on his shoulder. Yet he had no time to fix it.

AntiTrust   When Ryan Phillippe suspects his girlfriend is trying to poison him at dinner he tests his reaction to the food on a cut he makes on his wrist, pulling his sleeve up to the elbow. When she walks back into the room he pulls his sleeve back down to hide it. Then when he makes a toast the sleeve has magically jumped back up again.

Army of Darkness   Ash's hairstyle varies throughout the film. The scene where he gets the *Necronomicon* is the most obvious because in that scene he has very bushy hair.

Austin Powers in Goldmember In the first two Austin Powers movies, Dr Evil has brown eyes. In *Goldmember* he has blue eyes.

Austin Powers: International Man of Mystery When Alotta Fagina is changing, her hair is down, but as soon as she opens the door, her hair is twisted and pinned back in a complicated way – she couldn't have done it that quickly.

When Austin and Mrs Kensington are at the Swinger's Club and the waitress gets punched in the face her hat falls off. In the next shot he/she is still wearing it.

In the scene in the toilet, we clearly see that Austin's trousers are pulled down in one shot, but then when he's drowning the Irish guy, they are suddenly pulled up again.

Austin Powers: The Spy Who Shagged Me In the final scene with Dr Evil, he is giving Mini-Me a 'little prick', but, if you look closely, Mini-Me hasn't got his trousers down and he is bent over. When he stands back up he can clearly be seen to pull his trousers back up, which were never actually down.

Batman The young Jack Napier in the flashback has blue eyes; Jack Nicholson's are brown.

At the beginning of the movie when the police are standing outside Axis Chemicals, Eckhardt has very distinct facial hair. In the next shot, when they are inside the plant, he is clean shaven.

Batman Returns Towards the end, Batman is talking to Catwoman about sparing Max Shrek's life. He has his mask on, and his eyes are blacked out to add to the intimidating effect. However, just before he takes the mask off, there's suddenly no make-up around his eyes, so when we see his face, he doesn't have the panda eyes that he should have.

In one scene Catwoman is doing cartwheels through a store. She starts out in boots with high heels, but mid-air you see she has no heels on, then when she lands, she is in heels again.

Beetlejuice When Otho is going through the house suggesting changes he is wearing white sneakers in one room and red ones in the next.

Beverly Hills Cop II The construction worker Axel talks to at the beginning yanks off his hat, but it jumps back to his head a second later.

The sunglasses on the guard at the warehouse at the film's end disappear and reappear when Axel beats him up.

Blade Blade is in the room where the 'Vampire's bible' is and gets captured and stabbed by the vamp and starts to laugh. Blade is meant to have an ear-piece in his ear but there isn't one. In the next shot there's an ear-piece big enough to have seen it in the previous shot.

Blade II Towards the end Blade is strapped to a table and has spikes run through his wrists and thighs. Later he regenerates himself in blood and the wounds are healed. Fine, but there are numerous times after that (e.g. the fight with Nomak) when there are no holes in his trousers from the spikes in his thighs.

In the scene where they first encounter the Reapers in the rave (right after Reinhardt has shot the Reaper with the shotgun) Snowman is confronted by a Reaper wearing sunglasses. The camera goes back to Snowman then back to the Reaper who now does not have the sunglasses.

Blade Runner In the scene where the female replicant is shot and goes through the windows, her shoes change from high heels to flat from shot to shot.

The Blues Brothers   When Jake and Elwood talk with the record executive backstage, they are alternately dripping with sweat and not.

As Jake and Elwood stand up after the rocket shooting, their shoulders are clean. When they go upstairs in the next shot, stone debris falls off their shoulders.

The Bourne Identity   In the beginning of the film, Bourne is rescued by a fishing vessel. He is taken on board and examined. As Bourne's wet suit is cut away, there are two bloody bullet holes in his back – but no holes on the wet suit.

In the part of the embassy scene where Jason Bourne starts hitting security people, the marine's hat falls off no fewer than three times.

Braveheart   In the scene where Wallace first meets the future queen and is left alone with her in the tent, the wimple she is wearing appears to have a life of its own – first it's on her chin, then over her chin, and then under her chin.

During the scene in which Steven (the crazy Irishman) joins up with William Wallace and they converse about killing Englishmen and such, pay attention to Steven's forehead. It's very obvious that the scene was composed of multiple takes because of the way that Steven's hair changes repeatedly throughout the scene. There are a couple of locks of hair that go from being stuck across the middle of his forehead to being off to the side with the rest of his hair.

Bridget Jones's Diary   After Mark Darcy and Daniel Cleaver fight in the street and Bridget goes to comfort Cleaver, Darcy flings his jacket over his shoulder as he walks off. You can see very clearly the white lining of the sleeve, flapping around as he walks. When the camera cuts to his receding back, the jacket is perfectly flat and smooth down his back, and the lining is nowhere to be seen.

THE AMAZING CHANGING WARDROBE

🎥 **Can't Hardly Wait**   When Seth Green first walks into the bathroom he takes his coat off, but in the very next shot he still has it on.

🎥 **Casablanca**   In the famous train scene where Ingrid Bergman stands up Humphrey Bogart, his coat is soaking wet. He gets on the train after receiving his 'Dear John' note and his coat suddenly looks amazingly dry.

🎥 **Catch Me If You Can**   When Frank Jr is getting fitted for his pilot's uniform (because he lied and said he lost his other one), after the tailor finishes and tells him the cost, there are only two rank bars on his sleeves. Then, when he walks out in the uniform, there are three bars on the sleeves.

🎥 **Cats & Dogs**   In the scene after the soccer tryouts, Jeff Goldblum comes out of his lab with a bunch of wires all over him and a mask on. When the camera shows an outside view and you can see the parents' shadows on the curtain, you can see that Jeff has no wires on him, and no mask.

🎥 **Charlie's Angels**   Lucy Liu is climbing up to the castle with a rucksack. The next time we see her, a bow and arrow is suddenly sticking out of it.

🎥 **Chicago**   In the scene in which Roxie shoots her lover, he looks into her mirror while putting on his tie. He ties it, then puts down his collar. He turns away from the mirror and there's a shot of his back. His collar is up again.

Near the end of the film, after Roxie's audition, Velma is pitching her act again when Roxie puts on her coat and buttons it. The camera cuts back to Velma then when it's back on Roxie her coat is unbuttoned. Seconds later she is walking through a door and her coat is buttoned again.

When Velma is telling Roxie to keep her paws off her laundry, Velma's top keeps switching from straight to crooked.

Chicken Run   When Rocky's standing in the hut, he's clearly got no rucksack on – no strap over his shoulder or anything. Still nothing when he leans in and says, 'I was born to answer that call', but the second he dives out the door, and afterwards, he's suddenly got a rucksack on.

Clear and Present Danger   At the end, when Jack Ryan is arguing with the president, his 'A' tag switches from being over the lapel of his jacket to under it, without him moving.

Clerks   The length of Dante's beard changes throughout the movie.

Close Encounters of the Third Kind   At the end of the film, when those people dressed in red leave the 'church' on their way to the spaceship, watch the blonde woman just in front of Richard Dreyfus. She is not wearing any sunglasses, but after a shot of a walking Dreyfus you see the group walking again, and now she's wearing sunglasses, just like the rest of the group.

Clue   When everyone is searching upstairs and the lights go out, they all come running down. Yvette has on flat black shoes, but right after the running shot is over she is back in heels.

Clueless   After coming home from the party, Josh and Cher are talking while watching *Ren & Stimpy*. Cher's combing her hair and, before she has a chance to put any clips in her hair, she picks up the phone and a red clip magically appears.

When Cher and Josh are sitting on the stairs near the end, Cher's hair is loose. The angle changes, and suddenly it's neatly pushed back.

Cocktail   Tom Cruise's hair changes from long to short to long to short in some of the early scenes.

Con Air   When Duncan Malloy's car comes crashing to the ground, not only do John Cusack's arms rapidly change position, but also his sunglasses seem to jump rapidly on to, and off, his face.

Pinball is fighting the female guard on the plane and they are struggling. From one angle her hat has fallen off and from another angle she is still wearing it. It jumps between scenes like this with her hat being on and off.

Crossroads   Throughout the scene when the three girls are in the bathroom, Mimi has a pink toothbrush that keeps disappearing and reappearing from behind her ear.

The Crow   When Sarah is sitting at the hot-dog stand near the beginning of the movie, her hood changes from being up to down without her touching it.

Dante's Peak   The motel clerk has an on and off problem with his glasses when registering Pierce Brosnan. When seen full face, his glasses are in his shirt pocket, yet when seen from the back, he has his glasses on.

Daredevil   In the scene where Elektra is battling Bullseye there is a shot, right after Bullseye stabs Elektra with her own sai, where the sai is poking through her back making her top stick out. From another angle, just before he pulls the sai out, her top is perfectly flat.

In one of the last scenes, Matt Murdock is talking to his friend in a coffee shop. A woman walks through the door and Ben decides to leave to take a walk. He grabs his jacket from the chair. However, when he's walking, he is not carrying or wearing the coat. Where did it go?

Dazed and Confused   When Pink and Don are driving around at night in the orange car and throwing trash cans at mailboxes, there is an obvious mistake. First, Don throws a trash can and then encourages Pink to throw one. When it is Pink's turn to throw, it shows a rear view of the car and an arm reaches out to pick up the trash can. It should be Pink's arm, but, as you can tell by the green shirt with the rolled-up sleeves, it's actually Don's arm.

Deep Blue Sea   In a scene near the end of the movie, Carter is swimming back to the wet lab through flooded passageways. At the beginning of the swim his left shoe is completely untied – you can see both laces floating. In the next full-body shot (where his shoes show) the shoe is tied again.

Dirty Dancing   In the last dance scene of the movie, Patrick Swayze jumps down from the stage and the hair on his forehead, which was completely dry, is suddenly very wet and plastered to his head.

In the scene where Jennifer Grey and Billy first walk into the staff dance, watch the guy that is with the girl with the black shirt (that is hanging off on one side) – his shirt keeps going from on to off. When you see him in the background it is on, and when you see him close up it is off.

In the scene where Patrick Swayze is fighting Robbie, his belt breaks and is hanging down. Next shot it is fastened again. And then it is hanging down again.

Dogma   During Ben Affleck's 'Prepare to taste God's wrath' diatribe, you can clearly see the seam along the front of his shirt that he uses to tear his shirt open to reveal his armour. This seam is not seen at any other point in the movie.

Look carefully when they transport to the Mexican restaurant. Linda Fiorentino's nightdress is unbuttoned at the top but mysteriously closes in a matter of seconds.

After Jay and Silent Bob break Linda Fiorentino's car, angrily she leaves the car shouting 'Nobody is f***ing me.' Depending on what the camera angle is during that scene, the hair device used to hold her hair back is different.

Dr. No   When James Bond is waiting in a house, he grabs a pack of cards, sits down and screws a silencer on to his gun. Pay attention to his shirt – in the full-length shot he's wearing a tie, but when we see a close-up of the gun, his tie disappears.

Empire Records   There is a scene where everyone is dancing. It's towards the end but not at the very end. One of the employees of the record store takes his shirt off. Then the camera cuts back and you see the entire group of people dancing. You'll notice that he has his shirt back on. Then a couple of shots later he has it back off again.

When Eddie comes in to actually work, he comes into the back room, takes off his pizza shirt and puts on a button-down shirt that is already buttoned. Then he asks where 'Sexy Rexy' is and his shirt is unbuttoned. Then, after Debra says 'Better question, where's Gina?' his shirt is buttoned again.

In the scene where AJ tries to tell Liv Tyler how he feels about her and she is distraught over her episode with Rex, she puts her sweater on and her hair remains under the sweater. Then you see her hair out of the sweater, and then back in again.

Eraser   Arnie goes to the gay bar to solicit the help of the guy he saved at the beginning of the movie. The guy is wearing a white shirt and a black vest. During their conversation he takes off the vest, then the scene shifts to another bartender. When it comes back the guy has the vest on; another shot and the vest is off again.

🎥 **Erin Brockovich** When Ed Masry is taking his tie off in one part of the movie, he loosens it, then they cut to Erin, then back to Ed, and his tie is back to tight around his neck, and he's taking something out of his breast pocket. Then they cut back, and his tie is off.

🎥 **Evolution** At the beginning, when Seann William Scott is running from the meteor, he jumps to the ground with no jacket on, but when they show the wide view of the crater, he has the jacket on.

During the scene in the mall when the girl is in the dressing room, she keeps putting on more layers of clothing. But as they are shooting different shots she will have a hot-pink shirt on, then it is back on the hanger, and then back on again. It switches back and forth many times.

🎥 **Exit Wounds** DMX changes from a sweat suit into a shiny crimson suit and leaves his apartment only to come back in the same sweat suit.

🎥 **The Faculty** In the scene where Elijah Wood is walking up to the school, after his father drove him there, we see that his bag strap is backwards. Then they cut to the car and then back to Wood, and all of a sudden his bag strap is turned the right way. The next cut is when Robert Patrick and Casey's father look at him, and then Elijah Wood starts to walk up to the school again and his bag strap is turned backwards again.

🎥 **Father of the Bride** In the scene where Martin Short is looking at the house to see the changes for the wedding and they are talking about the menu, Annie starts with her hair in a ponytail, then for a split second her hair is half-up in a barrette and then it's back to a pony-tail (or vice versa).

When Steve Martin is going berserk in the grocery store he is wearing black socks. In the next scene, in the jail cell, he's wearing white socks.

🎥 **Ferris Bueller's Day Off**   When Jeanie meets Charlie Sheen at the police station his hair changes after every cut from her to him.

In the scene where Ferris is doing his dancing thingy to 'Twist and Shout' there is a cop wearing a blue jacket, and then he's not wearing it in the next scene.

When Mr Rooney goes to Ferris's house he is wearing a long-sleeved shirt and coat jacket. A shot of his arm ringing the doorbell shows a bare arm with dark hair. When they return back to a shot of Mr Rooney, his sleeve is touching his wrist and he does not have dark hair on the back of his hand.

🎥 **A Few Good Men**   During the trial at the end, Jack Nicholson struggles with Tom Cruise. After the struggle, his tie is all out of place, and its position varies between shots.

🎥 **Final Destination**   When Alex is talking to Clear in her garage, one strand of her hair keeps changing, first curled under, and then straight, back and forth.

🎥 **First Knight**   When Guinevere is about to meet Arthur for the first time, her hair is down when she's in the carriage and when she steps down to the ground. However, in the next shot of her walking forward, her hair is up.

🎥 **Forrest Gump**   In the scene where Jenny is supposed to be playing the guitar and singing nude in the club, you can see the nude-coloured thong she is wearing when they show her from the back.

🎥 **The Fugitive**   A couple of minutes into the film, at the bus accident bit, Richard Kimble is handcuffed. On the parts where the bus is falling, you can see that he has no handcuffs on, but then, when he asks the driver to uncuff him, he has them back on again.

🎥 **Full Metal Jacket**   Pvt Pyle is on the rifle range with Gunnery Sergeant Hartman right behind him. When filmed from Pyle's right side, he is wearing a white wrist-wrap/brace, but the shot moves behind him and it is gone. Back to the right side and it reappears.

🎥 **Ghostbusters**   The Stay Puft Marshmallow guy has a red bow tie on as he walks down the streets of NYC, then he doesn't, then he does.

🎥 **Gladiator**   When Commodus tells his nephew Lucius about Roman history, the hairdo of Lucius changes a few times during the scene.

🎥 **Gone in 60 Seconds**   When Angelina Jolie and Nicolas Cage are in a car, she finds a tube of red lipstick and puts some on. A short time later they get out of the car and her lipstick is back to the colour it was when they first got in the car.

🎥 **Grease**   Sandy walks over to meet the girls after doing a cart-wheel that sucked. They are telling her she did great. Anyway, if you look at Sandy's cheerleading uniform, she has a *long* red string right next to the letter on her shirt. Then, suddenly, the string disappears in the very next second.

🎥 **Grosse Pointe Blank**   In the scene where John Cusack goes into the DJ booth to talk to Minnie Driver, every time the camera goes back and forth to her, her necklace is twisted and then untwisted.

🎥 **Harry Potter and the Chamber of Secrets**   When Gilderoy jumps into the entrance to the Chamber of Secrets his cape goes flowing up above his head. In a short second shot, taken from above, it's not.

When Harry casts the charm on Malfoy in the duelling club, Malfoy falls on the floor with his hair messed up. When the camera cuts to the next scene as Snape pulls Malfoy up, his hair is neat again.

When Harry, Ron and Hermione are drinking the Polyjuice Potion, Harry leans towards the mirror and starts to gag, and you can see his shirt is half unbuttoned. There is another shot farther back, then it cuts back to him again and his shirt is nice and neatly buttoned.

Harry Potter and the Philosopher's Stone   In the Quidditch scene, Hermione's hair is crimped. Later, when you see the class looking at Neville after his fall, her hair is straight. The very next shot she's in, her hair's crimped again.

Hollow Man   Throughout the film, Kevin Bacon is seen with sticky sensor wires stuck to the top of his head and around his face. But we never see him get his hair cut off, even though we even see he has no hair when they first attempt to make him visible. Also, just a short time later, we see him swimming in a pool, with a full head of hair, and later it is gone again.

At the end of film when Elizabeth Shue and her lover are escaping from Kevin Bacon in the hall, Elizabeth Shue turns on the fire alarm and everything becomes wet. But after that, they and their clothes are dry.

Independence Day   The scene after Jasmine's no-show club pole dance, she is with her girlfriend in the dressing room. She is warning her girlfriend not to go to the alien rooftop site. She is undressed when she enters the dress closet, and comes out fully dressed within two seconds.

🎥 **Jerry Maguire**   In the scene where they are at Dorothy's house and Jerry Maguire is waiting to go to dinner with her, he has five buttons done on his shirt. The next shot he has only four buttons done, and then when the camera turns back he has five buttons done.

Before they go on their first date, keep an eye on Dorothy's dress. In some shots the straps are short and the top of the dress is close to her neck, in others they're longer, with the top further down.

When Jerry is at Dorothy's house, Renée and her sister bump into each other, and she gets pizza on her shirt. When she's changing, there's a shot of her sister handing her the black top, then about a second later it cuts to a shot of Dorothy with the top on, fishing her hair out from the collar – how did she get it on so fast?

🎥 **Lake Placid**   When Bridget Fonda is on the boat with Brendan Gleeson and the soon to be headless deputy, her green vest (life jacket) is fully unzipped. When we see her immediately after she's been knocked in the water, her jacket is zipped almost all the way up.

🎥 **Legally Blonde**   When Reese Witherspoon is at the beauty salon she has two flowers in her hair, one purple, and one pink. When the camera angle changes, the flowers also change position from shot to shot – one above the other from the front, and one behind the other from behind.

Reese Witherspoon is in the CULA counsellor's office to discuss getting into Harvard Law School. Her hair goes from in front of her shoulder, to behind her shoulder, to in front of her shoulder again.

🎥 **Legends of the Fall**   In the scene where Brad Pitt returns to see Julia Ormond at her new home with Aidan Quinn, her hair is down. But on every subsequent shot her hair is variously pulled behind her ear, then both sides of her face, then one side pulled back, and so on.

🎥 **The Lord of the Rings: The Fellowship of the Ring** When Frodo awakes in the bed in Rivendell, his shirt is open and the sheet low down on the bed in the first shot, and then his shirt's closed and the sheet pulled substantially higher in the next shot.

🎥 **The Lord of the Rings: The Two Towers** In the battle with the warg riders when Aragorn goes over the cliff his sword is not in its sheath. Yet later, as he drifts up on the shore, his sword is sheathed and safe. Did he return it to the scabbard as he fell?

When Theoden is spouting his poem about the horse and the rider, Gamling is putting the armour on his King but when the camera returns to a wide shot, he still only has his breastplate on.

🎥 **Mars Attacks!** At the end, just before Jack Nicholson is killed, he fixes his tie, but it keeps on getting fixed to messed, to fixed. Apparently this is an in-joke reference to *A Few Good Men*, where Jack Nicholson suffered a similar error.

🎥 **Mary Poppins** When Mary Poppins is reading the children's torn-up note to Mr Banks, she is wearing a pair of white gloves. The next shot is a close-up and she is wearing black gloves. And then finally a room shot, where she's wearing white gloves again.

🎥 **The Mask** At the beginning when Jim Carrey is talking to Cameron Diaz about his tie, the tie is down, then the camera switches to Cameron and then back on Jim. His tie is then on his shoulder and he drags it down.

When Cameron Diaz goes to the jail and meets Jim Carrey they almost kiss for the first time. She is wearing bright red lipstick. A few minutes later she is running from her boyfriend down an alley outside the prison. She is now wearing soft pink lipstick.

The Matrix When Neo and Morpheus are in the hallway to see the oracle, watch when they are in front of the door. Morpheus has his sunglasses on. They show a shot of Neo's hand on the knob and his sunglasses are still on. When the door opens and they both walk through, the sunglasses are off.

In the scene with Morpheus and the agent fighting after they are set up (exits get blocked off by bricks and they are fighting in a bathroom), Morpheus headbutts the agent and his glasses fall off. About one or two seconds after that it shows the agent (from behind) headbutting Morpheus back, but he has his glasses on.

Me, Myself & Irene When Jim Carrey and Renée Zellweger arrive at the train station in Rhode Island, Jim Carrey's dual personalities are having a 'fight'. During this fight Carrey unzips his pants to wiggle his 'thing' at a group of ladies sitting on a bench. Immediately after that he falls to the ground and his pants are zipped.

Meet the Parents When Robert De Niro is on the phone talking in Thai and Ben Stiller is on the roof grabbing the cat, De Niro is wearing a red shirt, but when the cat falls and they do a close-up of the cat on the floor, the person walking back into the house is wearing some kind of yellow jacket, which we see the bottom of.

Memento In the scene in which Guy Pierce writes on the back of his picture of Teddy, 'He is the one. Kill him,' we see a shot of him placing the picture on top of his tan jacket on the bed as he goes to write on it. Then it goes to a close-up of the picture and the jacket has disappeared – the picture is lying directly on the blue bedspread. It actually happens twice within that same scene.

Men in Black When Edgar/Alien is pulling the woman scientist out of the car she is wearing boots, but when she falls from the tower she is wearing shoes.

🎥 **The Mexican**   At one point Brad Pitt is fighting with the Mexican men who stole his car. In one shot he has on his sunglasses; in the next, they show him grabbing the sunglasses back off the thief.

🎥 **Minority Report**   In the part when Tom Cruise is in the greenhouse with the old lady, her hairstyle changes under her hat in every scene when she turns around, looks up or down or when they are talking.

When Tom Cruise is driving Agatha, a.k.a. the Pre-Cog, in his car after kidnapping her from the Temple, she is complaining that she is cold, so he takes off his jacket and puts it on her shoulder and body. The next shot is from outside the window and the jacket is down on her arm; the following shot is back to Tom Cruise and the jacket is on her shoulder again.

🎥 **Mission: Impossible 2**   When Ethan Hunt and Nyah are lying in bed after the chase, at the end of the scene, he leans in to kiss her. Nyah brushes back a very clear lock of hair that has come out of nowhere.

Throughout the film, Ambrose has relatively short hair (on the back of his neck). But at the horse-racing scene at the beginning of the film, you can see that his hair at the back of his neck is exceptionally longer than at any other point in the movie.

During the motorcycle scene near the end of the movie there is a shot of Ethan Hunt from the front. You can clearly see an earring on his left ear. A second later it's gone.

In the first scene Ethan is climbing – he makes a strange jump and he manages to move from one rock to another, but after that tremendous front-hit his T-shirt is perfectly clean ... what soap does he use?

At the racetrack, when the girl has the binoculars up and she's talking to Ethan Hunt, her hair is behind her ear, then down, then behind her ear again.

Monsters, Inc. Just after James tells Mike nothing matters, it cuts to a scene with Mike holding the ball from a snow cone and he has only two toes on his left foot. It then goes to James again and when it goes back to Mike he has three toes again.

The chef at Harryhausen's has a bandana with a Japanese symbol on it. The symbol in the first shot changes to another one for the rest of the scene.

The Mummy When the two groups are racing to the city of Hamunaptra, Evelyn takes the lead after Beni falls from his camel, and you can see her knee. Moments later her knee is covered by her clothes – obviously she was not able to set loose the camel's reins by herself. Her other knee's now come uncovered too.

When the warden who gets the beetle in his brain runs into the wall, his shirt is untucked. The camera changes angle and it is tucked in.

My Best Friend's Wedding When Julia Roberts is leaning against Dermot Mulroney's hotel door she is smoking a cigarette. When he opens the door she falls back and ash from the cigarette falls on her hair. Two scenes later it is gone and her hair is rearranged while she is still on the floor.

When Julia Roberts is in the bedroom in her underwear, Dermot Mulroney walks in and she pulls the cover around her. When she pulls the jacket in front of her she has her hands down by her side. In the next shot she has her left arm going across her stomach, holding the jacket up. The shot cuts away and cuts back, then Julia has her hands down by her side again (exactly the same way she had them to start with).

In the scene where Julia Roberts and Cameron Diaz are eating in a restaurant, Cameron's necklace goes from being outside her dress to inside it.

Mystery Men At the beginning, after Captain Amazing defeats the red eyes, a reporter tells him that he lost his Pepsi contract so, when he gets in his limo, he rips off the logo. However, when the Mystery Men are in Casanova Frankenstein's mansion, trying to save him, he still has his Pepsi logo on.

Notting Hill Hugh Grant heads out wearing a belt. When he is in the orange juice shop the belt is gone, but it reappears as he leaves the shop.

The Patriot In the scene where Mel Gibson's previously silent daughter runs to him and says that she loves him and wants him to stay, there is a continuity error with her pigtails. When that camera is at her back, they're behind her shoulders, and when the camera faces her they are in front of her shoulders.

Payback When Mel Gibson is tied to the chair being beaten up he is wearing boots and his legs are not tied to the chair. In the next few scenes when Mr Bronson shows up with his hammer, Mel Gibson has no boots on his feet and his legs are tied to the chair.

Pearl Harbor In the scene in front of the hotel on the night before Ben Affleck ships out to England, Kate Beckinsale puts a scarf around his neck. There is a camera shot from his back: no scarf; then another one from his front, and he's wearing the scarf again.

The Perfect Storm In the bar before the crew go on their fatal mission, Mark Wahlberg is drinking with his girlfriend. His goatee is thick and dark around his chin. When they are upstairs in their bedroom later that night, it is very light and slight. The next morning, when he is leaving to get on the boat and saying goodbye to her, it is thick and dark at the bottom again.

When the Black Hawk helicopter ditches into the sea, the pilot's night vision goggles clearly fall off, yet as the cockpit starts to fill with water they are still there and remain there for several shots.

🎥 **Pretty Woman** In the scene in the park when Richard Gere is reading to Julia Roberts, he has his shoes on, then off, then the camera pans back and his shoes are on again.

In the scene where Jason Alexander hits Julia Roberts she rips his watch off. You can see it fly off to the left. In the next scene (where she bites him) it's there. Then, when Richard Gere pulls him off her, it's gone again.

When Julia Roberts is watching *I Love Lucy*, she goes over to Richard Gere and undoes his tie, and then goes to get a pillow or something; in the next shot of him his tie is done again, then goes back to being undone.

🎥 **Robin Hood: Prince of Thieves** When Robin reaches his homeland, after he kisses the ground, he rolls over in the water. His coat is covering him then, in the next scene, it isn't, then it is, then it isn't.

When Robin and Little John fight in the river Robin's hair changes from being dry to wet to dry again despite falling in the river several times.

🎥 **RoboCop** In the scene where RoboCop and Lewis are at the steel mill, after he was all shot up by ED-209 and the police, RoboCop removes his helmet. All through the movie he has a black lining on the sides of his face and chin. When he removes the helmet they just disappear.

In the locker room at the start, a female police officer has just put a bullet-proof vest on when the boss walks in. While he's talking, no one's moving, but after a camera change she's suddenly got a shirt on too.

🎥 **The Rocky Horror Picture Show** When Magenta is undressing Brad, there is a shot of her unbuttoning his shirt, but in the next shot it's still buttoned.

Runaway Bride   In the scene where Julia Roberts and Richard Gere are talking outside at the luau, Richard Gere's flower necklace is in a different place every other shot.

Rush Hour 2   At the very end of the film when Jackie Chan and Chris Tucker are saying their final goodbyes, Jackie Chan is wearing the strap to his bag on his left shoulder. You will notice that in almost every scene, even in the mistakes during the credits, the rubber thing on his bag is alternately there and not there.

Scary Movie   In the scene where Buffy and Cindy get dressed in the locker room, a girl standing right next to Buffy drops her towel to get dressed and a few seconds later has the towel wrapped around again.

Scream   Tatum Riley is in the garage and throws beer bottles at the killer, getting him soaked with beer and lots of foam ... until he lands on the steps behind her, when he's suddenly bone dry and foam-free.

Signs   When the deputy sheriff comes out of the house, her ink pen is clipped to the outside of her pocket, not in the pocket. After she turns around at the car, her ink pen is visible through the flap but it is inside her pocket and not as it was just a split second before.

In the scene where Mel Gibson and the kids are returning home from town, and Morgan is holding his baby monitor to listen to the aliens, his fingernails are very long. When he gets out and climbs on top of the car to listen better, his fingernails are very short.

Smokey and the Bandit   When Sheriff Justice stops the kids in the van, his gun belt keeps appearing and disappearing.

Snatch   Brad Pitt's tattoos appear to smudge during the last fight.

Space Cowboys   When Donald Sutherland is getting off the roller coaster to talk to Clint Eastwood, he kisses the woman and then removes his glasses. You then see a shot of the back of his head and his glasses are still on. They then show a shot of his face and they're off.

Spider-Man   In the scene where Norman is getting ready to test himself he lies down on the bed, fastens himself in and the doctor goes to the computer. However when it shows him being brought in to the chamber he has several electrodes connected to his chest and head. Wow, self-attaching electrodes. What will crazy Oscorp think of next?

When Peter is taking out the trash, and begins talking to MJ, as MJ walks towards him you can see her underwear sticking out above her trousers. As the shots change, this underwear seems to appear and disappear.

In the beginning, when Peter runs out to catch the bus, he swings his backpack over his shoulder, but when he is seen running after the bus, the backpack has disappeared.

Steel Magnolias   During the scene when Dolly Parton is styling Julia Roberts's hair for the wedding, we see Dolly start taking the rollers out of the left side of Julia's hair. The camera then goes to another character and when it comes back she is again taking the rollers out of the left side of Julia's hair while the rollers on the right side are now out.

When you see Shirley MacLaine laughing in the mirror after she belches at Julia Roberts, you can also see that her hat is back on her head, after she's taken it off and laid it on the chair.

Swingers Near the end, during the scene where Trent is standing on the table at the pancake house, the camera cuts to Mike, and you can see Trent in the windows, with his shirt off, swinging it over his head. The camera cuts back to Trent and his shirt is still on, *then* he takes it off and swings it around.

10 Things I Hate About You When Cameron's friend is putting on his helmet before he goes on the motorbike you can clearly see the goggles strap over the helmet. He gets on his bike and is run off the cliff. After he gets up the strap is nowhere to be seen, but his goggles are still on.

When Michael is almost hit by Kat's car, his goggles are up on his motorcycle helmet, but a moment later when he pulls up to Cameron, the goggles are on his face. It's all one continuous sequence and he's in shot the whole time – there's no chance for him to pull them down without us seeing.

The Terminator In the scene where Arnie is blasting everyone in the office of the police station, if you look at the shirt under his jacket, it changes from blue to black as he swings around.

When Kyle escapes the department store he is not wearing a shirt, but in the next scene, when he is following Sarah, he is wearing a grey shirt and continues to wear it throughout the movie.

There's Something About Mary When Ben Stiller got his 'frank and beans' caught in the zipper, the friendly police officer thought he would assist with the problem. He unbuttoned his sleeves and rolled them up, but then the next camera shot showed them buttoned up, and they had to be rolled up again.

When Ben Stiller and Cameron Diaz are sitting on top of the car, Cameron looks at her watch to see what the time is but, if you look closely, her watch is facing the camera, so there is no way she could have seen what the time was.

When Ben Stiller sees Cameron Diaz for the first time in years, the hood on his sweatshirt changes from his back to his right shoulder.

Thunderball When James Bond is fighting underwater with an opponent, the opponent rips off James's diving mask (which is blue). Then James rips another mask off another opponent who is lying dead on the ocean floor. This dead opponent's mask is black. James puts on the black mask and then he turns around and the mask is blue again.

Titanic When Jack is asking Rose to dance, after dancing with the little girl 'Cora', you will notice that Jack's hair is down when first asking her when the camera goes to Rose and then back to Jack it is back up, all nice and neat.

When Rose is about to jump off the back of the boat there is a long shot of her and she is wearing black socks. But when Jack helps her back over she slips because her red shoes get caught on her dress.

Young Rose has green eyes, but old Rose has blue eyes. Later in the film, there is a fade between the faces of young and old Rose and this time old Rose's eyes have magically changed to match Kate Winslet's eyes.

Jack and Rose are talking on the deck and Rose is explaining why she considered jumping. Pay attention to Rose's hair. One second, her hair in perfectly curled with bangs, then it is behind her ears. It alternates back and forth: bangs, no bangs, bangs, no bangs until she grabs his portfolio and they sit down on the chairs to look at his drawings.

Tomorrow Never Dies When James Bond jumps out of the plane he has a diving rig that is somewhat different to the one he has when diving on the wreck of the *Devonshire*. In the water he wears a twinset manifold air-bottle rig. While skydiving the rig was not mani-folded and the bottles were in a different position on his back. To change between the two requires some work with a toolkit, preferably on dry land.

In the scene where Bond is trying to escape from Carver's headquarters, a black guy holds him over the newspapers being printed. In one shot the back part of his tie (that hides behind the larger front part usually) is hanging by his ears, then it cuts to a shot of the black guy and when it cuts back, the back part of the tie has risen back to its proper place against his chest.

The Chinese agent handcuffs Bond to the shower. When she is running away you can see her from the back, picking up a piece of clothing. Her hair is completely dry, although she was under the shower with Bond only a few seconds ago.

Top Gun   At the end, a victorious Maverick is hoisted on the shoulders of the guys. As he goes up, he isn't wearing sunglasses, his head goes out of the shot, and when he comes down, he's wearing a pair.

In the volleyball scene, Maverick can clearly be seen looking at his watch because he has a hot date with Charlie; however, while they are actually playing it is easily noticeable that he is no longer wearing his watch.

At the beginning of the film, the squadron commander enters CATTC with a chest full of ribbons – next shot, all ribbons are gone.

In the elevator scene with Maverick and Charlie, Maverick's hair keeps changing.

While in the trailer reviewing Maverick's flying, Charlie is wearing a grey skirt. In the next scene, while she is out by Maverick's bike, she is wearing a black skirt.

When the instructors are out on the flight line discussing Maverick's loss of confidence, in each shot Viper's sunglasses can be seen to alternate between Randolph (square type) and then Ray Ban (aviator style).

When Goose dies, Sundown (the black guy) acts as Mav's RIO. On the plane his helmet has a Sun with rays, and walking on the runaway it does not.

Toy Story 2   Near the end of the movie when the 'false' Buzz Lightyear is running along the air conditioning ducts his 'New Utility Belt' disappears then reappears again.

The Truth About Cats & Dogs   When Uma Thurman visits the radio station for the first time, she asks Janeane Garofalo if she can sit down by the microphone. She comes in wearing a sweater over her dress, but by the time she gets to the microphone, she's no longer wearing it. It simply disappears from one shot to the other, along with the bag over her shoulder.

Twister   After leaving Aunt Meg's the first time, Bill Paxton and Helen Hunt are in the red truck. Bill says, 'OK, let's get you wired.' When Helen looks over at him you can see that she already has the headphones around her neck. Then they cut to Bill and, when he goes to put the headphones on, her neck is bare.

Unbreakable   In the scene where Bruce Willis and Samuel L. Jackson first meet at the stadium, the man Bruce Willis suspects of carrying a weapon is wearing a camouflage coat. In the following scene where Samuel L. Jackson follows the suspect, he is again wearing a camouflage coat, but there are suddenly much brighter colours on it.

Vertical Limit   Chris O'Donnell walks into a tent where Monique tells him where to find Skip. The stubble he has when talk-

THE AMAZING CHANGING WARDROBE

ing to Monique is totally gone when he finds Skip, immediately afterward.

📽️ **What Women Want**   When Mel Gibson tries on the pantyhose, the hole in the left leg changes from large on the outside of his leg, to small with a run on the outside of his leg, to large on the inside of his leg.

In the scene in the bar, Helen Hunt and Mel Gibson are talking. During the dialogue the camera cuts from one face to the other. Helen Hunt's hair is sometimes in front of her shoulder, and sometimes behind.

📽️ **William Shakespeare's Romeo + Juliet**   Just before Romeo and Juliet jump into the swimming pool, Juliet's hair is in a braid that wraps around her head. But, when they jump into the pool, the braid is gone.

When Romeo is talking to the Capulet father at the party, his mask goes up and down depending on the shot.

📽️ **The Wizard of Oz**   During the scene when Dorothy and Scarecrow are fighting with the trees, Scarecrow says, 'I'll show you how to get apples', and he gets hit by the apples. The very next scene, if you quickly look at Dorothy's shoes, you can see that she is wearing black shoes, not her ruby slippers.

During the sequence where Dorothy meets the Scarecrow, Dorothy's pigtails are first short (above her shoulders) and then, as the song progresses her hair gets longer (below her shoulders), then short, and then long again.

📽️ **The World is Not Enough**   At the beginning, when James Bond jumps into the speedboat to chase after the assassin, he's not wearing a helmet. But when the speedboat hits the bigger one and rolls in the air, you can clearly see the driver with a helmet on. It's most obvious just before he lands – slow it down and you can see the curved helmet with a visor.

When M is imprisoned and is being spoken to by Renard, she is wearing a multicoloured scarf which is draped over her left shoulder and down the left side of her body. When Renard leaves the room, M turns around and walks towards the bed. The camera angle is reversed and the scarf has completely disappeared.

X-Men When we first see Wolverine, his sideburns are thick and full, but when he wakes up in Xavier's school, his sideburns are not nearly that thick, in fact, they look rather scrubby. They change back to thick at the end of the movie, when he puts on the X-men uniform.

At the end, when Rogue and Wolverine are saying goodbye to each other, she runs after him and stops suddenly, and there are several strands of hair stuck across her mouth. It cuts to Wolverine quickly, then back to her, seemingly in the same position, and her hair is straight.

In the scene right after Logan hits the hood of the truck, and Sabretooth is distracted by something, you can clearly see Storm's hair is pulled back in a ponytail (you can also see it when she gives Rogue a hand out of the truck). But when they are still standing out in the open, the camera view switches behind them, and her hair is blown forward around her face. Then it is back in a ponytail.

In the scene in the Statue of Liberty, where Toad has shot his slime at Jean Grey's face, we see Cyclops shoot his optic beam to free himself from the room he was trapped in. Then he rushes to Jean's aid. If you look closely you can see that the gloves he was wearing as part of his costume are no longer there when he takes the slime off Jean's face.

xXx When Xander throws grenades to make an avalanche he unzips his coat. He then fixes his goggles and jumps. In the next scene his coat is already zipped up, but he didn't have time to zip it.

WHAT WAS THAT YOU WERE SAYING?

Editing is a vital part of making a film – putting together the ideal shots and adding the sound effects can make or break the structure of a film. Trouble is, the right sounds might not fit over the right visuals, or the perfect take might involve a bit of overlap with an earlier shot. If nothing else, using multiple takes means that the same extras might crop up slightly more often than planned ...

American Beauty   Lester is in Janey's room looking through her phone numbers. When he gets to Angela's number it starts with 555 but when he dials it on the phone the first two numbers are a similar beep but the third is a different tone. It looks as if he is hitting 553.

American Pie   In the scene where Jim's father gives the son the magazines, right before he's about to leave, he taps his hands together, but a loud clap is heard, like he really clapped his hands hard, while he just touched them together.

Anaconda   In one shot when the boat is pulling away from the waterfall, you can clearly see that the shot is the same one they used earlier in the movie. The water from the waterfall now is going up the cliff! They have just put it in reverse.

Austin Powers: The Spy Who Shagged Me   When Dr Evil is singing 'Just the Two of Us', as he says 'C'est la vie' Scott Evil walks past him. Dr Evil looks at him (he walks to the right). Then Dr Evil turns around about four seconds later and Scott is back standing by Frau and Number 2. He couldn't have moved that fast.

Bad Boys   When Tea Leoni and her friend enter the fancy hotel room, they make a point of saying they will only be there for a couple of minutes. It is daylight when they go in. The visit is cut short (the one that's supposed to be a few minutes long) because of a gun battle in which one of the women dies and the other escapes. The escapee gets out through the roof into a late night's sky.

Batman   After Batman rescues Vicki Vale he has a voice remote for the Batmobile. As the car approaches he orders the car to stop by speaking into the remote and then lowers it to his side. When the camera shot changes, showing the car stopping right in front of him, he is still holding the remote to his mouth.

Batman & Robin   When Robin is being pulled underwater by Poison Ivy's plants he surfaces for air and gets pulled under again. It's obvious the film was just rewound. Then when he finally gets free we see the shot that was rewound was the same shot used when he escapes. Really bad editing.

Batman Returns   When the Penguin dies, and is slowly sinking into the 'pool' in the sewer, you can see that, while he is rather round, the shadow at the bottom of the pool is definitely rectangular, i.e. the platform on which he was being pulled was removed, but the shadow missed.

Just after Bruce Wayne has spoken to Alfred about him letting Vicki Vale into the Batcave in the past, we see him pulling his jacket on from behind. He puts his right arm in, then starts to reach behind himself to get his left arm in. The shot then cuts to seeing him from the front, and we see him reach behind himself again.

Beverly Hills Cop   In the scene where Axel Foley throws the art dealer's henchman on to the buffet table, if you watch carefully (or use slo-mo) you can clearly see the stunt double pulling off that manoeuvre.

Blade Runner   Deckard investigates the maker of artificial reptiles, an Abdul somebody. It's obvious that the dialogue was added, as neither actor is in sync with the sound. The end of the scene has the storekeeper's voice telling Deckard the information he was seeking, and Deckard's mouth is the one moving. Deckard's mouth continues to move even after Abdul's lines are finished and the scene cuts.

Braveheart   In the first battle, the cavalry are charging. During the charge, there's a very brief shot of the Scots, and we can see them with raised spears, a few seconds before they actually raise them.

Clue   In one ending, Mrs White is responsible for Yvette's death, yet when Yvette rushes downstairs to meet her killer, Mrs White is still heard screaming upstairs.

Days of Thunder   In one scene Tom Cruise's accelerator gets stuck – you see him pounding on the accelerator while telling his crew chief Harry Hog 'The accelerator is stuck' – but Tom Cruise's mouth never moves when he speaks.

Dazed and Confused   In the scene where O'Bannion gets paint dumped on him by the freshmen, he gets in his car and squeals his tyres while driving on grass – it wouldn't sound like that even if it's wet.

Die Hard   When Al gets his car shot up you hear him say, 'I'm at Nakatomi Plaza; I need back-up assistance now.' Later, when Thornberg is listening on the police scanner, Al says, 'I'm at Nakatomi Plaza; they're turning my car into Swiss cheese; I need back-up assistance now.'

Die Hard: With a Vengeance   When they're at the payphone, several extras seem to be doing laps – a man in a red shirt with a bag strap across his shoulder passes behind John McClane when he says, 'I'm the only one here on official police business', bearing round to the left. In the reverse camera angle exactly the same man is seen again, coming in the opposite direction from around to the right – too far away and in the wrong direction to have just turned round for no good reason. Behind him is a man in a patterned shirt, and heading past him is a woman with a bag strap over her shoulder. Reverse angle again, and the man with the patterned shirt is suddenly coming out of a shop (too quickly for him to have gone in, bought something and come out again). Then, when they pick up the phone, just as the terrorist says 'rats and mice', we see the woman with the strap heading in the same direction that she was the first time.

Dirty Dancing In the scene where Penny and Patrick Swayze are teaching Jennifer Grey their dance routine, you see Penny putting on a record. If you look closely you can see that Penny moves the arm to put the record on, then right away you see her taking the arm away, even though the music has started.

In the scene where Jennifer Grey sees the staff dancing for the first time, Patrick Swayze asks her why she is there and she answers, 'I carried a watermelon'. In the next shot you see her mouthing it to herself in disbelief, but then in the shot after that you see it again but from a different angle and you hear it this time.

At the end-of-season show Patrick Swayze has the record put on to dance. The guy puts the record on the turntable and goes to place the needle on the record, but then you can see him move the arm back off it.

Dumb and Dumber In the scene when Jim Carrey and Jeff Daniels pick up the hitchhiking natives, when they were playing the mockingbird song, the guitar was playing but his hands weren't moving at all.

📽 **E.T. The Extra-Terrestrial** While the kids are huddled around the kitchen table, Elliot is saying his lines while Drew Barrymore's character is actually moving her lips, saying those same lines on the right side of the screen.

📽 **Galaxy Quest** When Tim Allen and Sigourney Weaver have to negotiate the chompers you can hear Tim Allen giving instructions of when and when not to go. However, his mouth is clearly not moving.

When Tim Allen and Sigourney Weaver first see the hallway with the chompers, she says, 'Oh, screw that!' but if you watch her lips she clearly uses the 'f' word instead of 'screw'.

In the beginning scene at the Galaxy Quest conception, the crowd is clapping and shouting to see the actors but, when they cut to the back of the audience, you clearly see they are not clapping and shouting, or even moving yet, but the sound of the clapping and the shouting is still there.

📽 **Goldfinger** The bomb is disarmed with 007 seconds left on the conveniently placed timer with big white numbers. Then, James Bond says, 'Three more ticks and Mr Goldfinger would have hit the jackpot.' How does three ticks equal seven seconds? Well, originally the timer would have stopped at 003, and the line would make sense, but later the powers that be decided to stop it at 007 instead for a good old Bond joke, and apparently never forgot to delete that line in editing.

📽 **Harry Potter and the Chamber of Secrets** When Harry, Dumbledore, and Lucius Malfoy are in Dumbledore's office and Harry says he will be around to save the day, his face is clean. Later, when Harry gives Malfoy Tom Riddle's diary, his face is as grimy as it was in the Chamber.

Home Alone   When Kevin is remembering what his relatives have said to him, he remembers his brother saying something about feeding Kevin to his tarantula. Kevin's brother never said that.

Home Alone 2: Lost in New York   At the start of the film, Kevin tapes his uncle Frank singing in the shower, but he doesn't tape all of the singing. When Kevin is in the hotel in New York, he plays back the tape when the blow-up clown is in the shower, and all of the singing is on the tape, including something his uncle said when Kevin ran away from him.

Jurassic Park   When the group is first entering Jurassic Park at the huge door, Jeff Goldblum says, 'What have they got in there, King Kong?' but, if you look closely, his lips do not move. This happens again later in the movie where Tim and Alex are in the car when they encounter the T-Rex. Lex has the flashlight and Timmy tells her to turn it off. She then says 'I'm sorry', but her lips don't move.

The Lord of the Rings: The Fellowship of the Ring   When Arwen and Aragorn are talking on the bridge, you see Arwen's lips moving while Aragorn is speaking.

The Lord of the Rings: The Two Towers   In Edoras, when Wormtongue is 'charming' Eowyn, his hand is clearly on her face and his body is only inches away. When Eowyn retaliates with words and gets Wormtongue's hand away from her, the next shot shows that they are over six feet apart from each other.

The Matrix   Trinity flies through the window, tumbles down the stairs and then looks back up at the window. You can hear the light squeaking while it swings, even when it's not swinging.

Men in Black   When Will Smith is looking at the two space ships at the MIB headquarters, if you look in the background Zed and Tommy Lee Jones are there typing on the computer. But if you look closer you can tell that they're not even touching the keyboard and the sounds are just added into the movie. It's not a new kind of keyboard because in a later scene he definitely makes contact with the keys.

Monsters, Inc.   Near the end of the film, when the identity of 0001 of the Child Detection Agency is revealed, number 0112 is shown both standing next to 0001 as she enters the room and behind Sully and Mike on the opposite side of the room.

When Sully and Mike first speak to the geeky monsters in the lobby, there is a sluglike monster in the background just entering one of the corridors leading to the Scare Floors. When Mike is talking to Celia a short time later, the same slug has yet to enter the corridor.

In the first shot of all the monsters entering the Scare Floor, there is a broad-chested purple monster without eyes. In his next two shots he has three eyes. Then, in the following shot, his eyes are gone again until his assistant gives him a whole bunch.

Ocean's Eleven   When Casey Affleck is walking through the casino with the balloons, he bumps into Steve Caan. Watch when he first bumps into him and their argument ensues: their mouths are not moving.

The Patriot   Heath Ledger writes a letter home in the snow. The voiceover says his friend was killed at Elizabethtown, but in the written letter you can see that it states his friend was killed at Monmouth. When it shows Ledger writing the letter, you can see 'Monmouth' above the line he is writing.

Pay it Forward   In the taping of Haley Joel Osment's interview, he stutters at one point, but when they replay the interview he does not stutter.

Pulp Fiction   At the beginning, Amanda Plummer screams that she's gonna kill 'every last mother f***in' one of you.' In the last scene it's changed to 'every last one of you motherf***ers!'

Road to Perdition   When the young Sullivan boy goes to get Rooney's overcoat, he walks into the room where the coat is and a man is lying on the couch. When he starts talking to the boy, his cigarette is nearly gone; a few seconds later it flashes to the man again and he has an almost full cigarette.

RoboCop   When RoboCop play back his recording of Clarence Boddicker spilling his guts about Dick Jones, the words he says are different to the ones that were recorded.

Sleepy Hollow   In the starting scene, when Peter van Garret sees the scarecrow from the carriage window, a lot of time passes until he jumps out of the carriage (about two minutes). When he flies through the maize field, he reaches the scarecrow in a few seconds. I don't think that an old man is faster than four horses.

Smokey and the Bandit   Every time they show how fast the car is driving, there are fewer miles on the odometer.

Speed   There's an extra click near the beginning when the lift numbers are changing.

Spider-Man   During the scene where the apartment building is on fire, the lady whose baby is still inside points directly up and asks 'what's that?' Spider-Man is, however, still swinging towards the fire from several blocks away, around corners.

At the beginning of the movie when Peter is chasing after the school bus there's a bridge ahead of the bus. But neither the bus, nor Parker, go under the bridge.

The Terminator The telephone message left by Sarah Connor's roommate changes the two times we hear it. The second time, there is no delay between 'Hi there' and 'ha ha ha, fooled you', while the first time has a delay of over a second.

Terminator 2: Judgment Day In the scene where John Connor is on his bike and is being chased by T-1000 in the semi, if you listen very closely, that bike has over fifteen gears.

Tomorrow Never Dies Gupta, Carver's gadgetman, proves that Paris, Carver's wife, knows James Bond extremely well by showing Carver some secret footage taken at the cable TV launch party. In that footage Paris says to Bond, 'Tell me, James, do you still sleep with a gun under your pillow?' As she asks him this question, Bond can be seen looking down over the railing at the crowd below. Yet if you rewind a few minutes to the actual moment in the movie when she asks him this question, Bond is not looking down; he is, in fact, regarding her fixedly. They clearly reshot it (even her intonation of the question is different).

Twister After Bill Paxton and Helen Hunt chase the first tornado they switch to Bill's new truck. They look at the speedometer once then they look at it again about three seconds later and the odometer is hundreds of miles different from what it was only three seconds before.

Wayne's World When Benjamin is playing the video for Noah Vanderhoff in his office, Wayne says, '... put that thing on your ... on your melon,' stuttering a bit. However, earlier in the movie, during the 'live show', he does not stutter.

The Wizard of Oz You see a bird-monkey flying with Toto before he gets picked up.

X-Men When Rogue is riding in Wolverine's truck and he gives her the beef jerky, you can hear her lips smacking as she eats, but she is actually chewing with her mouth closed.

xXx In the scene where Xander drives the Corvette off the bridge after being chased by the police at the start of the film, the shot changes to a far away shot where the whole bridge can be seen. If you look closely you can see Xander's first parachute emerge. However, when the shot then changes to one looking down from above him you can see Xander has not released his parachute and does not do so for at least another three or four seconds.

LIGHTS, CAMERA, ACTION!

This is cast and crew partly giving the game away, but enough films suffer from it to warrant a section. This is devoted to any film-making equipment getting on-screen when it shouldn't, whether it's cameras, special effects or the old classic, boom microphones . . .

Air Force One In a scene midway through the film, where Glenn Close receives the fax from the plane, the tracks for the camera can be seen on the floor.

American Beauty After being beaten up by his dad, Ricky is looking at his injuries in the mirror. Look closely at the mirror – you can see the edge of the camera for about a second, then the shot is adjusted slightly so you can't see it any more.

American Pie When Jim walks to Nadia the first time – right after he trips on the couch – a light stand is seen right at the left edge of the screen.

Army of Darkness When Ash emerges from the Vortex, he falls on what look like mats. When he coughs, the mats are gone.

Beetlejuice When Geena Davis tries to leave the house and falls into the sandworm's world, you can clearly see her knee pads.

Blade In one of the final fight scenes, Blade throws a vampire, and you can see the mat the stuntman falls on.

Blade Runner When Deckard shoots the snake woman, as she is crashing through the glass windows you can see the blood pouches strapped to the stunt woman's chest.

🎥 **Braveheart** At the end, Wallace's friend is charging in slow motion, and if you look closely you will see his battle axe flopping around like it's made of rubber.

🎥 **Clear and Present Danger** When the lone Huey helicopter comes to rescue Jack Ryan from a rooftop, the reflection of the filming helicopter can be seen in its window.

🎥 **Cliffhanger** This mistake is visible during the 'grand finale' fight scene, which takes place on the underside of an overturned helicopter that hangs from a cliff. If you look carefully, a few frames show the rigging that is holding the helicopter in place.

🎥 **Coyote Ugly** During the scene between Violet and Gloria, outside Violet's apartment in Chinatown, Gloria is wearing sunglasses on her head. Looking closely, you can notice the overhead lighting reflecting in her sunglasses. Apparently, the sunglasses were not dirtied enough for the light to disappear.

🎥 **Cruel Intentions** In the swimming pool scene between Reese Witherspoon and Ryan Philippe, a positioning mark can be seen quite clearly on the floor.

🎥 **Evil Dead 2** During the scene when the evil Henrietta flies up from the basement to attack the girl, while she is in the air you can see the wire holding her up, a split in the butt of the latex costume and, as she turns to see Ash, sweat pouring out her ear.

During the first scene where the 'evil force' is chasing Ash through the house, you can see above the rafters, showing that this is not actually the house but a set.

When the eye is flying towards Bobby Jo, you can see the rig holding the eye as it flies and the wire when it enters her mouth.

🎥 **Face/Off**   In the shoot 'em up scene in the hangar at the beginning of the film, Pollux Troy shoots an agent in the stomach and the agent flies back – and you can see the rope pulling him.

When Pollux falls through the glass roof, you can see his harness pulling him back.

🎥 **Ferris Bueller's Day Off**   When Ferris has just picked up Sloan from her school, he looks over at the camera and says, 'The question isn't what are we going to do. The question is what aren't we going to do.' While he is saying this you can clearly see a boom mike moving back and forth in the car reflection.

When Ferris and gang are driving into the city (Chicago), you hear a song being played and they show an aerial view of Chicago. When they do a flyby of one of the buildings, you can clearly see the helicopter, and the cameraman who is doing the filming, in the reflection of the building's windows.

🎥 **Frequency**   In the scene when the fuel tanker crashes and flips, you can see a cable attached to the end of it, pulling it along.

🎥 **Ghostbusters 2**   When they gather around to watch what happens when you put the slime in the toaster, you can clearly see when the toaster starts popping that it has little springs attached to the bottom, making it jump.

🎥 **Gladiator**   In the battle with the Barbarian Horde one of the chariots is turned over. Once the dust settles you can see a gas cylinder in the back of the chariot.

In the scene where the Roman legion attacks the gladiators' quarters and the gladiators are forced to fight in order to hide Maximus's escape, the big German gladiator is shot full of arrows. Note the blocky silhouette of his torso area? What kind of padding is he wearing under that canvas jerkin?

GoldenEye   At the beginning, James Bond is running along the clearly empty dam. After he jumps, we see a side shot of him falling for a few seconds, then it cuts out to a wider shot as we follow him down. At the very beginning of that wider shot, look at the top of the screen. We can see the top of the dam, and it's suddenly sprouted a white van, another truck, and some other equipment which obviously wasn't there earlier.

Gone in 60 Seconds   When Nicolas Cage is speeding up to take the final jump on the bridge, you can see the camera crew on the other side of the road filming. If you look closely you can make out the shading devices used to block out the sun from the camera. Look to the left of the jump just before he hits it.

When they enter the shipyard during the final chase scene, you can clearly see the camera mounted inside the police car as it jumps and crashes into the frontloader.

Gone with the Wind   Scarlett is seen walking on the main street on the way to the hospital. You can clearly see a light bulb in one of the street lights.

In the scene where Ashley is brought back wounded from the raid where Scarlett's husband Mr Kennedy was killed, Melanie grabs a lamp to follow the man carrying Ashley to the bedroom and you can see an electrical cord hanging down from it.

Grease   In the soda shop scene, where Sandy and Danny are at the jukebox, the reflection of the boom mike is clearly visible in the chrome part of the jukebox.

Hannibal   Near the beginning, Clarice is being debriefed about the messed-up take-down. At one point there's a shot of the floor, and we can clearly see an actor's mark (a black T-shape). A few shots later someone comes into the room and stands squarely on it.

During the scene in which Krendler shows the fake Lecter postcard, look closely and you can read the line 'Sounds like him to me', although this line is part of Krendler's speech, and not part of the message itself. Forgetting your lines, Mr Liotta?

Harry Potter and the Chamber of Secrets   After Errol delivers the Howler to Ron, he flies very close to Hermione's head, and the wire attached to the owl is visible as it passes her hair – it actually looks like it hits her in the face.

Highlander   There is *no* invisible magic power lifting Connor MacLeod in air at the end – there are two wires clearly fixed on his shoulders.

Jurassic Park   In the scene where the T-Rex is knocking the Jeep with Lex and Tim in it, it knocks it once, and then again, making the vehicle flip over. If you watch that exact scene in slow motion, you can see a big wooden pot containing one of the fake trees for the set and a stage light. Not only that, when T-Rex spins the Jeep, you can see the firm cable that holds the Jeep coming from the left edge of the screen to the Jeep itself, the purpose of which is, of course, to control the Jeep's spinning.

Jurassic Park III   When the group is flying on to the island, there's a shot of the plane flying in front of the cloud, and there's the obvious shadow of the helicopter that filmed that shot!

Kingpin   When Woody Harrelson is guiding Randy Quaid's bowling, he tells him to step two boards to the right. Quaid then gets a strike, but you can see a stick being used to knock over the pins, making sure he gets a strike.

A League of Their Own   After the Peaches are introduced at their first game, they run on to the field. If you watch the background carefully, Rosie O'Donnell clearly trips over a production wire.

Legends of the Fall   In a scene that occurs after the confrontation in the bar, Brad Pitt is riding his horse. At one point, he rides off very quickly, and the horse's hoof kicks up a fluorescent orange traffic cone. It can be seen at the bottom of the screen, but only in the VHS version.

The Matrix   When Neo is going to open the door to enter the oracle's house, you can clearly see a camera on the doorknob. Look more closely and you can see that they've thrown a green sheet over it, and painted a tie on the sheet to line up with Morpheus, who's standing behind it.

When Neo flips away from the subway train, pay attention to his arms. They are obviously holding on to the digitally removed wires.

Men in Black II   When agent K is in the elevator with the little worm dudes he swings down and starts shooting at the robot. But as he swings down you can see the safety harness between his legs.

Mission: Impossible 2   When the cars flip over as they blow up, you will see a circular object underneath the vehicles, about the size of a tyre (very obvious in slow motion). This is the device that 'lifts' the vehicle for it to flip on one side, timed with the appropriate explosion.

In the scene where Ethan Hunt is riding his crotch rocket after escaping from the island with the virus, he slams on his brakes to make a lot of smoke. The shot goes from a close shot of the bike to a shot where Ethan is coming at us. If you look to the sides of the screen, you can see two thin poles, which would be about waist height, giving off smoke.

When Ethan's pal is in the helicopter and Ethan is escaping on the motorbike, he fires a grenade launcher at the car – he misses the first time, gets the car the second time, but you can clearly see the bridge is made of wood – where the car gets blown up there's a big concrete/steel plate to support the bridge.

In the rock-climbing scene, just after Hunt does his flying jump, he falls, slides down a smooth rock face and grabs a hold at the last minute to stop him plummeting to his death. When he pulls back up and over, he grabs a handhold on the smooth surface, which wasn't there before. If you know what you are looking for, you will also see that it is a bolt-on hold which has been attached to the rock face.

In the scene where Nyah and Ethan have a race with the Porsche and Audi-TT, at the end, after the camera shows Nyah's feet, you see both cars from in front. Now, in the lower right of the screen you see the shadow of the filming helicopter.

A Nightmare on Elm Street   When Freddy falls over the banister on to the stairs near the end, notice the mattress he lands on.

When Nancy is running up the stairs in her house to escape Freddy for the first time, her foot hits the step and goes through into some goop. Look at the steps above that step and you can see the pre-cut holes where the next sets of goop will be.

The Patriot   In the last battle Col. Tavington races towards Mel Gibson (flag in hand) on his horse. Mel Gibson kneels and stabs the horse, sending the horse flying. If you watch the shot of the horse coming towards Mel, you can see that the horse is on tracks. You can tell this because the horse's legs don't move. The shot is quick, so you have to be ready to watch the horse slide along.

🎥 **The Perfect Storm**   In the scene where they are getting ready to leave, it's dark and George Clooney is checking the equipment – you can clearly see a face in the depth-finder of a crew member.

🎥 **Reservoir Dogs**   The boom mike's shadow is visible when Joe gives out names. It is easily seen moving to the left when he says, 'Let's go to work!'

🎥 **The Rock**   When Nicolas Cage is driving through the warehouse in his yellow convertible and then smashes through the big glass window, you'll notice that it's simply not possible. The window is about a foot off the ground, which means there would have to be a ramp. If you look closely there are two hinges at the bottom of the window which show where the ramp ends.

🎥 **Scary Movie**   When the teacher jumps off the ledge on the side of the school he sinks into the ground and bounces up a little, like he landed on a padded mat with leaves and grass laid on top.

🎥 **The Shining**   In the first scene, when Jack Nicholson is driving to the Overlook, the shadow of a helicopter can be seen.

🎥 **Smokey and the Bandit**   There is a scene that is filmed with a camera mounted outside the passenger door of the Trans AM as it is being driven. Frog is in the passenger seat, the Bandit is driving. Look at the bottom of the screen at the reflection in the car door. The camera is clearly visible.

🎥 **Speed**   After the bus explodes, there's a 4×4 very obviously towing it – there's a chain visible in several shots.

Spider-Man   After rescuing MJ and leaving her at the church, Spider-Man (apparently) uses a trampoline to jump off the ledge. MJ then walks forward and carefully walks around the hidden trampoline.

Sudden Impact   At one point Clint Eastwood is out in the woods practising his shooting with his new .44 auto-mag pistol. While he's doing this, a car pulls up and a black male begins to get out with a shotgun. (We later learn that this is his partner.) As the man with the shotgun is opening his door, if you look at the reflection in the car window, you can clearly see the reflection of a man with a camera and another man standing next to him.

Swingers   A boom mike appears from the bottom of the frame for a few moments during a scene at the Hollywood Hills party, when Mike and his friend Rob look at a woman who passes by them and one of them says, 'There's so many beautiful women here'.

The Terminator   At the end of the film, just before the tanker truck explodes, you can clearly see the tow rope pulling the tanker forward.

Titanic   When Rose says, 'Yes, I would like to see my drawing', when she is in her stateroom with Lizzie, the shadow of what appears to be a boom mike (behind her and to the left) can be seen dropping down prior to her line and then going back up afterwards.

When the ship is sinking, there is a shot of Thomas Andrews leaning against the wall in deep contemplation. The camera angle is very tilted and a few things slide off the shelf in front of him. Look carefully on the DVD and you'll see a wire just under his elbow pulling the china cup off the shelf!

Twister   About halfway through the film, as they all take shelter in the garage near the drive-in movie, when the 'Drive-In Movie' sign goes crashing through the garage wall you can clearly see a large metal chain pulling it through.

Vertical Limit   Throughout the film, many of the climbers are wearing dark, black reflective sunglasses. If you watch them, the whole camera crew can be visible in them – a few people standing where there shouldn't be anyone, cameras visible, reflectors, you name it...

A View to a Kill   When James Bond and Patrick MacNee are pushed into the lake in the Rolls-Royce, you can clearly see the wire pulling the car into the water. It leaps out of the water as it takes the strain.

The Wizard of Oz   Several times you can see the wire that makes the Lion's tail wag.

X-Men   The 'copper' straps used to restrain the heroes in the Statue of Liberty are actually made of foam or some other malleable material. They flex considerably as the characters struggle.

SUSTENANCE FOR THE SOUL

The classic line goes 'Never work with children or animals'. After reading this collection, a lot of directors might start thinking they should never use food in any scenes, ever – if a character's eating, but you need to do multiple takes, you'd better make sure someone's on standby to rebuild their plateful . . .

American Beauty   When Kevin Spacey's talking about the car he's just bought, the beer on the table has its label facing the camera. On the reverse shots, it's still facing the camera. The label doesn't wrap round – later on we see that there's one front label and nothing on the back. Shameless advertising.

When Kevin Spacey is drinking from the blender in the kitchen, the amount changes . . . the wrong way. First it's half full, then a third full, then half full again.

American Pie   In the bedroom scene at the beginning the girl is holding a clear cupful of beer. The camera goes off her and when it comes back she is holding a blue cup. The camera goes back off her then on her and the cup is clear again.

In the scene where Stiffler and the girl are in the bedroom at his party, the amount of beer in the cup changes frequently. Before he picks it up, it's about half full; when he picks it up, it's about three-quarters full.

Animal House   In the cafeteria, John Belushi puts stuff on his tray. Before the cut his bunch of bananas is on the side of the tray. After the cut the bunch is on the other side.

Austin Powers: The Spy Who Shagged Me   In the scene when Mini-Me and the young Number 2 grab for the cookies, when

Number 2 grabs there are two, one that looks like chocolate chip and a plain one. When Mini-Me grabs, there is just one.

Beverly Hills Cop   When Axel is getting the bananas from the waiter in the hotel, the bananas he gets are straight. When he places the bananas in the tailpipe of the detectives' car, they are curved.

Big   Billy and Josh go to a restaurant and Billy orders Josh a birthday cake. During the meal, the level of cola in Billy's glass goes down and then up again.

Charlie's Angels   In the party scene, when Bill Murray is talking to the president of Red Star, he is offered blowfish (1 in 60 chance of death etc.). When the dish is first brought out there is nothing over it – but when Bosley takes one he pulls clingfilm off the dish.

Clerks   After Dante helps the customer remove the Pringles can from his arm, he places it on the counter. In the next shot the Pringles can has gone.

Clueless   When Cher and Josh have dinner, Cher is eating a long green asparagus, or something like that. In the next scene it's suddenly short (although she didn't eat it) and then it gets longer again.

Dances with Wolves   The piece of meat that Kevin Costner offers the wolf changes shape and size dramatically throughout that scene.

Die Hard   When the terrorist breaks into the candy rack, he reaches his hand into a box marked Nestlé and later he is eating a Hershey bar. Then in the next shot he is eating a different type of candy bar.

Dumb and Dumber   In the scene where Jim Carrey is talking to the person at the bar, the barman gives him another beer. In the first shot there are two bottles on the desk; however, when he gets another, there is only one bottle.

E.T. The Extra-Terrestial   During the dinner scene at the beginning of the film, Drew Barrymore has half a hamburger on her fork. The next time you see her the hamburger is full.

Ferris Bueller's Day Off   When Ferris is talking with Cameron on the phone and playing on the computer there is a no Pepsi can on his desk. A second later one appears next to his hand. The can then disappears in the next shot.

From Dusk Till Dawn   In the motel scene with the hostage, Quentin Tarantino is eating a burger and drinking a beer, mixed up with different camera angles.

Ghostbusters   When the eggs pop out of Sigourney Weaver's bag and start cooking on the counter, they're in different positions depending on whether it's a close-up or wide shot.

The Godfather   When they're drinking wine, watch Kay's glass. When the camera's on Michael Corleone she's holding the stem, but when the camera's on her she's holding the body of the glass. The major mistake though is that, just after he stands up, the amount of wine in her glass suddenly doubles.

Grease   At Frenchie's sleepover, when they are talking about piercing Sandy's ears, it shows Sandy holding the wine bottle and passing it to Jan. It cuts back to Sandy and she is still holding the wine, then it cuts back to Jan and she has the wine again.

Grosse Pointe Blank   In the scene in the bar, three glasses arrive – John Cusack pushes one over to Minnie Driver, so she has two and he has one. But keep an eye on them, because occasionally two are on his side.

Independence Day   When Jeff Goldblum is getting drunk and he's talking to his ex-wife, at one point he slams the bottle down on the counter and a little liquor sprays up out the opening. They then talk for a second and he picks the bottle back up to pour himself more, but he now needs to unscrew the cap, which was lying next to the bottle just a moment previously.

Jerry Maguire   The morning after their first date, Jerry sits down to breakfast with Ray. He pours out a bit of cereal for Ray, then himself, then puts the box down, but in the next shot Ray's got about three times as much cereal as he had before.

Jurassic Park III   In the scene where Dr Grant gets rescued by the kid and they are sitting in the water tank (truck) eating candy bars, they show the kid eating a Crunch bar with no wrapper, just in the tinfoil. In the next scene you see him eating the same candy bar but the Crunch wrapper is now on. After a few more seconds the Crunch wrapper disappears again.

Legally Blonde   When Reese Witherspoon is eating chocolates after being dumped, look closely at the box. When she finds one that she likes, there are two white ones one row in from the back. Two seconds later, just before she throws the box at the screen, there's only one white one, and it's moved forwards a row.

The Matrix   In the scene where Neo comes back from the conversation with the oracle, a part of the cookie, which he has got from the oracle, is bitten off. A few seconds later he wants to eat the cookie and there is no sign of a bite any more.

In the scene where Cipher is making the deal with Agent Smith, he cuts off a big piece of steak. A few seconds later, when he actually puts it in his mouth, it has changed shape and shrunk considerably.

North by Northwest   While Cary Grant is talking with Eve before dinner on the train, his glass mysteriously changes places several times. When shot from behind, he's holding the glass; from the front, it's on the table.

Ocean's Eleven   Matt Damon and Brad Pitt are standing in the Botanical Garden at the Belagio going over Damon's observations. Pitt has a cocktail glass of shrimp in his hand; when the angles change he has a plate in his hand . . . change back, glass.

Near the beginning, when George Clooney raises $2,000 in the poker game, there is a water bottle in front of Topher Grace. When Joshua Jackson calls, it's gone. When Brad Pitt calls, it's back again. It's gone when Topher calls, and back when Danny shows his cards.

Panic Room   When Jodie Foster kisses her daughter good night she opens up the fridge and gets a bottle of water. The fridge is clearly stocked with insulin, water and orange juice. Later, when she goes back and gets the insulin for her daughter, there is no orange juice at all, only water and insulin.

During the first meal in the new house, the level of Coke in the daughter's glass keeps changing as the camera cuts between her and her mother. The Coke can revolves as well. Sometimes the Coke logo is visible; at other times the list of ingredients is facing the audience.

Pay it Forward   Early in the movie, after Haley Joel Osment befriends a bum, they are sitting at the kitchen table and the bum pours Haley a bowl of Captain Crunch and fills it over the rim of the bowl. In the next wide shot the bowl of cereal is below the bowl's rim level as they pour milk into it.

Pretty Woman   The morning after Julia Roberts's first night at the hotel, room service brings breakfast. She is eating a croissant in one scene but in the next it's a pancake, and the pancake goes from being half done to being a whole pancake again.

When they are sitting down with David and his dad in the important business meeting, they all get served ice cream in goblet-shaped dishes. The waiters take them away. When they stand up to leave, those dishes are still there.

Road to Perdition   When Jude Law is first talking to Tom Hanks in the diner, he orders a cup of coffee. They talk for about thirty seconds with the camera going back and forth between Hanks and Law. In one shot, there's nothing on Law's table, then in the next shot of him he has a cup of coffee in front of him.

The Rocky Horror Picture Show   Near the beginning of 'The Time Warp', we see the fat male Transylvanian handing a tray of snacks to someone off-screen to the left. In the very next scene, he is holding the tray of snacks.

Scary Movie   During the scene where they are driving in the car, when they run over the guy, keep an eye on the Jack Daniels bottle. The quantity continually changes.

Scorpion King   When Memnon is conversing with the sorceress in his palace, he talks about the dangers of her being outside 'his care'. Memnon takes some meat and throws it to the tigers. The next shot shows his hand empty, then holding meat again and then empty again.

🎬 **Shanghai Noon** When you look at the bottle of whiskey during the Chinese drinking game, you can see the bottle's contents shrink and grow.

🎬 **The Shawshank Redemption** When Warden Norton first receives the pie, it is in an aluminium (crinkled edge) pie pan. Later, when Morgan Freeman is eating from the pie, it is in a solid tin pie pan.

🎬 **The Shining** At the beginning, when Danny is talking to his mom and eating a sandwich, the sandwich gets about five bites smaller in a split second.

🎬 **Shrek** When a glass of milk is poured during the torture of the gingerbread man, if you look closely, the glass is filled but the level of milk in the bottle doesn't seem to lower.

🎬 **Signs** When Mel Gibson goes to meet his family for pizza, he sits down and they all stare at Ray Reddy. As the camera pulls back out of the doorway, you can see that Gibson's slice of pizza is half eaten already, although he couldn't have been eating as he was staring at Reddy as he arrived.

🎬 **Steel Magnolias** At the wedding, Darryl Hannah's glass of Coke is full when it's poured, but the level's lower when it's handed to her.

When Julia Roberts has a diabetic attack in Dolly Parton's shop, she is given a glass of orange juice, and she shakes so much that she spills about half the glass. But when Daryl Hannah grabs some paper towels and goes to clean it up, there's at least two glasses' worth of juice on the floor.

🎬 **There's Something About Mary** In the scene at the fairground, Cameron Diaz is holding a stick of very abundant cotton candy. The camera pans away for a few seconds, and when it returns the cotton candy is almost completely finished.

📽 **The Thomas Crown Affair**   In the first scene in the gallery, when Thomas Crown is admiring the *Haystacks* painting, he is preparing to eat a bagel, or something like that. In the shot looking at him face-on he manoeuvres the bagel into position in the bag it is in so that he can begin to eat it. However, in the next shot – a longer-distance profile shot – just after he answers Bobby's question, he is already chewing on a mouthful and starting to tear another piece off.

📽 **Three to Tango**   The first time Matthew Perry is in Neve Campbell's apartment, before he realises she thinks he's gay, he fills two glasses of wine in two very different glasses. He hands one to her and holds the other himself, but in the next shot they hold different glasses.

📽 **Top Gun**   At Charlie's, she and Maverick are having dinner and he asks for the wine. Throughout the entire scene the bottle of wine is rotating.

📽 **Unbreakable**   In the scene where Bruce Willis is sitting at the table with his wife and son, there is an orange juice container on the table, the type of container that is a carton but has a screw-on cap on the top. When Bruce's son is about to sit down at the table, the screw-on cap on the orange juice carton is facing Bruce. When the camera focuses on the child, the screw-on cap is facing the boy, and no one had touched the carton.

📽 **The Wedding Singer**   At the cakeshop, Adam Sandler is feeding a stranger some samples of cake. First you see two pieces of cake on the plate. Then he feeds one to that weird person, and in the next frame featuring the plate, it's empty. Then, after that, there is still one piece of cake on the plate.

You've Got Mail When Tom Hanks and his dad are on the boat, and Tom is making martinis, keep an eye on his olive-adding. He puts an olive in one of the glasses, the camera cuts away, then when it returns the glass is empty and he puts an olive in again.

TAKE 14

Quite hard to define, this category. Every so often you'll be watching a film and you'll notice something that reminds you it's a film, not reality (beyond the fact that Natalie Portman exists in few people's reality, more's the pity). Movie-making relies on a willing suspension of disbelief, of course, but sometimes you'll notice something that cuts the strings and brings your disbelief crashing to the ground again . . .

Animal House The scene where Flounder tosses the box of marbles into the street to trip the ROTC cadets during the parade. Look at the background parade audience as they go into fast forward along with the action of the marbles. It's very quick (about half a second), but easy to see if you're looking for it.

Apocalypse Now In the major helicopter scene, when 'Ride of the Valkyries' is played, the actual tape isn't going over the playing heads.

Armageddon There's grass on the edge of the cliff when the *Armadillo* finally lands – look just under the *Armadillo* while the astronaut's pulling himself up the road. Considering this is an airless, waterless asteroid, it doesn't really fit.

Austin Powers in Goldmember Right before the opening dance number begins, Gwyneth Paltrow and Steven Spielberg do back flips – the person doing them as Gwyneth was wearing a blonde wig that falls off after the first flip.

Austin Powers: International Man of Mystery In the scene where Austin and his allies burst through the big blue door, right before 'Secret Agent Man' begins playing, the door explodes, and you can clearly see that it's made out of wood, even though it's painted to look like, and is meant to be, metal.

🎥 **Batman & Robin** When Mr Freeze is freezing the town, the cop car that crashed into the store has flexible icicles on the driver-side door.

🎥 **Batman Forever** When Two-Face and the Riddler enter Wayne Manor and knock Alfred down, Alfred, supposedly unconscious, pushes the dinner tray aside, so the thugs can carry him into the closet.

🎥 **Batman Returns** When the Penguin goes into the cemetery, he bumps a tombstone and it moves. Apparently this was a nod to hack director Ed Wood – admired by *Batman* director Tim Burton. In *Plan Nine From Outer Space* (and recreated in Burton's film *Ed Wood*), someone bumps a tombstone and it moves.

🎥 **Beetlejuice** In the part where Geena Davis and Alec Baldwin are asked to draw a door on a wall in case of an emergency, there is already a chalk outline of where a door would be.

When Geena Davis is moving the little plastic horse in front of the mirror to prove that she's invisible, the 'reflection' of the horse is not synchronised with the actual horse.

🎥 **Blade II** In one scene Whistler has a thermal scope on a rifle and looks at Blade walking with a group of vampires. Blade is red (warm) and the other vampires are blue (cool). Later Whistler is walking in the tunnels with two vampires from the earlier group that were blue in the scope. They give him a night vision headset so he can 'see in the dark'. When he looks at the vampires with the night vision they are both red (warm).

In the scene where Nyssa and Reinhardt are fighting the Reapers after Blade has detonated the UV bomb, Nyssa takes a deep breath before diving under the water – yet vampires don't breathe.

🎥 **The Bourne Identity** When the first assassin runs out of bullets shortly after coming through the apartment window, his gun makes a series of rapid clicks as if dry firing full-auto, but real guns, even full-auto ones, don't keep on clicking when empty. It should either make a single click or a nearly inaudible one.

🎥 **Braveheart** After William Wallace kills the Scottish noble in bed, he jumps out of the castle window into a river, while astride a horse. As he is falling, you can see that the horse is a model and, when they fall into the water, one can see the fake horse bobbing around.

When his wife gets attacked, Wallace jumps over a roof and you can clearly see him wearing modern-day black briefs.

🎥 **Bring it On** In the scene where Kirsten Dunst is in the living room trying to call her boyfriend, her brother is shown playing a PlayStation. When she gets mad at him for making a comment about her boyfriend being gay, she comes over and pulls the controller out of his hands and out of the PlayStation, but when the camera changes angles it shows the PlayStation open and no game inside.

🎥 **Catch Me If You Can** In a phone conversation between Leonardo DiCaprio and Tom Hanks, Leo is using a phone that has a plug-type receiver. The phones in that era were all hard-wired.

When Leonardo DiCaprio is arrested in France, Tom Hanks bends over to look at him through the rear window of the police car. You can clearly see the lines of the window defogger on Hanks's face. Cars did not have electric defoggers like that in the 60s.

Charlie's Angels   When the Angels are driving through a tunnel and decide to turn around to get to the marina, there are distinct skid marks the exact same way the girls U-turn. Evidence of previous takes.

Chasing Amy   When Ben Affleck is driving in the car with Alyssa while it is raining (right before he tells her he loves her), if you look at the speedometer in front of him, the needle is on 0. The car is obviously on a track to look as though they are driving.

Chicago   As Roxie is being escorted into the murderers' row, Mama and Roxie pass Velma's cell. The dollar Velma gives Mama is a modern one.

Clear and Present Danger   In the scene in Colombia when the convoy is attacked, Jack Ryan is running away from the last car and falls as it explodes. In his left hand, you can see that he is pressing the switch that makes the last explosion as he is falling.

Con Air   When Nicolas Cage is shot in the arm on the plane, you can clearly see that blood is shot out of the back of his arm, then a split second later you see the hole in the front of his arm appear.

Daredevil   When Daredevil kicks Bullseye off his motorcycle, Bullseye has nothing in his hands as he's flying through the air but, when he lands, he's holding Daredevil's baton. Watch closely when Daredevil's kick connects and you can see they never come close enough for Bullseye to grab the baton or for him to snatch it if it were dropped.

In the fight scene between Daredevil and Elektra, some of the sheets hanging to dry still have crease lines from taking them out of the package, meaning they have never been on a bed or ever laundered before, just bought for the movie and immediately hung up.

🎬 **Days of Thunder**   During many of the races shown in the movie, shots from the wrong track are shown. For example, the caption at the bottom of the screen for one race claimed they were at Martinsville speedway, but a shot was shown from Daytona speedway (in one shot you can even see DAYTONA USA painted on the wall).

🎬 **Deep Blue Sea**   When Samuel L. Jackson is attacked and killed by the shark, you can clearly tell that he is CGI. His arms and legs are segments and it looks really corny.

🎬 **Die Another Day**   In the scene where Bond is in the rocket sled being chased by the huge beam of light, Graves uses the laser to cut a huge section of ice out of the cliff and it cuts about 100 metres without a problem. But, when the laser is used on the ice palace, it just melts slowly instead of being completely annihilated.

When Bond and Jinx are trying to escape in the helicopter they open the door and start the conveyor. The red car drops. Quite a few seconds later, the yellow car is dropped. Yet, later, both cars are nose down in the mud about twenty feet apart. How did this happen when the plane was moving at such speed?

The red sports car is sticking nose down in the ground after falling hundreds of feet down out of the aeroplane, without a singe crack in the windshield, in mint condition. The yellow one only has the right door open.

When Bond is driving the Chevy in Havana, look at the speedometer – it's at zero.

🎬 **Die Hard**   When Alan Rickman discovers the first bad guy lying dead in the lift ('Now I have a gun – ho, ho, ho!') and slaps him over the cheek, the corpse is moving its head before it is hit (watch carefully!). He also blinks.

Die Hard 2   In the scene where Richard Thornberg is in the aeroplane bathroom giving his live report, in a number of the shots he is holding the phone upside down.

In the skywalk scene, when John McClane pushes the paint stand on the terrorist, you can clearly see that they use a dummy when the paint stand falls.

Dogma   When God destroys Ben Affleck, she goes out into the street to clean up the mess. When she gets there she is standing right next to Matt Damon's dead body, but look closely at his legs – when the camera moves up to God, you can see Damon's legs moving out of the way.

Dumb and Dumber   In the scene where Jeff Daniels and Mary are making the snowman, there are three pre-formed holes where Mary puts the charcoal and carrot.

Eraser   When Arnie jumps from the plane, notice the stunt double. He weighs about half of what Arnie would, and has no muscles.

Eyes Wide Shut   In the newspaper that Tom Cruise is reading, the same sentences are printed over and over – clearly a fake newspaper, without too much thought being given to the keen-eyed reader.

Face/Off   When the speedboat crashes at the end of the film, the two actors flying through the air look absolutely nothing like John Travolta or Nicolas Cage. Obviously stunt doubles will never look identical, but in this case it's just ridiculous.

The Fifth Element   Right after they 'create' Leeloo and she is lying in the plastic cage with the little straps on her, the guy approaches her and says, 'If you want out, you are going to have to work on your communication skills.' She gives him a dirty look and then, if you put it in slow motion, you can see a huge hole, pre-cut in the glass, that she busts her hand through.

Fight Club When members of Fight Club are starting fights, watch *very* closely when the guy with the hose sprays the vicar – you can see the camera wobble slightly (looking on the left of the screen at the top of the fence is a good reference point). This happened because the cameraman started to laugh.

In the scene where Brad Pitt is cutting out newspaper articles about Project Mayhem's mayhem, the headlines refer to their deeds but the actual writing in the articles has absolutely nothing to do with the movie. They seem to all come from one article about some town council meeting.

Near the end, when Brad Pitt and Edward Norton are fighting in the garage, the fighting carries into a stairwell. Edward Norton gets pitched down the stairwell and it is very clearly a stunt double.

Near the end of the film, when Brad Pitt throws Ed Norton down the steps, we get the view from a security camera; however, we can see the camera we are supposed to be looking through in the top right-hand corner.

Final Destination When they look at Todd's dead body in the morgue, you can see him open his eyes a little bit.

First Knight When Lancelot is chasing the horse, it gallops through a field and you can see a telegraph pole.

Gangs of New York During the first fight scene, the snow is obviously fake. One shot zooms in on a man's foot and, as he lifts it, the snow is lifted as well, like a sheet of cotton.

Ghostbusters   There's a scene where Sigourney Weaver's building is falling apart and stones and stuff are falling to the street below. One of the huge boulders bounces off a wooden police barricade in the bottom left-hand corner of the screen.

Gladiator   In the scene where Maximus quickly kills all his opponents, when he stabs the third to last man in the stomach, you can clearly see him 'stab' to the side of his stomach. Even more visible when you slow it down.

Near the end of the movie, when Commodus and Maximus are in close, struggling for the knife, take a good look at the knife. Both of the actors' hands are gripping it and it's clearly rubber because it's bent at a serious angle.

When Maximus falls over after his fight with the emperor, slow the tape down. You can clearly see that Russell Crowe remembers that the woman has to kneel on his left side, and so quickly pulls his left arm in.

In the battle of Carthage, towards the end and just after the repeater crossbow has been fired, we see one of Maximus's friends running towards one of the fallen chariot riders. You can clearly see the spike that he kills the guy with moving as he runs, suggesting that it was made of a softer, safer material.

As Maximus approaches his home after he should have been killed, the grain fields clearly show marks which are only caused by a tractor during crop-spraying.

The Godfather   Vito Corleone is unconscious, yet he jerks his hand out of the way when it's scraped past a door frame. Michael Corleone and the nurse seem to notice this, but carry on regardless.

One of Sonny's punches clearly misses Carlo, yet Carlo reacts as if hit. The punch was wrong for the camera angle.

Godzilla   In the scene where Matthew Broderick gets into the elevator in Madison Square Garden, he presses the 'close doors' button, but if you look at the button to the left of his hand the picture shows the 'close doors' sign, so he would be pressing the 'open doors' button (handy for keeping the doors open and maintaining tension . . .).

GoldenEye   Near the start, when James Bond climbs out of the manhole, he leans against the stone corridor walls while preparing his next move. Look closely at the wall as he touches it – it bends.

Goldfinger   When Oddjob first demonstrates his lethal bowler hat by decapitating the statue, the stone statue's arm bends as the head falls on to it.

Gone with the Wind   The shadow scene in which Scarlett and Melanie care for the wounded in the Atlanta hospital was filmed with two doubles. Since the stars were standing at the wrong angle to cast the shadows, two stand-ins were positioned in front of the high-intensity light. The shadows of the doubles were reflected on the wall behind the stars, and the result was a stunning visual effect. Yet upon a closer look, the gestures of the stand-ins are not totally synchronised with the movements of the stars. Most noticeable is when Melanie leans down, and her shadow is about half a second behind her.

In the scene showing guests arriving at the Wilkeses' barbecue, you see buggies and carriages driving through the front gates and up the drive toward the Wilkeses' home. The carriages clearly create shadows on the ground, but not on the stone pillars of the gates. This is because when the movie was filmed, there were no actual gates. The gates were later 'painted' into the frame. Proving someone forgot to 'paint' shadows on to the pillars.

GoodFellas   In the scene where Karen is too afraid to accept free clothes from Jimmy and speeds off, the yellow NY state licence plate falls from the parked car to reveal the modern white one underneath.

When Samuel L. Jackson is shot by Joe Pesci, the blood spatter very clearly comes from off-screen to the right.

Grease In the soda shop, the waitress turns off the lights with her elbow because her hands are full, but she misses the light switch by six inches. It still turns off though.

Halloween: Resurrection After Michael kills Laurie at the beginning, he hands the knife to the inmate with the clown mask. Next he uses the tripod ends to kill the cameraman. A few scenes later Michael is shown holding a knife with fresh blood on it. He hasn't killed anybody with this knife yet so where did the blood come from?

Harry Potter and the Chamber of Secrets At the beginning of the scene with Lucius Malfoy fuming at Dumbledore in his office, Malfoy's hair is fanned back behind his shoulders. The lighting in the room illuminates the back of his neck, where you can see his real, short brown hair.

In the quidditch scene, Harry breaks his right arm but, as he sits up after he falls off his broom, he leans directly on it.

When Harry is fighting the basilisk on top of the skull in the Chamber of Secrets, there is clearly a safety tip on the end of the sword.

In the many and lengthy dialogue scenes between Harry Potter and Dumbledore, with countless facial close-ups, neither of them have glass in their spectacles.

Harry Potter and the Philosopher's Stone When Harry receives his first letter in the mail, Dudley snatches it from him and gives it to his father (Uncle Vernon). Uncle Vernon asks, 'Who'd be writing to you?' and, if you watch Dudley carefully, you can see him mouth what Uncle Vernon is saying.

When Harry, Ron and Hermione rush to Hagrid after end-of-the-year exams and Harry says something that ends with 'why didn't I see it before?', Hermione is mouthing his lines.

Highlander At the end when the car is being driven by Kurgan, it bashes into the railings on the bridge several times, but by watching in slo-mo you can see that the sparks fly out of the railings about a metre in front of the car.

The Hunt for Red October In the scene where Jack Ryan is brought aboard the USS *Dallas* after releasing himself from the helicopter, two crewmen drag him inside. One of them backs into a metal valve but the valve bends and snaps back as if made of rubber instead of metal, as it should be.

Independence Day When Jeff Goldblum is throwing a tantrum in the hangar housing the captured alien craft, he knocks over several plastic garbage cans, one of which is clearly labelled 'Art Dept' – kind of odd for a top secret underground government military research facility.

Jurassic Park In the scenes where there's a video link to the docks shown on computer, there's a bar moving along the bottom of the screen, showing us that it's actually a video that's just playing on the computer.

When the T-Rex has a Raptor in its mouth at the end, the Raptor disappears completely from the T-Rex's mouth, then reappears in the next frame.

📽 Kingpin   In the middle of the movie, Woody Harrelson is flossing his teeth by himself. In the mirror, as well as when he turns around, if you look closely, you can see his hand holding the hook.

When Woody Harrelson and Vanessa Angel are fighting in the car park, Woody's rubber hand somehow manages to grab her ankle.

📽 The Last of the Mohicans   Near the very end of the movie, when Magua has taken Uncas's love interest and he is taking a path through the mountain, Daniel Day-Lewis runs up a path and brushes against what seems to be a rock. But the grey coloured 'rock' seems to be a prop and moves like a piece of cloth.

📽 Legally Blonde   In the scene where Reese Witherspoon is entering the elevator after being harassed by her mentor, you can see Selma Blair's reflection in the plaque right before her cue. You see her reflection right before the doors close, so you know she was waiting for the cue.

📽 The Lord of the Rings: The Fellowship of the Ring   When Boromir is killed, he's shot twice. You can clearly see the hole for the third arrow between the first two, before the third arrow appears.

Hobbits go barefoot, but when Frodo and Sam are first walking through the fields, Frodo's leg comes above long-grass level and the sole of a boot is clearly visible.

📽 The Lord of the Rings: The Two Towers   When the men are retreating into the halls of Helm's Deep, an archer in the bottom right corner is repeatedly shooting his bow without an arrow on the string.

When the riders break out of Helm's Deep, the hooves on the last horse pass straight through the orc corpses on the bridge.

🎥 **The Mask of Zorro** In the ending shots, when Antonio Banderas and Captain Love are fighting, when Captain Love falls down the hill, Alejandro grabs a shovel and slides down the hill. If you look at the shovel, you will see the strap that holds his feet to it.

In the opening scene when Anthony Hopkins is freeing the peasants and jumps down from the top of the mission to the small balcony, you can see that the bricks where he lands are actually made of, or mounted on, some type of rubber, as they give way and bounce back under his feet when he lands there.

🎥 **The Matrix** When Agent Smith is fighting with Neo in the subway, Neo's back is against a pillar. The area of the pillar which Agent Smith punches away with the first punch is visible before Neo ducks, and then he punches it away. You have to look carefully, because it only appears for a very short time.

In the scene where Neo is on the ledge outside the office, trying to follow Morpheus's instructions, he wraps his hand around the pillar to attempt a pass. If you look, you can see multiple hand prints from where Reeves had repeated the shot over and over.

🎥 **Minority Report** When Burgess is talking, on the flip-up transparent panel on his desk, to Tom Cruise in his car, the word Nokia is the correct way round to the people in the cinema, therefore it would have been a mirror image to Burgess who was using it.

In the final scene of the movie, as the camera pulls back from the cabin, where the three Pre-Cogs were taken after leaving the Temple, there is a tractor to the left of the cabin. Between the tractor and the cabin is a small bush that is moving like it is being blown by a strong wind. However, the smoke coming from the cabin is more or less rising straight up into the air, if anything drifting a little to the right; the bush is being blown to the left by the helicopter that has the camera.

🎥 **Ocean's Eleven** When Bruiser (the guy who's supposed to beat up George Clooney) is faking the noises of a beating, the two thugs can hear him through the door. But earlier, when he punched George Clooney by accident then started to talk to him, the thugs should have been able to hear their talking through the door as well.

🎥 **Panic Room** After the intruders flood the panic room with propane, Jodie Foster's character gets a lighter and ignites the propane causing it to burn along the ceiling. This would be impossible as propane is heavier than air and would sink to the floor rather than rise up to the ceiling. Lighting a flame in that room should have caused anyone in the room and on the floor to be engulfed in flames almost instantly.

🎥 **Pretty Woman** The scene where Richard Gere offers Julia Roberts the necklace and shuts the box on her fingers wasn't scripted – Richard Gere just did it for a laugh. You can tell because, when he does it, Julia Roberts laughs and looks up and around (i.e. at the film crew) – in the context of that scene there wasn't anyone there for her to look at.

🎥 **Red Dragon** In the scene where Will Graham is teaching his wife to shoot, there is absolutely no muzzle blast as she takes each shot. Muzzle blast is always present when a gun is fired.

In the scene when Will is opening the drawer of films from the Leeds home, there is a copy of *Mrs Doubtfire*. How can that be? As the caption says, *Red Dragon* is set 'several years' after 1980, but before the 1991 *Silence of the Lambs*, so probably late 80s. *Mrs Doubtfire* came out in 1993.

🎥 **Reservoir Dogs** When Mr White and Mr Pink are together in the bathroom, Mr White tries to light his cigarette. He doesn't get it lit, but he still pretends to smoke it anyway.

Mr Pink continues shooting at the cops even after his pistol locks back, indicating he is out of bullets.

🎥 **Road to Perdition**   When Tom Hanks first drives into Chicago among all the 1931-era cars, a giant, modern, swing-arm, stationary crane is reflected in his car window.

In the diner scene, Jude Law pours sugar in his coffee and the bottom of the sugar dispenser is exposed to reveal the bar code label. Bar codes were not used in 1931.

🎥 **Road Trip**   When Tom Green is feeding the snake, there is clearly visible plastic tape around its mouth. With this tape the snake wouldn't be able to open its mouth.

🎥 **RoboCop**   When RoboCop is fighting Clarence Boddicker in the cocaine factory, he throws Boddicker through a plate-glass window. If you watch closely, you can see the window shatter about 1–2 seconds before he goes through it.

When ED-209 is being demonstrated for the first time and it goes out of control, repeatedly shooting the young executive, you can see packets of fake blood strapped to his back, under his suit.

🎥 **The Rocky Horror Picture Show**   When Riff-Raff and Magenta burst in after Frank's song, Janet steps away from Frank's side into Brad's arms. Watch Brad's face – you can clearly see the look of pain as Janet steps on his foot in four-inch spike heels!

The saxophone Eddie plays in 'Hot Patootie' has no reed.

🎥 **Scooby-Doo**   At the end of the movie when Scooby jumps into Shaggy's arms and knocks him down, Shaggy is already falling backwards before Scooby actually lands on him. The CGI animators did not quite synchronise the jump.

When the reporters are all gathering around the gang as they exit the park near the end of the film, the reporter on the viewer's right asks a question while the reporter beside her, in green, is also mouthing the words at the same time.

🎬 **Scorpion King**   One of the first times you see Balthazar you can see the adhesive for the fake scar on his right cheek is coming loose.

🎬 **Scream**   When Dewey enters the house where the party is held, calling out for Mr Prescott and holding his gun, he passes a table with a vase on it. If you look closely, you'll see the table and vase are knocked by someone off-screen twice; Dewey is nowhere near it.

🎬 **Shanghai Noon**   At the end, when Jackie Chan is fighting the bad guy, he jumps up on to a window sill and then jumps down when the bad guy tries to hit him with a spear. If you look at the spear when it hits the wall, you can see that the spearhead is made of rubber – it bends when it touches the wall.

🎬 **Smokey and the Bandit**   When the Bandit first pulls over and picks up Frog, he then screeches off. If you look at the road you can see all the skid marks from where they practised it, even down to the bit where the van pulls out of the junction and the Bandit brakes suddenly and then speeds off.

🎬 **Speed**   The bridge that the bus jumps has had a section digitally removed, but look closely, because on the ground you can still see the shadow it would cause.

When the bus is speeding up in one shot, we can see the flat trailer in the background with policemen on it. Watch them closely – they've speeded up the film so the bus seems to be going faster than it really is, but a side-effect of this is that the policemen are moving about incredibly quickly!

When the subway train's sliding along the ground at the end, the sparks, supposedly caused by the metal scraping on the ground, are obviously being artificially generated, because they're nowhere near the tarmac.

Spider-Man   When Peter Parker first discovers he can climb up walls (while in normal clothing), he tests it out by climbing up a building in an alley. During this scene, you can see his clothes hanging out forwards, indicating that the scene was filmed with him crawling along a floor horizontally.

Superman   When Superman lets out a scream after discovering Lois Lane's body, you can clearly see his tooth fillings. Not strictly in keeping with his invincible image!

Superman II   When Superman puts the flag back at the White House, you can see that he is flying against a picture of the White House. The way you can tell this is because the water in the fountains is frozen in mid-air.

When Superman lifts General Zod in the Fortress of Solitude, you can clearly see a sweat stain under his arm.

10 Things I Hate About You   In the scene where Joey parks his car behind Kat's, you hear him coming up really fast and then you see him stop, but if you look in the window across the street you can see in the reflection that the car was still and then it just moves up a little bit, giving the impression of having just stopped from speed.

The Terminator   During the first few minutes of the film, the future shows a flying HK travelling through the air; look closely at it and you can see it 'clip' through a large piece of foreground.

Terminator 2: Judgment Day After the T-1000 steals the truck and throws the driver out there is a big action sequence where the truck hits a lot of cars. In one scene the truck hits two cars which, if paused, shows that those cars were both parked across the main road, front bumper to front bumper, blocking the main road in the process, making it impossible for the truck to miss them.

When Arnie's arm is caught in the wheel and he rips his own arm off and stands up, if you look closely (slo-mo can help) you can see his real arm stretched behind his back under his leather jacket.

In the bar fight scene Arnie gets stabbed by one of the bikers – if you put it in slow motion you see the rubber knife bend in a few frames.

When the T-1000 follows them in the helicopter, we can clearly see that he has three hands – he is loading his gun with two and steering with the third. OK, it might be able to generate arms at will, but worth a look.

In the scene where Sarah Connor hits the hospital guy with half a broom, you can see it bend like rubber in slo-mo.

There's Something About Mary When the investigator takes Ben Stiller's head and starts slamming it on the table, after Ben got finished telling them about the hitchhiker, Ben Stiller's head never hits the table but his own hand.

The man kissing Cameron Diaz in that last shot (when the homeless guy shoots the singer) is *not* Ben Stiller, noticeable by his much taller, slender figure.

Titanic At the end when Rose is lying on the wooden door, she is looking at the sky singing 'Come Josephine'. When you look hard you see that the stars in the sky are symmetrical. You can actually draw a line in it. Some people have said that if you look *very* carefully, you can see that the stars form the outline of the famous necklace, the Heart of the Ocean.

In the scene where the ship tilts to a vertical position, you see people falling and hitting objects on the deck. In a close-up of that, you can see that a black metal cylinder thing has wrinkles in it and bends when someone hits it.

When Jack is handcuffed to some pipes and the ship is sinking, Rose finds an axe to save him. Check out the few frames where Rose is actually swinging at Jack's handcuffs. You can see she never even came close to hitting them – or Jack – or the pipes he was handcuffed to.

In the scene on deck where Rose is checking out Jack's portfolio, and Jack is teaching her to spit, for a split second you can see the breakers rolling in to shore through the ship's railing.

Tomorrow Never Dies   In the scene with the helicopter chasing them down the street, apart from the fact that the rotors should catch on something and hurl the machine into a wall, when it finally hits the wall at the end, the pilot and crew quite clearly become crash-test dummies. This wouldn't be so bad if it weren't for the fact that they are unpainted and all sit in their seats looking straight ahead with their hands in their laps while they are driven into a wall. You'd think they could have at least posed the arms over their faces or something.

Top Gun   In the final battle scene, which takes place way out over the water, in some of the F-14 shots, mountains can be seen in the background.

Unbreakable   In the final scene, the headline on one of the newspaper clippings on the killer's office wall reads something like, HUGE MUDSLIDE IN MEXICO: ALL KILLED EXPECT NEWBORN. The penultimate word should be 'except' – obviously a faked paper. Unless a lot of dead people are all pregnant with the same child.

Waterworld   Right before the Smokers show up, you can see land on the left-hand side of the screen.

When Harry Met Sally   When they are in the museum and Harry says, 'For the rest of the day, we are going to talk like this . . .', the last thing he says is ad libbed. 'But I would be proud to partake of your pecan pie' is not in the script. You can see Meg Ryan look off-camera at the director and say 'Oh, no', but she continues with him. It's obvious that she wasn't expecting it.

The Wizard of Oz   When the wizard is getting ready to take off in the balloon, while most people watch Dorothy climb out of the basket and go after Toto, the Tin Man is unravelling the thing holding the hot-air balloon down, then he 'accidentally' lets go.

When the group is waiting to see the wizard, the Lion sings the 'If I Were King' song. The Tin Man grabs a flowerpot and breaks it to make a crown. When the crown falls off the Lion's head later, it bounces around like plastic.

At the end of the movie, when Dorothy is confronting the 'wizard' about going home, Toto goes over to the curtain and you can see him tied up to it as he opens it. Dorothy then goes over there and automatically has him in her arms – she didn't even need to bend down and pick Toto up.

Zulu   Some of the Zulu warriors are wearing the wristwatches they were paid with – not strictly the right time period.

A separate branch of standard continuity mistakes, this. Spotting mistakes can be tricky enough if you're following the action, but when you're watching your favourite film for the twentieth time, your gaze might start wandering to whatever's going on behind the stars. That's where you might notice something interesting . . .

American Pie   When Jim is setting up his computer to take a photo of himself for the dating site, we see shots of him trying to look good for the camera. However, in the supposedly live shots of him gurning at the camera on the monitor the blinds are open, whereas in the wider shots of him in the room they're well and truly shut – the webcam footage was obviously taped.

Animal House   During the classroom scene, Donald Sutherland writes the word 'Satan' on the board. In the first shot, the 't' in Satan is directly over the crease on the chalkboard. In the next shot, it is clearly on one side of the crease.

Austin Powers in Goldmember   When Austin is beating up Mini-Me, he smashes him through the glass table and it shatters (even though there are two tables in the room it's the glass table that can be seen through the screen door). But then there is a shot of the 'mole' talking to Basil on the phone – with the table, on the right side of the screen, perfectly intact.

When Austin enters the room with the fountain in the factory, he kicks out the power cord. In every following shot that features the power cord, the cord is in a different position.

Austin Powers: The Spy Who Shagged Me   When Austin Powers spits the chess piece and breaks the vase, it flies over Ivana's shoulder, who is sitting across from him. In a shot soon afterwards, the broken vase has somehow moved 'behind' Austin. His multicoloured jacket is a good reference point.

The Bourne Identity   Before the car chase, there is a police car behind Bourne and Marie; then, when they pull away, the police car isn't there any more.

When Bourne and Marie are in the car before the car chase, they have a conversation with camera angles switching back and forth in the car. From shot to shot the window glass is alternately covered with a lot of rain droplets, a few rain droplets, or even completely dry.

When Jason Bourne is on top of the hotel, waiting for the CIA agent, he's standing right under the big letters on the roof that spell out the hotel's name. When it cuts to the agent waiting for Bourne on the bridge, the hotel's roof can be seen in the background but without Bourne standing by the letters. When it goes back to Bourne, he's there again.

When Bourne blows up the tank at the farmhouse, the wide shots show a solid wall of black smoke. In the closer shots there's nowhere near as much.

Braveheart   When the princess visits Wallace, the guard leaves the room, almost closing the door. When the camera cuts back, it's suddenly much more open.

Broken Arrow   When the helicopter on the train blows up, the boxes that John Travolta is hiding behind are on fire. When he stands up, the boxes are not even touched.

Casablanca   When Ingrid Bergman is in Laslo's bedroom, she is shown from behind looking out the window at the street below, then after an edit she is shown looking at the street from outside the window. The problem is that the first shot showed her looking through a roll-type window shade, and the second is a slat-type venetian blind.

Cast Away   The final sequence of the film has a whole load of stuff different. Just before Tom Hanks reaches the crossroads, we see there's a solid double yellow line on the main road, a dirt track to one side, and another road on the other side – that one has one solid and one dashed line on it. It cuts to a wider shot, and the dashed line has suddenly become solid, the Texas state sign has moved closer to the stop sign, and a big shadow (of a telegraph pole or similar) has appeared next to the stop sign. There's then another cut looking down the adjoining road – Tom Hanks's shadow's done a complete 180, the shadow of the telegraph pole's disappeared, the line's gone dashed again, and the Texas sign's moved away. Basically, in one twenty-second clip at least four things change significantly – they used two very similar, but not identical, junctions, for no good reason.

Commando   In the scene where Arnie is fighting Cooke, they smash a few square panes of shower glass, then as Arnie tosses Cooke over his shoulder he knocks the pink lampshade over, but it is standing back up soon after.

Crossroads   Towards the beginning of their drive, while the girls are singing 'Bye, Bye, Bye', the position of the window behind Mimi keeps changing. Sometimes it is all the way up, then it is partly down, then back up again.

Daredevil   Close to the end of the scene where Elektra is practising in her room with the sandbags, she throws a sai into the sandbag with Daredevil's face painted on it. The camera then switches to behind her looking down the length of the room, showing the same sandbag without a sai in it.

Die Another Day   When M leaves Bond's bedside, the doors close but the LED of the security computer lock stays green. It should have turned into red to show that the door had been closed, as happens shortly afterwards when Bond locks the medical staff in.

Towards the end of the film as the helicopter tumbles through the sky after it has fallen out of the plane, Jinx looks back from the cockpit and sees the diamonds in a neat pile spilling out of the door. Surely if the helicopter has been tumbling through the sky, they would be scattered all over the place?

As Bond and Jinx are in the helicopter after being dropped from the plane, Bond is starting the engine. The caution/annunciator lights turn off three times in three different shots for no apparent reason whatsoever.

Dogma The writing on the second book from the left on the right of Linda Fiorentino's bed changes colours in different scenes.

Eyes Wide Shut When Tom Cruise is going into the same room as Marion, there are two tables visible – each one has a sculpture on it. When Carl arrives a few minutes later, the sculpture on the first table has vanished.

When Tom Cruise is reading a paper, keep an eye on the small pictures behind him – they change depending on the shot.

Forrest Gump In the scene where Forrest visits Jenny (and is introduced to his son) there is an iron on the ironing board in the background. It is standing up, then down, then up. The child's artwork in the background also disappears.

When Forrest firsts meets Jenny on the bus to school, a girl is sitting behind them, then disappears.

Harry Potter and the Chamber of Secrets When Harry first meets Dobby, Dobby is bouncing on the bed. There is a bulletin board of some kind with a Gryffindor flag on it. A couple of minutes later, the flag is still there, but the board itself is gone.

Mrs Weasley might as well knit like a muggle because she's not making any progress with magical knitting. In the Weasley's home when the magic knitting is seen, the needle goes into the hole but no wool loops around and it is not advancing. The amount that has already been knitted is magic indeed since all the motion shown in the film produces no results.

Jurassic Park   Jeff Goldblum, Sam Neill and Laura Dern are in the same car, but when Jeff Goldblum talks to Richard Attenborough through the camera you can see that Sam Neill is not sitting in the back seat. In the next scene, when Goldblum sits down again, Sam Neill is now sitting there.

The Lord of the Rings: The Fellowship of the Ring   When the Fellowship meets in Rivendell, and the Dwarf tries to break the ring with his axe, the axe breaks into many pieces on the platform upon which the ring is laid. At first, the pieces are there in the close-up view. When the camera pans back for a long-range view of the Fellowship, the pieces of the axe on the platform are gone. In the following close-up, the pieces magically reappear.

The Lord of the Rings: The Two Towers   After Aragorn, Legolas and Theoden and his men have just come out on the bridge outside Helm's Deep, there's a wide shot of Gandalf and the Rohirrims charging down the mountainside. The bridge is in the background, where the King and Aragorn and the riders should be visible, but they're nowhere to be seen.

In the scene in the storeroom where Sam is suggesting Frodo use the Ring to escape, Frodo is initially sitting in front of a barrel. Then

Faramir arrives and Frodo and Sam are sitting on a cloak and there are no barrels in sight.

When Gandalf, Aragorn, Legolas and Gimli enter the King of Rohan's chamber, Aragorn, Legolas and Gimli start knocking down soldiers to protect Gandalf. When they have finished, there is a shot taken from behind and one of.the beaten soldiers is lying on the floor playing with his hair, curling it around his finger.

The Lost World: Jurassic Park When they're in the shack, and the Raptors are making the walls shake, something like an animal's muzzle falls off the wall and lands in front of the door. We then see a close-up of the Raptors starting to dig under the door, and there's no sign of the muzzle. We then cut back to a wider shot of the door, and the muzzle's back there again.

The Matrix When Neo is out on the scaffolding and loses his phone, in one shot you see the phone falling towards an empty street, then you cut to Neo, and then back to the falling phone. This time the street is filled with people and a big parade.

When Neo comes to work he glances at the name of his company. The sign says Metacortex. When Neo is running from the agents there is a sign on the back wall which says Meta Cortechs.

Minority Report At the beginning of the movie, Tom Cruise is working on the case with the jealous husband (case number 1108). During this scene, there is a shot of Cruise taken from behind the transparent screen and in the upper right corner of the screen there is the case number – 1108. Later in the movie, Cruise starts working on the case where he himself turns out to be the killer. This is case number 1109. There is again a shot of Cruise taken from behind the transparent screen. However, the case number is still 1108.

During the jet-pack escape scene, Cruise scales the side of a building followed by a group of Pre-Crime officers who fly up to catch him. When Cruise jumps and catches the officer directly below him, there is a cut to a shot of the pair falling directly towards the camera. If you look to either side of them, you'll notice that all the other officers – including the one hanging from the rail without a jet pack – have disappeared.

🎥 **Monsters, Inc.** When a green monster named Frank walks out of Monsters, Inc. on the second day, take a look at what's behind the door – it only shows passages to Scare Floors but, when Mike and Sulley (holding Boo in costume) walk in, the Child Detection Agency is all over the place.

Just before they go into the scare room, a sluglike monster is mopping up a spill. When he has finished, he leaves his own trail of sludge. When all the scarers walk to their doors a little later, the slug is there but the floor behind him stays clean.

🎥 **Notting Hill** In the scene where Julia Roberts first goes to Hugh Grant's flat, there's a chalkboard that's telling Spike to clean up. It's quite small writing, but in a close-up of Hugh Grant when he's directing her upstairs it's clearly larger. It then goes small again until she comes downstairs, when it goes large and stays that way.

In one scene in the bookstore at the end, there are three copies of a guide to Germany on the table next to Hugh Grant. In one clip, there are three spines, but in the next shot two of the books have been turned round.

When Hugh Grant is interviewing Julia Roberts in the hotel suite, the trim around the door handle behind him is light brown, with no screws visible on it. A second later, it goes a much darker colour, and there are a couple of screws clearly visible in it. After the publicist leaves, it changes back again.

Ocean's Eleven   The two guards outside the vault doors get gassed and then bound by their hands and feet. Afterwards, while Matt Damon and George Clooney are putting batteries into the bomb detonator outside the vault, the two guards behind them on the floor are unbound.

Se7en   The amount of the name that is left on the door when the janitor is scraping it off changes – it goes from being Some to Somerset.

Spider-Man   In the scene where MJ is being mugged by four men, Spider-Man throws two of the men into two windows behind MJ. Then the camera goes back to Spider-Man beating up the other two guys. When the camera goes back to MJ the two windows behind her are intact.

When Peter shoots his web at his bedroom lamp and pulls it across the room, it smashes against the wall and breaks. But when Aunt May is talking to Peter from the door seconds later, the lamp is back on the dresser in one piece.

Titanic   When Rose is trying to rescue Jack she spies a fire axe. Smashing all the glass out from the holder she grabs the axe and turns round. The next camera shot shows Rose standing in front of the case with almost all of its glass intact.

Tomb Raider   The day after the battle between Lara and all the troops, the UPS man arrives. He steps through the open front doors into Lara's mansion, then it cuts to his feet. When it cuts back to him, the doors he just came through are closed.

What Women Want   Mel Gibson is in the doctor's office and, after reading her mind, he comments on the lamp that she has bid for on eBay. She also has the auction page up on her computer. If you look closely you will notice that the auction is not an eBay auction, but rather a Yahoo! auction.

When Harry Met Sally When they are playing win, lose or draw, Sally is trying to draw baby talk and, if you keep your eye on the drawing, the baby looks different all the time – it has eyes, and then doesn't have eyes, etc.

William Shakespeare's Romeo + Juliet During the wedding, we see the nurse in the background – can't miss her in bright red, with a large guy in black behind her. Cut to a wide shot of the altar and we see them both sitting down. Then back to the original shot, and they're still standing in the aisle.

xXx When Xander ejects the roof of the car towards the end of the scene, the windows of the car are wound up. There are no windows attached to the roof when it flies off and, immediately after the roof is ejected, the windows are no longer wound up either.

DAYLIGHT ROBBERY

Every film needs to be lit properly – when it comes to recording actions for posterity, mother nature just can't quite cut it. However, start moving light sources around and you could end up with some unforeseen events . . .

Batman Returns In one scene, the Penguin (Danny De Vito) is making a 'bat' shadow puppet on the ceiling. But there's no light behind his hands. If there's no light, there can be no shadow.

The Bourne Identity The climax scene of the movie is at night. Conklin looks into a room to see if Bourne is in it and daylight is streaming through the windows like it is morning. The next shot has dark windows again.

For Your Eyes Only When Bond (Roger Moore) and company attack Kristatos's warehouse, it is in the middle of the night; however, as Bond runs up the stairs to chase the escaping bad guy, he reaches the top in broad daylight.

From Dusk Till Dawn At the end, Kate is shooting holes in the walls in order to let the sunshine in. Then, sunbeams come in from all sides. That's impossible. The sun, especially in the morning, is shining in only one direction.

Gladiator After the final fight scene, Maximus is on the ground and Lucilla is kneeling above him. When her face is shown, it is blocking out the sun. And yet, when they show Maximus's face, there is no shadow.

At the end, when Maximus goes to Elysium to meet his wife and kid, both the wife and the son put their hands up, as if to shield the sun from their eyes. You can clearly see that their hands are not blocking out the sun, because the shadows are not over the eyes.

🎥 **The Hunt for Red October**   At the end of the movie, in the scenes with Ramius (Sean Connery) and Baldwin on the tower of the sub, the light of the moon is obviously shining on their faces but the reflection of the moon stretches out across the water behind them.

🎥 **Jurassic Park III**   After Sam Neill gets done talking with Laura Dern near the start, he backs up in his car. As he pulls away, we can see that the interior dome/map light is blaring down on his hand that is on the steering wheel. After the instant angle change, however, the light is now suddenly turned off.

🎥 **Keeping the Faith**   In the scene in the karaoke shop, watch the light through the window. Sometimes it's daylight outside, sometimes it's dark.

🎥 **Me, Myself & Irene**   When Charlie is shooting the cow, the wide shots with the bike are really sunny, but in the close-ups (fingers in the nose) it is overcast or studio lighting.

🎥 **Meet the Parents**   When Ben Stiller is being questioned by the police at the end, the table he is sitting at has a square beam of light shining down on it. When the cop brings Robert De Niro in, the beam is a circle, but it becomes square again when Robert De Niro sits down.

🎥 **Mission: Impossible 2**   When Ethan finishes showing Nyah the pictures of the aeroplane crash, so she can see what kind of man Ambrose is, she puts out a candle with her hand. Then when they show her from the front, it's lit again, from the side it's out, then lit from the front again.

At the rock-climbing sequence, after he slips and is hanging by one hand, in the wide shots, the sun is directly behind him, but in the close-up shots, he is in the shadow.

A Nightmare on Elm Street Keep watching for the lighting when Glen sneaks through Nancy's bedroom window. When the exterior shots are shown the light is always on, but it is sometimes off inside.

North by Northwest When the plane crashes into the truck, the bystanders walking towards the scene have shadows, which change angles as you see the next shot. They took these shots both in the morning and in the afternoon.

Pay it Forward At one point late in the movie, Arlene McKinney is at the kitchen sink. If you look through the window, it is daylight. She then goes outside and it is night.

Scary Movie When the six characters are imitating the scene of *I Know What You Did Last Summer*, they get out of the car after it has spun round. All the headlights are on, the two yellow and the two white. Later, if you look behind them, the left headlight is off.

Shanghai Noon In the scene in the desert when Roy is buried alive, Jackie walks up and casts a shadow over his face. In the next camera shot, the shadow is facing a different direction. It continually changes throughout this scene.

Shrek When Farquaad turns round, we see a fairly dull reflection in the back of his armour. The angle changes, and the sun's suddenly shining right on it.

Sleepy Hollow When that boy lights the spinning lamp that casts shapes on everything, we can clearly see the shapes on the wall behind him, but they never shine on him or his mother.

The Terminator   When the terminator says 'I'll be back', he walks out of the police station. The cop inside the building looks out the window – he looks very surprised – and you can see the headlights from the car shining on the cop's face. But when the car comes crashing through the building the headlights aren't on.

Titanic   In the scene where one boat rows back to search for survivors, you can see the lightspot of one lamp turn round faster than the man who holds this lamp, so you know that the lightspot is not from the lamp but from a studio lamp. The man sees it himself, and he then turns round very quickly to hold the speed of the spotlight.

Toy Story   When Buzz is in Sid's sister's room, Woody comes up to it disguised in the Christmas lights. He then leaves them beside the door before he goes in. When they leave the room, the lights are gone. Later the lights return when Woody goes to get them, but there are fewer of them.

RUN THAT PAST ME AGAIN

A category devoted to things in the movies that just make no sense. Not really a continuity mistake, nothing related to editing, just a combination of things that the film-makers got wrong, or that bear no relation to any kind of logic whatsoever . . .

Air Force One   When the lead MiG-29 is about to fire its missile, before it is countermeasured by the flares, the pilot flicks the A/G missile switch, which stands for air–ground, even though he had a full air–air load.

Aladdin   The animators have clearly tried to make all the writing in the film look Arabic. However, in one scene we see the faces of Jafar and the Sultan as they read a scroll. Their eyes move from left to right; Arabic is read right to left.

American Pie   In the scene where the lacrosse team is in the locker room, right before Oz comes in singing, Stiffler (Seann William Scott) is talking to his friend, saying, 'Man, that cheerleader, she wants me, man, she called me up last night asking for my number . . .' If she called him up why would she need his phone number?

Army of Darkness   When Ash falls through the portal he has his gun, but after the king's men seize him he doesn't, even though you never see them take the gun. After the king draws his sword to challenge Ash to combat, Ash shoots the sword with his gun. How did he get it back so fast?

Austin Powers in Goldmember   Austin Powers left school in 1959. He would probably have been eighteen then. This means that the family holiday in Belgium, when he was a baby, would have been about

1941. Continental Europe would have been an odd choice for a family holiday that year, what with World War II going on.

📽 **Batman**   When the Joker enters the cathedral, Batman is the next person inside. Later he ends up fighting Joker's goons, but where did they come from and how did they know the Joker was in there?

When the Joker is having the party with all the balloons, Vicki Vale tries to escape from the gas by getting into a car. If you look at the back window while she is driving off, it is rolled down – surely she should be dead?

📽 **Batman Forever**   In the scene where Batman uses one of the gadgets in the Batmobile to drive up the side of the building to escape from Two-Face's henchmen, where does he go from there? Does he just hang there until all is quiet and then let himself down?

In the scene where the Riddler invades Two-Face's lair, he has nothing but his cane with him. But when he proceeds further into the lair, he picks up two of his 'boxes'. They were there before he got there.

📽 **Beetlejuice**   When Barbara and Adam are digging up Beetlejuice's grave, you can see that a piece or cardboard states FRAGILE, or something in small print which is proportional to Barbara and Adam at that time. However, the lettering should be ten times larger if the cardboard was proportional to the actual model.

📽 **Blade Runner**   When Deckard visits the Tyrell corporation, he prepares to test Rachel with the 'VK' machine. He is shown putting his briefcase on the table and lifting the machine out and on to the table. If you look closely, the 'VK' machine is already on the table and Harrison Ford is miming the lifting – there is nothing in his hands.

📽 **The Bourne Identity**   Throughout the movie, there are countless references to the incident early in the movie at the US Embassy in Zurich. Neither the US nor any other country maintains an embassy in Zurich as the capital of Switzerland is Bern. Since most of the characters in the movie work for the US government, they would surely know the difference between an embassy and a consulate.

The scene where Bourne dyes the girl's hair is sexy, but why does he go to the trouble to change *her* looks when he does absolutely nothing to his own? He doesn't even put on a hat!

Braveheart   At the beginning of the film we see Murron hand William the thistle; they are both children and, he is probably 5–6 years older than her at most. Fast forward to when they meet again as adults and William is now a craggy, weather-beaten fortysomething Mel Gibson, while Murron is a baby-faced, youthful twentysomething Catherine McCormack. How did he age faster than her?

Casino   At the beginning of the film, where Sam (Robert De Niro) gets into his car and it explodes, you can clearly see a cut, and they replace him with a dummy.

Catch Me If You Can   There is a scene in which Tom Hanks and Leonardo DiCaprio are on board a plane at LaGuardia Airport. This particular scene takes place in 1969 and, at one point, there is a shot of the New York City skyline with the Twin Towers intact. However, the towers were not completed until 1973.

Charlie's Angels   After the Angels come out of the sea, they start walking towards a cave, dumping their rucksacks behind them and stripping to their waists. Very attractive, and a dramatic view, but in the next shot they're crouched on the beach, getting equipment out of the backpacks they just dropped. If they needed stuff from them, why did they dump them and keep walking?

Chasing Amy   When Silent Bob starts to tell his Amy story, Jay (Jason Mewes) tells Bob he never knew of any chick, but when they are leaving Jay yells at Bob, saying, 'Why do you always tell that stupid story?'

Close Encounters of the Third Kind   In the climactic scene at the end of the movie, when the alien mothership flies over Devil's Tower and the base, there is a shot of the mothership's shadow creeping along the ground, enveloping the shadows of the crew there. It's a dramatic shot, but since the mothership was not between the ground and the light source (the stadium lights of the base) it should not be blocking out the light, or creating a shadow.

Clue   In one of the first scenes in the study, Mr Boddy hands each guest a weapon and then proceeds to turn out the lights. The room is thrown into complete darkness. Unfortunately, there is a roaring fire in the fireplace that would have illuminated the room enough for everyone to see what was going on.

Daredevil   When the audience sees the burning 'DD' in Urich's glasses it is not a reflection. The DD should be backwards in his glasses.

When Matt Murdock first loses his sight, he is woken in the hospital room by the sound made by an IV drip, amplified by his new Daredevil senses. Terrified by the noise he gets out of bed and creeps around the room. There is no sign of a needle in his arm and there appears to be no one else in the room, so what was the IV connected to? Same goes for the heart monitor.

In the scene where Elektra's father is killed, she picks up what appears to be a Glock 19 and empties it in the direction of Ben Affleck. The weapon clicks a few times indicating it is out of bullets, but the slide is still in the closed forward position, and it should be locked back when it goes empty.

In the courtroom scene, Murdock, a defence lawyer, cross-examines the alleged rapist even though he isn't a government attorney, i.e., a prosecutor. Additionally, the victim is sitting at the table with Murdock's partner, Nelson, which would only occur at a civil, not a criminal, trial.

Diamonds Are Forever   In the scene where Bond escapes from the Willard Whyte facility in the desert in the moon buggy, a car that is chasing him goes over a ridge and turns on its side as the buggy speeds by. A wheel rolls back into the shot, all on its own. It doesn't belong to the car, or the three three-wheelers also chasing, but looks like it belongs to the buggy, which has its full complement of wheels all through the scene.

Die Another Day   During the final Ice Palace action sequence, as Bond is getting into his Aston Martin just prior to his 'automotive duel', he crouches and manages to hide behind the invisible car, even though Q was clearly seen through the car when it was introduced.

When James and Jinx sneak on to Graves's plane, Jinx heads for the cockpit. The pilot gets out of his seat and leaves, making it easy for Jinx to knock out the copilot and take over the plane. But what happens to the pilot? He never comes back, not even when Frost is pointing a sword at Jinx, nor when Jinx is fighting to keep the plane flying.

In the pre-title sequence, James Bond travels in a hovercraft along the dirt road that is full of land mines. Soon after reaching the waterfall at the end, trucks drive up along the road he just drove in on. As there was only one road in to the waterfall complex the landmines must have all disappeared, as earlier on in that sequence it is confirmed that the *only* way the North Koreans can avoid the mines along that road is by hovercraft.

In the opening sequence in North Korea, when James Bond detonates the C4 in the briefcase carrying the diamonds, the diamonds fly into the air and some are embedded into Zao's face. When the C4 is detonated, however, Zao has the back of his head facing the case with the diamonds in and when the case explodes he lands face down on the floor. How come he has diamonds embedded in his face – surely they should be in the back of his head?

🎬 **Die Hard 2**   The payphone McClane uses in Washington's Dulles airport has the 'Pacific Bell' logo. Pacific Bell is a West Coast phone company.

When Holly's plane finally lands, the cockpit shot shows the pilot with his hands on four engine throttles. But Holly's plane is an L-1011 TriStar, which only has three engines.

🎬 **Die Hard: With a Vengeance**   When the collected bad guys are at the North of the Border truck stop, a subtitled henchman tells Simon Gruber (Jeremy Irons) that they can leave in ten minutes. But he actually says '. . . in zwanzig Minuten,' which means *twenty* minutes!

🎬 **Dogma**   When Rufus falls out of the sky and reads that message from Jesus, he says it is written in Aramaic. Aramaic is written from right to left, but he read it left to right as if it was written in English.

🎬 **Enemy of the State**   At the end, when Will Smith is watching TV, he's watching his own face. The camera is supposed to be in the ceiling, but it must be right in front of him.

🎬 **Entrapment**   At the beginning, Sean Connery says that he stole five superchips at Cryptonik, each worth $4 million. At the end, when he gives the chips to the FBI agent, he says that these are four chips worth $5 million each.

🎥 **Erin Brockovich**   In the second scene of the movie Julia Roberts is standing on the street, and in the background at the top left there is a billboard with an ad for www.quepasa.com. The movie was set in the early 90s, but the web wasn't even around then (well, not like we know it now). That website came out in 1998.

🎥 **Ferris Bueller's Day Off**   The movie supposedly takes place in April. However, based on Chicago's climate, it is quite clear that the actual filming was conducted well into the summer months, based on how full and leafy all the trees are, not to mention the ivy on the outfield wall at Wrigley Field which does not become fully developed with leaves until late May at the earliest.

🎥 **Fight Club**   When Bob is shot in the head, he is shot in the back of the head. But when you see Bob laying on the table back at the headquarters it is the back of his head that is missing. The exit wound of the bullet would have left a huge hole in the front of the head, not the back.

🎥 **First Knight**   In the scene towards the end where Richard Gere kills the leader of the bad guys, he steps back and at the bottom of the screen you can see that the sword hasn't got a proper blade – it has one that is about an inch long.

🎥 **Forrest Gump**   Jenny shows Forrest a clipping of him in *USA Today*, but the date on it is later than March 1982 – the date of her death, which we later see on her grave.

When Forrest is running the football field and passing all the players, he passes everyone except the referee, who can be seen moving down the sidelines at a faster pace than Forrest.

🎥 **Frequency**   The past segments take place in 1969, but when

Shep and his partner are looking for Frank on the docks, the camera pans to the left and we see a flash of the World Trade Center just before the cameraman catches his error. It was built between 1970 and 1977, not 1969.

Full Metal Jacket During the training scenes, which are supposed to be at the US Marine Training Base, Parris Island, when the recruits are shown running along the roads, the give way markings are for vehicles that drive on the left, not the right as in the States. The scenes were shot at Bassingbourn Barracks, Hertfordshire, England; in fact, the whole film was shot in England.

Galaxy Quest Why are there chompers coming from the sides when in the 'historical documents' there are only chompers coming from the ceiling?

Laredo drives the ship out of the starship docking station and scrapes the main hull on the walls. This would not be possible without either scraping the wings first, as they are much wider than the main ship, or turning nearly sideways, which they clearly don't.

The crew are escaping the enemy ship by holding a boost button down. By doing this they blow an engine and come to an abrupt stop. Why? There is no force to stop them in space.

Considering the pains the aliens went through to reconstruct the ship, why do the chompers vary in speed so much from the TV show to the real ship?

After Dr Lazarus and his Thermian admirer free the suffocating crew members the Thermian is shot. Problem is, he's shot directly through the chest, but the soldier is down the hall to his left.

Gangs of New York In a scene set in 1862 or 1863, Bill the Butcher says, 'An Irishman will do for a nickel what a n****r will do for a dime or a white man for a quarter.' The first nickel five cent piece was coined in 1866. At the time of the scene the five cent coin was a small silver coin called a half-dime.

When Bill the Butcher is lying in bed with the naked women, one woman has a noticeable tan line from a bikini – a bit early for the bikini . . .

Gladiator In the scene where the four soldiers are taking Maximus into the woods to kill him, the swords don't add up. Maximus grabs the first guy's sword and kills him with it. Then the next one tries to draw his own sword, but the frost makes the sheath stick to the blade and then he is killed. Maximus yells for the third, and when he comes closer, Maximus throws his sword at him, so he dies. He yells for the fourth and last soldier, and suddenly he has a sword in his hand – where did it come from? The only other available sword was stuck in the scabbard by frost.

In one scene, where you see a view of the coliseum and its flags, all the flags are pointing towards the middle – that's strange, keeping in mind the wind comes from one direction.

Goldfinger Oddjob drives a car to the junkyard to get crushed. When it gets lifted up, look at the front end – it's got no engine!

Halloween: Resurrection In the abandoned house, Michael breaks through a wall and smashes a mirror to kill a boy, causing the boy to scream for his life; however, no one else in the otherwise quiet house hears him . . .

Freddie was stabbed three times in the shoulder/upper back by Michael and left for dead. Yet, five minutes later, he arrives at the storage room able to swing a shovel perfectly and fight Michael again.

Hannibal   When Hannibal attacks Francesco after the lecture, they show their shadows on the screen at the same time as the picture of the man hanging. This is not possible, as the picture was projected from a slide projector behind them. In other parts before that scene you can see their shadows blocking the picture.

Highlander   In the initial fight scene in the stadium car park, MacLeod's opponent is seen doing back flips all over the place, but what does he do with his sword when he's doing all that gym-foolery? He's not holding it in his hands and if he shoved it inside his clothing, it would impale him while he's bent double.

Hollow Man   Kevin Bacon shouldn't be able to see anything – the cornea refracts light rays to the back of the eyeball to the optic nerve, a central point. If the cornea was invisible, light rays would go straight out the back of his head and he would have no vision.

When Elizabeth and her boyfriend notice the nitro in the mixer machine, she wants to take the top off but her boyfriend says, 'No, we gotta go.' Why didn't they just unplug the machine?

Home Alone   Kevin's dad calls the neighbour's house and leaves a message. How can he when he and the neighbours live on the same block and the phones are supposed to be out?

Independence Day   The three helicopters hover by the alien space ship. The ship then shoots a beam to destroy all three of the helicopters. But the two smaller helicopters start to explode from the inside before they are hit with the ray.

Jurassic Park   The correct spelling of the dinosaur is 'stegosaurus', yet when Dennis Nedry steals the embryos, the freezer says 'stegasaurus'.

Jurassic Park III   When the Navy picks up the survivors, the person on the radio says that they have six souls on board. They only picked up five people.

The spinosaurus breaks through that huge great fence with almost no problems, but as soon as the heroes are in a shack with a little bolt across the door, it can't get in!

The Living Daylights   At the beginning, Bond (Timothy Dalton) sees the bad guy get into a truck and drive off – he chases after him, about 20 metres behind. They're travelling on parallel roads, Bond running and the bad guy driving (quite fast), but when Bond's road runs out he manages to jump on top of the truck, having miraculously caught up with him.

After the plane runs out of fuel, Bond says, 'There's no place to put down'. They then get into the jeep and out of the plane in a complex move, ending up on a huge flat desert, right next to a long straight road.

Mallrats   When Jay and Silent Bob are running away from Lefours and hide by the table that Brodie and TS are sitting at, check out the positions of everyone – Jay and Silent Bob run on from the right side of the screen, across to the left side of the screen, and duck down behind the table, just as Lefours comes on from the right side of the screen, where he looks around, failing to see them. The layout of everything means that he would have been able to see them the whole time they ran across the screen.

The Magic Eye picture which 'that guy' is looking at throughout the movie is *not* a sailboat. If you pause the movie and find the image it's actually three rows of 3D shapes.

Mary Poppins   In the scene after they have finished cleaning the children's room and are leaving to go to the park, half of one of the beds is missing.

Supposed to be set in London, at one point Mary says something like, 'Oh look, there's a robin'. The bird shown is an American robin (a stuffed one at that).

The Matrix   Neo gets a FedEx envelope containing a Nokia phone. He takes out the phone and it starts ringing, but if you look at the cellular display then you can see that it's turned off, but still ringing.

Meet the Parents   When Jack is about to read his poem at the dinner table, his reading glasses are on his face instantly. The camera does leave his face for an instant, but paper is heard shuffling the whole time, so he wouldn't have had time to put on glasses.

Men in Black   When 'Edgar' walks into the morgue, he's carrying a shotgun. He sets it down by the side of the window. Later, J walks in and starts ringing the bell. You can clearly see there is no shotgun there. Also, when he has the revolver to the lady's head, he doesn't have the gun. So where did the shotgun go?

Minority Report   In the beginning, when Tom Cruise arrests the jealous husband, he notes that he is being arrested on 22 April – that day – for the future murder of his wife and her lover. Later, while Cruise is jogging, there are clearly billboards advocating a 'Yes' vote on Pre-Crime on 22 April. The next day, Cruise's boss Lamar notes that the vote is in a week, which would make it 15 April that day, and the day that the jealous husband was arrested 14 April.

The time period of the movie is 2054. There is an election day (22 April) that is announced as a Tuesday. However, 22 April 2054 is actually a Wednesday.

In the scene where school children are given a tour, they are told that Pre-Crime has been running smoothly for nine years. Tom Cruise's son has been missing for six years. Why, then, when John was talking to Burgess did he say that, if the company had been around six months earlier, his son's death would have never happened, when the company had been around three years earlier?

📽️ **Mission: Impossible**   In the scene where Ethan is in the NOC list room, Krieger starts to drop him and Ethan is hanging there for a little while. Suddenly some sweat starts to drip down his glasses and he catches the drop with his hand. If you look at how close he is to the floor, this move would be impossible.

In the final sequence, how is it that the blades of the helicopter attached to the first train don't strike the second?

Max@Job 3:14 is an illegal e-mail address because of the space and the colon.

📽️ **Mission: Impossible 2**   The first night that Nyah is in Ambrose's house she meets with Ethan outside the house and they talk. Then we find out that 'Ethan' was really Ambrose with one of those 'high-tech' masks. Devious, except that Ambrose is about five inches taller than Ethan, so it would be blindingly obvious that he was disguised.

When Nyah is informed that the disc is in an envelope in Sean's pocket, she takes it out and puts it under her arm with part of it sticking out on the back side of her arm. The scene changes to a half-body shot of Nyah and you can tell there is no envelope under her arm, and as she turns to walk away, Sean would have seen the envelope sticking out from under her arm.

📽️ **The Mummy Returns**   When Rick sees Izzy, Izzy runs through the door, shuts it, and we hear three bolts clearly go across. Rick then fires one bullet into the lock (which from the audio wasn't locked anyway), and then manages to open the door. Er . . . what about the bolts?

In the beginning when Brendan Fraser is looking around the tunnels, he turns round to see his kid and they scream. As they are screaming they are at eye level but a few seconds later, when they are standing, the kid is two feet shorter then Brendan Fraser, and if you look around there is nothing for the kid to have stood on.

Never Been Kissed In the montage sequence showing Drew Barrymore hanging out with the math club, they have a pi poster with 3.1457869986. Only the first three digits are actually correct.

Ocean's Eleven Where do the flyers, which are in the bags that are carried out of the vault and into the van, come from? George Clooney and Matt Damon couldn't have taken them down there, there is no room with the Chinese guy and they are carried out to the van before the SWAT team appears, so they had to be in the vault to start with.

To get into the vault, the team need the amazing Yen to pull fancy acrobatics because of the elaborate alarm system, including lasers covering the floor. For some reason, exploding the doors does not set off the alarm. If they could kill the alarm, why didn't Yen just walk across the room?

On the tape of the stage robbery, three men can clearly be seen in the vault: Yen, Matt Damon and George Clooney. But, up until Clooney was 'burned', there were only going to be two people in the vault – Yen and Clooney. Damon was a last-minute replacement for Clooney. Regardless, there were only ever meant to be two people in the vault, as far as Damon knew, at least – he would have been a bit suspicious while filming the fake robbery with three people there.

Road Trip When Beth is in Josh's room she picks up the card that says 'Love Tiffany' and then asks, 'Who is Tiffany Henderson?' She wouldn't have known her last name.

Robin Hood: Prince of Thieves Isn't that Hadrian's Wall where Freeman and Costner first encounter the sheriff's men? So what happened? Did they land at Dover, walk all the way to the Scottish border and then backtrack to Nottingham?

The Rocky Horror Picture Show The criminologist describes the events of the movie as taking place 'on a late November evening'. In the very next scene, Brad and Janet are driving in Brad's car and Nixon's resignation speech is playing on the radio. Nixon resigned in August 1974.

Saving Private Ryan Before the final attack in the village, we can see a wall with an advertising for Byrrh, an aperitif drink made from a blend of wines. The ad reads, 'Byrrh, l'ami de l'estomach', which basically means, 'Byrrh, stomach's friend'. In French, the correct spelling is 'estomac', not 'estomach'. This is quite a big mistake since the ad and the building are three or four storeys high.

Scream At the beginning, when Billy (Skeet Ulrich) is leaving Sidney's (Neve Campbell's) room, he climbs out the window and walks away, which isn't possible because all the roofs on the house are slanted and it's at least a two-storey house. If her bedroom's on the ground floor, why the next night does she go upstairs to get to her room?

The Shawshank Redemption When Andy finally breaks the sewage pipe with a rock, a huge gush of sewage rushes upward from the hole. This would indicate that the pipe is completely full and under pressure. A moment later, however, when he looks into the pipe with a flashlight it is only about a third full, and remains so all the way to the creek.

When the warden comes into the cell the morning after the escape, the poster covering the hole is fastened down on all four corners – impossible to do after squeezing into that small hole.

After Andy escapes through the tunnel and Red is doing the voiceover on the post-escape search, Red comments on how Andy swam through 'five hundred yards of the most foul-smelling stench imaginable . . . five hundred yards, the length of five football fields, just shy of half a mile.' 500 yards is 1500 feet, and a mile is 5286 feet. Thus a half mile would be 2643, a far cry from 1500.

The Silence of the Lambs   When Dr Lecter was introduced to the police in Tennessee, their names were Sergeants Boyle and Petrie. When he escapes from his cell, he says, ' Ready when you are, Sergeant Pembry'. That name is repeated later when Sergeant Tate says, 'It's Jim Pembry, now talk to him'.

Snatch   Look closely at the character list in the end titles: it reads 'Gyspy Kids' instead of 'Gypsy Kids'.

Spider-Man   When Harry is talking to MJ on the phone, she hangs up on him and his mobile phone produces a dial tone. Mobile phones do not have a dial tone.

Peter Parker practises web shooting for the first time in his bedroom. When Aunt May checks on him the webs crisscross the room from wall to wall. Think about it . . . he's shooting the webs from his wrist so it should have been several strings hanging from the walls. To get the room as it is, every time he shot a string he would have had to have walked to the other side of the room and attached his end to the opposite wall. Not likely.

When Peter is learning about his new, improved eyesight, he takes off and puts on his glasses a few times. When he puts them on, the whole screen gets fuzzy – only what is seen through the glasses would be fuzzy, not the area around the glasses too.

The Sum of All Fears   At the football game it appears that the football stadium is domed. Baltimore doesn't have a domed stadium and this is evident a few minutes later when there is a panoramic view of the city and the two stadia are side by side and both are open.

The Terminator   The Terminator runs his finger down the phone book to look up Sarah Connors. Why would a cyber with enhanced vision need to do this?

The Thomas Crown Affair   How does Thomas Crown fold the Monet in half to fit into the briefcase? Originally I thought he'd separated it from the wooden frame (i.e. just a canvas), but when he takes it out back at his house he holds it up, and the wooden frame's clearly still in one piece. Also, surely folding it in half would crack the paint, but despite the painting clearly being twice the width of the briefcase (it fits snugly when the case is open), he then shuts the case down to a 'normal' size. Any ideas?

Rene Russo is reviewing the tape showing the room with the painting to see who stole the painting, and the tape is blank because of the heat generated from the suitcase – why doesn't she just back up the tape completely to see who put the suitcase there in the first place?

In the opening sequence, when Crown decides to walk and has 'Jimmy' meet him at the office, he is almost run down by a truck. First of all, the truck has to skid to a stop, yet there is a car no more than ten feet in front of it when they change camera angle. Why was the truck going so fast in the first place? Second, when Crown motions for the driver to pass, the same car is still stopped directly in front of the truck, yet the truck speeds off in a way that it should smash into the car in front of it.

🎥 **Titanic**   The lake that Jack told Rose he went ice fishing on, when she was threatening to jump, is a man-made lake in Wisconsin near Chippewa Falls (where Jack grew up). The lake was only filled with water in 1917, five years after *Titanic* sank.

When Rose is arriving in New York half asleep, she looks at the Statue of Liberty, which is the same colour as now (green). But if you visit the Statue of Liberty, you'll find a plate telling you that the original colour was brown, and it took over 35 years for it to change colour. The Statue of Liberty was placed there in 1886, so in 1912 it should have still been brown.

In the scene where Jack and his friend are standing on the bow looking at the dolphins swimming ahead of the ship, the dolphins are Pacific white-sides, not any Atlantic species.

🎥 **Tomorrow Never Dies**   As Bond is preparing for the high-altitude skydive, he is warned that he has to freefall for five miles and, without oxygen, he will be asphyxiated. However, he jumps from a non-pressured aircraft. Surely when the back hatch opened, the other people standing around would either also start to suffocate or be sucked out?

In Bond's hotel room, after Dr Kaufman has killed Carver's wife, he takes out the tape that has just been playing, holds it up, and it's somehow been fully rewound.

🎥 **Toy Story**   At the petrol station when Woody is almost run over by that huge lorry, you can see the wheel stop just before him. But you see that the wheel is one of the middle wheels on the truck, meaning that the front wheels must have already gone over him. But he wasn't run over. How?

🎥 **Waterworld**   When the mariner questions the woman about the little girl's drawings, she says, 'She's like a mirror; she draws what she sees.' Later she claims the mariner 'has things no one else has seen', like 'that reflective glass'. What do you think a mirror is, woman?

The Wizard of Oz   After the Scarecrow gets a brain, he states the Pythagorean Theorem. However, he incorrectly says it applies to an isosceles triangle when it applies to a right-angled triangle. Guess he got a defective brain from the wizard.

X-Men   Wolverine's claws are sometimes drawn with the curved effect of an in-motion slash. But they are not curved and the effect of him doing a 360 on the statue's tiara spike was really cheesy and even comic book impossible. His claws can cut through anything and he didn't have the momentum to do that move. If he was holding on with his fingers, that would be more believable.

Senator Kelly makes a phone call while he's in the helicopter, unaware that Guyrich is really Mystique. Before she transforms to her normal form, Kelly hands her (still in the form of Guyrich) his phone, which is placed in a pocket. Mystique transforms and . . . the phone is gone. Where would it go?

When you see the X-ray of Logan's body, you see the solid metal blades that shoot out of his hands. In the X-ray, they go from just before his elbow, up his wrist to the middle of his hand. But later Logan bends his wrist. How does he do that if the blades don't bend?

xXx   Xander puts a load of sticky bombs on a line of motorbikes outside the bad guy's house. These bombs have a detonator switch, which Xander has. When he eventually sets them off, the motorbikes blow up in the order that he put the bombs on; without timers on them why would they blow up one by one and not all at the same time?

Similar to editing problems, although with a specific twist. Ever noticed that in a book, if the word at the end of one line is repeated at the start of the next line, your brain ignores it and seems to fuse them together? Sometimes editors bank on that phenomenon when putting takes together, but it doesn't always work . . .

Almost Famous   When Russell and William (Patrick Fugit) are walking together to 'find something real', the VW bus containing the 'real Topeka people' drives by behind them twice over their left shoulder (it almost reaches them, then after a cut is a lot further back, then gets closer, then disappears) before pulling up to them a third time on their right side, but pointing the same way as it was when it was on the other side of the road.

American Pie   In the scene where Stiffler's mom (Jennifer Coolidge) seduces Finch, you can clearly see Finch playing with the balls on the pool table. The camera cuts to another shot, and when it's back to Finch, the balls are back in the original place.

Austin Powers: The Spy Who Shagged Me   When Austin is about to be sent back in time in the Bug, he reverses into some shelves with computers on them, knocking them over. He then pulls forwards. When he reverses again, the computers are back up, and he hits some barrels. When he pulls forwards again, the barrels are back up, but the computers have now disappeared again.

Beetlejuice   When the Deitz family first check out the house, Otho shakes up a can of spray paint, takes off the cap and hands it to Delia. When it cuts to the next scene, you can see Delia take off the can's cap again.

Beverly Hills Cop II When Axel is chasing the armoured truck that has all the money from the race track in it, the police light on the car falls off, but then in the next shot it is on again.

Big Josh turns back into a boy and the two 12-year-olds walk down the middle of the road. Josh has his red jacket on and Billy is carrying his skateboard. The footage used is identical to that used five minutes into the film. The cars are in the same position and the same lady walks across the street in front of them.

Blade After Whistler (Kris Kristofferson) applies the serum to Blade, he is holding Blade's hand. The doctor is watching all of this without their knowledge, until Blade senses her and looks up. You can still see Whistler's left hand holding Blade's left hand at the wrist. Suddenly Whistler turns to pursue the doctor, and lets go of Blade's wrist. When they show it from the doctor's view, as she is running away, you still see Whistler's hand holding on to Blade's wrist.

Blade II Towards the end of the film, after Blade beats up a lot of vampires, Whistler throws Blade's sunglasses to him. He is seen throwing them in one shot; in the next shot Blade is seen catching them. But if you look in the background at Whistler, he doesn't have the glasses, but is moving his arm like he is throwing them; the glasses must have been computer animated and bad editing showed it up.

The Blues Brothers During the scene at Bob's Country Bunker, when the band is playing 'Rawhide', a bar patron is dancing on top of a table. In the background, on the stage, John Belushi gets the bullwhip from stage left. In the next camera cut Belushi walks to the end of the stage and picks up the whip again.

The Bourne Identity   When Bourne is escaping from the embassy, he drops the bag, which hits something metal on the way down, making it wobble. The camera cuts away while it's still moving and the marines are coming up the stairs. When Bourne climbs under the fire escape, looking down to the ground the metal thing's stopped moving. All well and good, except that, after the marines leave, Bourne looks down and, in that shot, the metal thing is moving again, then stops – obviously the rest of the shot from before.

The Breakfast Club   After Molly Ringwald does her trick, she puts the lipstick away twice. It has a shot of her putting it away from the front and then another one from the back.

Bridget Jones's Diary   Near the start of the film, when Bridget is in the bar with her friends, watch the guy called Tom. First shot, he is holding his new phone next to his chest, he then puts it down and opens the box. Second shot, the phone is now next to his chest again; he puts it down again and once more opens the box. Third shot, he puts the phone down once more and opens the box, this time he empties a phone facia out of a plastic bag. Fourth shot, the facia is back in the bag, which he takes it out of once more!

Charlie's Angels   When Lucy Liu is fighting the thin man in the tower, the bell falls. Soon afterwards he heads towards her, sword swinging, and we can see the bell again on the right.

Clue   The same footage of Ms Scarlet screaming (when the cook falls out of the freezer) is used both when the cook falls out and when Wadsworth falls out. You can tell by looking in the background. It shows Mrs White standing on the landing by the door next to Prof. Plum. But when the shot changes, Mrs White is standing next to Ms Scarlet, leaning up against a cabinet.

Clueless   When Josh and Cher are driving home from a party, they show a shot of the car. It's a blue sports car that passes a Hertz car rental sign. When Elton is driving Cher home from the party in the Valley, they show the exact same shot of the blue sports car passing the Hertz car rental sign.

Coyote Ugly   When the real 'manager' comes outside to yell at 'Mr O'Donnell', you see the manager walk back into the club. If you look in the background of the next shot, you can see the manager walking through the door again.

Die Another Day   In the scene where Gustav Graves is demonstrating the power of Icarus, the audience has their sunglasses on to block the sunlight. After Icarus is shut down everyone has their sunglasses off. However, in a quick shot of Bond soon after Icarus shuts down, a woman is seen taking off her sunglasses after she's already been seen without her sunglasses on.

In the pre-credit sequence, Colonel Moon demonstrates the power of his shell launcher by blowing up Bond's helicopter and the soldier behind him lifts up his AK-47. It cuts to the helicopter exploding, then comes back to Graves firing the shell launcher a second time. The soldier also lifts up his AK-47 a second time, with identical movements.

Die Hard   When the terrorists launch the rocket at the RV, they break the same window of the building twice.

After the terrorists blow the roof and McClane jumps off with the fire hose, he hits the window. After kicking the window for a while, he decides to shoot at it. As he pushes off the window you can see that his gun is out and pointed at the window, yet in the next scene he pulls the gun from his side and then starts shooting.

Dirty Dancing   In the scene where Patrick has just given his speech about how wonderful 'Baby' is, he finishes, walks to the side of the stage, puts down the mike stand and takes off his jacket. In the very next shot, he puts down the mike stand and takes off his jacket again.

Dogma   Towards the end of the film, Jay takes off his pants in order to have sex with Bethany, as she promised. Then in the next scene, from Bethany's angle, he is taking them off for a second time, when they had previously been around his ankles already.

When Ben Affleck opens the church doors near the end, we see a flash of light. Then it cuts to God and the Metatron. They walk out and the light fades away completely. But when we cut back to Ben Affleck, the light has just begun to fade away.

Empire Records   When Debra is making the buttons, they focus on her making one, and you can see the stupid one already in the basket. Then they focus on her making the same stupid button next, when it was already in the basket before.

Fatal Attraction   Alex takes the cigarettes out of her bag twice when she and Dan have lunch in the restaurant.

Ferris Bueller's Day Off   When Ferris is trying to con his way into the fancy restaurant he greases the maître d's palm with a dollar. The maître d then drops it and we hear it hit the table. Then the shot changes to his hand and he drops the dollar again.

A Few Good Men   In one scene, when Sam and Joe are leaving Danny's apartment, there is a wide shot showing Daniel opening the door, then there is a close-up of Daniel and Sam, and Sam opens the door again.

🎥 **Final Destination** At the memorial, when Billy is telling Alex about his driving test, if you look closely behind Alex you can see someone walking towards the sculpture holding some flowers. This move is then repeated shortly afterwards.

🎥 **Gangs of New York** After Cameron Diaz gets mugged at the dock, the shot shows her pulling herself to a standing position on a crate. In the next shot, from farther back and up high, she is crawling over to the crate she just pulled herself up on.

🎥 **Gladiator** After Maximus and Titus's battle, Titus falls to the ground and we see that his mask is already up. Maximus then pulls the mask up, which has magically come down over Titus's face again.

🎥 **The Godfather** The waiter fills Tom Hagen's glass twice within seconds during his dinner with Woltz.

While Sonny, Michael, Clemenza, Tessio and Tom are discussing waiting till Don Corleone can make a deal after he is better, the humidor on the desk where Sonny sits is closed. After Sonny says 'We'll wait', he closes it.

Michael is talking to Apollonia's father after he has given her the necklace. The same two people pass by twice (one in red, one in white) – once in a close-up of Apollonia and again in a wider shot.

🎥 **Gone in 60 Seconds** When Cage's character offers the money for his brother and the brother is in the car about to get crushed, the back window gets broken out twice.

🎥 **GoodFellas** When Tommy shoots Spider in the foot and he goes down, Henry is playing cards at the table. Then in the next scene Henry is helping Spider up. Then in the very next scene Henry is back at the table watching Spider crawl on the floor.

Grosse Pointe Blank   When the Ultimart store is blown up you see the store on fire without the Ultimart sign. When they go back to the store the Ultimart sign is shown falling off. The two scenes are the wrong way round.

The Hunt for Red October   When Ramius tells the crew about sending the letter making their plans clear, Captain Borodin (Sam Neill) undoes the top button of his uniform twice.

It's a Wonderful Life   In a scene near the end of the movie, George enters the Building and Loan with a Christmas wreath on his arm. On hearing that he has a phone call from his brother Harry, he tosses the wreath on a table behind him and picks up the phone. In the next second, the wreath is back on his arm.

Jaws   In one of Richard Dreyfus's first scenes, Brody asks him to help with the group of men crowding into a small boat. Hooper says that the officer wants him to tell them that they're overcrowding the boat. They show the men climbing in and there's a fat guy in a blue jacket climbing down the ladder into the boat. He waves his arm and says 'What do you care?' They then show Hooper asking if they know a good restaurant or hotel on the island. When they show the men again, uttering the line 'Yeah, walk straight ahead', the man in the blue jacket is on the deck again and is again descending the ladder.

Jurassic Park   In the scene where the helicopter is landing, you see the jeeps waiting for them, yet in the next scene the jeeps have to drive up to meet the helicopter. From the overhead shot, you see the parked vans; when the copter lands, you see them drive up again.

In the scene where the lawyer jumps out of the jeep (just before the T-Rex approaches) he leaves the jeep door open. In the next two shots the jeep door is closed, but when the T-Rex shows up, the boy moves to the door and closes it.

Jurassic Park III   Near the beginning, as Sam Neill is giving his speech, the MC woman is standing, then sitting, then she is standing again but then sits down.

Legally Blonde   After Reese Witherspoon's first day at Harvard she gets her nails done. When she sits down she places her hands on the table and her fingers in the manicure bowl. The next shot is of her back, and her hands are not even on the table. Then back to Reese Witherspoon's face and her hands are back on the table, and finally we see her back and she places her hands on the table again.

The Lost World: Jurassic Park   Towards the beginning, where the girl goes to photograph the stegosaurus, the scene cuts back to her boyfriend and the guy with the video camera. In two cuts to their scene, while the girl is photographing and interacting with the stegosaurus, the guy with the video camera opens the flip-out LCD on the video camera and starts shooting the action.

Magnum Force   When Callaghan is in the car with Lieutenant Briggs, after they pick up the bomb, they drive by the 76 service station three times in about 30 seconds.

The Matrix   In the scene where Neo is waiting under the bridge to go into the car with Trinity, Switch and Apoc, watch when the car pulls up – you see the back door open completely and then it cuts and you see Trinity open it again.

My Best Friend's Wedding   Julia Roberts and Dermot Mulroney are looking for Cameron Diaz at the train station. Dermot is sitting at a bench and Julia comes to him. Behind you can see two railway employees walking; one of them is pulling a small metal suitcase, the other's holding a newspaper. A few seconds later, as Julia is standing at Dermot's side, the same employees walk behind them again.

Ocean's Eleven   The grey-haired casino guy is standing next to Carl Reiner as he's watching his briefcase being put in a safe. A couple of minutes later the same man is standing in a hallway when Andy Garcia asks him to escort Ramon out of the building. A couple of minutes after that he's next to Carl Reiner again. Plus, Andy Garcia told him to stay with Carl Reiner because he doesn't trust him. So, why was he in the hallway?

Panic Room   When the two remaining thieves are in the panic room with the young girl, one pulls back the carpet to reveal the safe. The shot changes and, when it changes back, he pulls back the same bit of carpet again.

The Patriot   When Mel Gibson comes down the steps out of the meeting, he walks towards his eldest son, who is signing up. Mel approaches him and he is facing away; the shot cuts to face Mel and his son is facing him. They cut back to the son and then he turns round to face Mel. He was facing another way before he actually turned round.

Pulp Fiction   In the pawn shop, when Butch comes down to the rescue, he slashes the first man, steps in front of him, then stabs him. Zed steps forward and the sword swings up to Zed's face. In the next shot of Butch, it shows him bringing the sword up again.

Reservoir Dogs   In the 'Mr Blonde' segment, Vic takes a cigarette from a case on Joe's desk and puts it in his mouth. Soon after, he takes it out. Then there is a shot from the hallway and the cigarette magically appears back in his mouth, where he takes it out for a second time.

There is a scene where the cops are chasing the 'gang'. It shows the guys running past some stores and then it cuts to the cops running past a hardware store (I think). But in the next scene, the guys run past the same store. Aren't the cops supposed to be chasing them, or are they just doing laps?

The Rocky Horror Picture Show   At the beginning of the film, just after the wedding photo is taken, we see the father of the bride run up the church steps. Seconds later, we see him running up the steps again.

Scream   At the beginning of the movie Casey (Drew Barrymore) locks the same door twice. Once before she finds out that it's a psycho on the phone and another time after he says, 'I wanna know who I'm looking at'.

Shanghai Noon   When Chon and Roy meet in the bar, the thing holding the cards on Roy's wrist starts to go back under his coat. Then there is a cut to someone else and back to Roy's hand, which still has the card-holder sticking out.

Spider-Man   When Peter and his uncle are talking in the car, almost every time the shot changes to Peter you can see the same blonde walking by (three times) and the same redhead (twice). One of the female extras even stops and looks in the direction of the car, only to have a male extra appear to tell her to keep walking.

Terminator 2: Judgment Day   In the scene where John and his buddy hack into the ATM machine and get cash, John is telling his friend his mother is a psycho. Watch closely as John puts on his backpack twice.

The T-1000 punches his body through the window of a helicopter to get inside. After the helicopter pilot jumps out, the door slams shut. The T-1000 then reaches over and shuts it again.

When Sarah is escaping from the hospital there is a scene where the T-1000 walks straight through a metal-barred door. If you look where the doctor is standing you will notice that the T-1000 clearly walks past him after he walks through the door. However, in the next sequence when the T-1000 is shooting his gun, he is way behind him.

🎥 **There's Something About Mary**   This is during the scene on the outside steps of Mary's office, when Mary and Ted see each other for the first time. A suit-wearing businessman comes from the left side of the screen behind Mary twice. This happens when Mary is saying 'Ted? Is . . . Is that you?' and the camera goes back and forth between Ted and Mary.

🎥 **Tomorrow Never Dies**. Bond and M are travelling in the motorcade. The privacy barrier is lowered to reveal that Moneypenny is in the front-passenger seat. The shot changes to an exterior shot of the limousine. You can clearly see the privacy divider rising during this shot. The shot returns to the interior of the limousine for more dialogue. Then the shot returns to Moneypenny for her to say that James will have to decide how much 'pumping' is required. Once again you can see the privacy divider rise.

🎥 **Top Gun**   After the class where they meet Charlie for the first time, and Maverick reveals that he's 'the one', he's confronted by Iceman. The Iceman asks him who was watching Cougar while he was 'showboating' with this MiG. If you watch Iceman, you'll see that he puts his watch on twice.

In many scenes when missiles are fired, the rockets are shown sailing away from the same racks – which should be empty. The Navy allowed only one live missile shot for the filming of the movie. Maybe that is why we see so many missiles fired from an empty rack.

🎥 **When Harry Met Sally**   When they stop at the little diner (on the trip to New York at the beginning), Sally opens her menu twice.

The World Is Not Enough   When James is chasing the other boat at the beginning, he fires the top torpedo first. Then when they show him fire the second torpedo, the bottom hole is empty, and he fires the same torpedo (the one on top) again.

xXx   Xander arrives at Yorgi's mansion and there are girls in the water fountain out at the front. Yorgi's large bodyguard, the one that sports five or so earrings and a large beard, takes a girl out of the fountain. A split second later the shot changes on to Xander and, in the background, the large bodyguard is taking the same girl out of the fountain again.

You've Got Mail   In the scene where Tom Hanks and Meg Ryan are at an outdoor cafe near the end of the film, a woman with a red cart walks by twice.

When Kathleen is waiting for her online friend at Cafe Lalo, and Joe comes in, he takes off his overcoat twice.

BLOOD STAINED

There's often no way round some of these. If a scene needs someone covered in mud, and a few different versions are filmed, you're never going to get the mud in the same shape each and every time. Sometimes though, it's beyond a joke ...

 Air Force One   When the president (Harrison Ford) tries to enter the conference room when he comes upstairs from the lower level, he first struggles with the guard to the conference room door. While fumbling with the keys, the guard 'wakes up' and fires two shots toward James Marshall, who turns round and shoots back. Those two shots from the guard leave bullet holes in the conference room door (the left door), and no one in the room gets shot from the bullets. Anyway the mistake is that, when James finally enters the room, the bullet holes disappear. Whenever the bad guys return, the bullet holes are gone.

In the scene when the Russian is shooting the three doors, on the second door, if you look in slow motion, you see two muzzle flashes before a hole is made in the door. The same on the third door. Also, when he shoots the third door, he puts five bullet holes in it, but when he opens it to check, there are six holes in the wall.

When the traitor first begins to shoot the three people, we see a close-up on one of the victims (the one who gets shot in the head). If you look behind him in slo-mo, you'll notice that the furniture is already red (from the blood).

 American Beauty   In the scene when Ricky's father rushes to his room and punches him, Ricky is bleeding before he is hit.

 Anaconda   When Paul Sarone (John Voight) throws a bucket of monkey blood over his captives, you can see the blood make-up on them before the 'blood' is supposed to hit them. In fact, the 'blood' doesn't go near them – it is thrown diagonally so that it does not hit the supposed target.

🎥 **Armageddon** When the military bods come to get Harry from the rig, you see the shot going between the two. In the initial wide shot his nose is clean. Then in three close-up shots Harry has a large speck of oil on the tip of his nose but on the fourth it has disappeared.

🎥 **Babe** When Babe is walking through the house, you will notice that several times his feet switch from muddy to clean as the camera angle changes.

🎥 **Batman** When Joker is at the top of the building, taunting them, his chin is red (presumably from his blood when Batman socked him on the jaw). After he falls off the building, and we see him lying on the ground, his chin is not covered in blood like it was before.

In the scene where the Joker's henchmen are trashing the museum, one guy puts purple handprints all over a portrait. Later, the Joker walks by the same portrait and the handprints are gone.

🎥 **Big** Billy and big Josh (Tom Hanks) fire silly string at each other. They didn't get the action right first time to the director's satisfaction, and you can see the evidence. There are bits of silly string attached to a piece of furniture and also dangling from something on the wall behind Josh – all there before they start the fight.

🎥 **Blade** The bloody make-up on Whistler's face and neck changes constantly throughout the scene when he gives his last words.

In the big fight scene at the end between Blade and Frost, the blood smear on Frost's face changes sides a few times.

🎥 **The Blues Brothers**   At the end, the number of bullet holes in the door of the assessor's office changes once it's opened.

🎥 **The Bourne Identity**   When Jason Bourne is on the boat, his gunshot wounds are on his left shoulder blade in a horizontal line. In the hotel scene, when Marie is taking off his shirt, they are diagonal between his shoulder blades.

🎥 **Braveheart**   At the end, when William Wallace is being led to be executed, he is pelted with food. Much of it sticks to his face and hair. A few moments later, when they are standing him up, he is completely clean.

🎥 **Bridget Jones's Diary**   After Bridget sprays the contents of the blender all over herself, there's a splodge on her right cheek – it changes shape when she answers the door.

The snow at the end occasionally sticks to their faces and you see it fluttering about – clearly fake.

🎥 **Bring it On**   During the carwash scene, when Cliff drives up in his dirty car, there are clumps of grass on it. In the next shot of the car, there is only dirt, no grass.

🎥 **Broken Arrow**   In the big fight scene at the end, Deakins gets hit in the face and has blood all over his face and the front of his shirt. This keeps disappearing.

🎥 **Cast Away**   When Tom Hanks is attempting to start a fire, his hands are so badly scratched/blistered that he ties a piece of fabric around one of them. Once he has started the fire and is doing his little dance on the beach, his hands face the camera and there is not a mark on them.

Catch Me If You Can   When Frank's mother spills red wine on the carpet, the stain has disappeared altogether by the next shot that shows his parents dancing.

Chicago   In the final scene when Velma and Roxie are performing, there is lipstick on Roxie's teeth. In the next shot it has disappeared.

A Clockwork Orange   In the film's opening scenes, Dim has a black mark on his leg, which is clearly visible. When he and Alex start fighting, it has disappeared.

Commando   At the end of the movie, Arnie puts on his flak jacket then his camouflage paint, but when he takes off his jacket, he's got paint on his chest. There's no time for him to reapply it between times.

Dances with Wolves   When Timmons and Dunbar get to the deserted camp, Timmons has pieces of egg all over his face in the close shots, but none at all in the further away shots.

Daredevil   Near the beginning of the movie Matt Murdock has many visible scars on his back. But when Matt and Elektra are having sex in the bed there's a shot of Matt turning over on to his back and almost all of the scars are gone.

When Daredevil throws his stick and it hits Bullseye on the forehead, there is a red mark where it hit, but the next time he is seen, Bullseye has no mark.

Days of Thunder   Multiple times in the movie one shot of the cars will show them covered with blackness from smoke, while the immediate next shot will show clean race cars.

🎥 **Deep Blue Sea**   The man with the cross has a wound on the left-hand side of his head. Later in the movie it has moved down.

🎥 **Diamonds Are Forever**   In the opening sequence, when Bond runs over and pulls the chain to release mud on to the guy rising up to shoot him, mud clearly splatters all over him as he dives to the floor. When he gets up, his suit is spotless.

🎥 **Die Another Day**   In the final fight scene on the plane between Jinx and Agent Frost Jinx is slashed across her stomach, drawing blood. In a later scene when Jinx and 007 are pouring diamonds over one another in the hut on the cliff her stomach is unblemished.

🎥 **Die Hard**   When McClane shoots Hans Gruber, Gruber falls through the window and grabs Holly's arm to pull her with him. He has a good grasp on her arm because of her watch. When Bruce Willis is trying to release the clasp on her watch, you see blood on her face from his arm. The shot then cuts to Hans Gruber, and when the camera goes back to Holly and John, there is no longer any blood on her face.

When John and Karl are fighting and Karl reaches for the gun lying on the floor, John legs it out of an open door. Karl fires two shots – the first hits John and the second sprays blood all over the door.

After McClane kills the first terrorist, he writes down the names of the other terrorists on his arm in thick Sharpie pen. It's permanent ink, but for the rest of the film, those names are not on his arm.

🎥 **Die Hard 2**   John McClane and Major Grant (William Sadler) are fighting on the wing of the aeroplane, and Major Grant's mouth gets extremely bloody. The shot switches to McClane and then back to Grant, whose mouth is still bloody. However, after the shot switches back from McClane to Grant, Grant's mouth is no longer bloody.

Dirty Dancing   In the last dance scene, Patrick Swayze jumps down from the stage and starts dancing. He goes down on his knees and when he lifts one knee, it is extremely dusty; however, when he stands up his knees are completely clean.

Face/Off   When Sean Archer is flying the helicopter to keep the plane from taking off, Castor Troy shoots the helicopter windshield three times, but there are four bullet marks.

The Faculty   When Stokely and Casey are chased into the swimming pool area, the alien pulls Stokely to the floor. You can see a trail of blood from her mouth, then in the next shot the blood has changed into a small neat circle.

The Fifth Element   When the police confront Leeloo on the side of the building, she raises her hands and we can see that they're covered in soot. She jumps off and lands in Korben's cab. When she comes to, she presses her hand against the glass, and her hand is magically clean.

Fight Club   When Brad Pitt is fighting with the bar owner, he has a lot of blood in his mouth; in the other scene there's no blood. Then the blood returns by magic.

From Russia With Love   When Bond (Sean Connery) is driving the white truck and being bombed from the helicopter, the truck gets smoke blackened, but when he arrives at the speedboat all the marks have gone.

Gladiator   In the first gladiator fight in the coliseum, when Maximus picks up the arrow from the ground, his hand is covered in blood, but when the camera shoots his hand for a second time, no blood at all, and the third time, you can see the blood again.

🎥 **Gone in 60 Seconds** The young kids go to steal the SUV at the party and when they are leaving a cop turns round and they start running from the cops. The camera shows another cop who has blocked the road and he pulls out his gun and points it at the SUV. When the camera pans back to the SUV, the window already has two bullet holes in it way before the cop fires his gun.

🎥 **Harry Potter and the Philosopher's Stone** The three children get past Fluffy because the harp is playing but, as Fluffy wakes, he dribbles on Ron's shoulder. However, when they fall down into the Devil's Snare, Ron's shirt is completely dry.

🎥 **Heat** In the shoot-out scene in the streets of downtown LA, the driver of the getaway car is killed when shot in the head by a single bullet. In the shot prior to this event, the bullet hole and blood on the windshield appear prior to the shot being fired.

🎥 **Hollow Man** When they're pouring the 'goo' on Kevin Bacon to make the mask, some of it gets on the end of his breathing tube. When they change shots, it is clean again.

Kevin Bacon gets blood thrown on him and it disappears within seconds. Ever try washing your hands after a nosebleed? It isn't that easy.

When they try to make Kevin visible, they use a blue spray to see his vein (like they did to the gorilla), but you never see the blue mark again.

🎥 **Home Alone 2: Lost in New York** There is a moment in the movie when Kevin is throwing bricks at Marv and Harry. If you watch the moment of the first throw in slow motion, you can see that Marv has blood on his forehead before the brick hits him.

🎥 **Kingpin**   Munsen's nose starts bleeding *before* Claudia hits him.

At the petrol station, the oil on Roy's mouth keeps changing position.

🎥 **Legends of the Fall**   When Samuel dies in the movie, if you watch closely there is blood running down his face in only every other scene.

🎥 **The Lord of the Rings: The Two Towers**   After Merry and Pippin escape from the Uruk-Hai, Merry has a deep cut over his right eye. The cut starts out over his right eye all bloody, then it changes to his left eye and it is still bloody. Then it goes back to his right eye but is clean, then it disappears entirely and comes back later to over his right eye and not bloody.

🎥 **Mission: Impossible 2**   During the fight between Ethan and Sean, Sean cuts Ethan's face with a knife and it's bleeding. A little bit later it is not bloody and it looks as if the wound is closed, then open and bloody again.

Near the end of the final fight scene, Ethan Hunt has some blood coming out of his nose. That blood disappears and returns several times during that scene, and it's clearly visible with all those close-ups of him.

🎥 **Pulp Fiction**   When the head explodes in the car, Jules has his back turned (he is driving) and so you see him with a relatively white shirt, yet later his shirt is covered in blood.

When John Travolta and Samuel L. Jackson are fired at in the apartment, the bullet holes are already in the wall before the gun is fired.

In the part where they are giving Mia Wallace the adrenaline shot, they mark her chest with a red magic marker. When the shot has been given, the red mark has disappeared.

Red Dragon   When Dolarhyde fires the shotgun in his house, blood spatters on Reba's face. When this happens, Reba is sitting in the middle of the couch, and there is an end table with a phone on it between her and Dolarhyde. You'd think at least some of the furniture would get blood on it too, but as the camera pulls back, there is no blood anywhere on the couch, the table, or the side of the phone.

Before the face of the Red Dragon is revealed, he is seen flipping through his book of news clippings. He focuses on the face of the *Tatler* reporter and puts red markings through his face. When he closes the book, the face of the reporter can be seen before the book fully closes – it has no red marks on it.

Road to Perdition   In the end of the diner scene Jude Law fires after the car with Tom Hanks and his son in it. A bullet goes through the rear window but not through the windshield. The bullet path goes by Tom Hanks's head, but there's no bullet hole anywhere in the car afterwards.

After the shooting at the diner, Hanks is driving away with his son. At some point Hanks drives off the road into a farmer's field. In the over-head shot of the car driving off the road you can see another set of car tyre tracks from a previous take.

At the end when Tom Hanks is shot in the back while looking out of the window, blood comes through the front of his shirt meaning the bullets must have exited his body, yet the window he is standing in front of isn't shattered by the bullets that had passed through him. Also when he is shot, blood squirts on the window. Afterwards, when he dies and his son is holding him, there is no blood on the window.

Robin Hood: Prince of Thieves   When Robin is burying his father he cuts his hand, saying he will avenge his father's murder – 'I swear it by my own blood'. We clearly see the blood dripping over his fingers. Suddenly the camera shot changes and Robin's hand has miraculously healed and the blood has washed away.

🎥 **The Rocky Horror Picture Show** After Dr Frank-N-Furter gets out of the pool, and is being threatened by Riff-Raff with the Anti-Matter Laser, the tattoo on his left arm seems to have mysteriously washed off. It's running and illegible.

After Frank kisses Janet's hand, as she puts it back by her side you can see his lipstick on it. When she reaches out to take the shirt from Brad, Frank's lipstick mark is gone.

After the 'Hot Patootie' number, when Frank is chasing Eddie into the freezer, there's already blood in the freezer as Eddie crawls in.

🎥 **Scooby-Doo** In the scene where Scooby-Doo falls down the hole to the cavern below Shaggy follows him a few seconds later. When Shaggy hits the sand below he has to roll when he hits the ground. In doing so, his back and knees are covered in what appear to be thick sand deposits. When he stands up in the next shot and turns around he has no sand on his knees or on his back, even though he has not made an effort to brush his trousers or shirt off.

At the start of the film, once they have caught the ghost, the mystery machine drives through the wall and the front becomes all dented. A few scenes later it's perfect again.

🎥 **Scream 3** In the scene where Gale and Dewey find the killer's voice changer, Gale's hands are clean, but when it shows her hands picking up the device, there's dried blood on them. But when it shows her hands again, the blood's gone.

🎥 **The Shining** When Jack Nicholson swings the axe into the black guy's chest, it is covered in blood in the next shot (as you might expect). However, when he is chasing Danny through the maze only moments later, the axe is clean again.

🎬 **The Terminator** When Arnie gets shot in the club, after he gets up again there are no bullet holes in his chest or blood on his shirt.

🎬 **Terminator 2: Judgment Day** When Sarah, Arnie and John escape from the hospital, Sarah orders the policeman to leave his car, and he shoots the windscreen. Later on, during the night, the windscreen has miraculously reverted to normal, with no trace of the gunshot mark.

When the T-1000-controlled helicopter bears down on the SWAT truck, Sarah tries to gun it down. The T-1000 shoots back and, while Sarah hides, three splatter marks appear on the door, marking where the bullets have hit the door. However, in the next few scenes the splatter marks are replaced by normal-sized bullet marks.

🎬 **There's Something About Mary** Ben Stiller's character gets 'hooked' with Warren's fishing line, getting a hook that quite noticeably has the prongs sticking out of his cheek when they are removing it. In the next scene, however, no scar and no sign of the injury exists.

🎬 **Titanic** When Rose is running in the hallways, trying to find help for Jack when he is handcuffed, she finds a man and asks him to help her free Jack. She gets frustrated with him and says 'Listen', then hits him. In shots before (you can put it in slow motion to see it) you can look at the man's hand and it already has blood on it before he touches his face.

🎬 **The Wizard of Oz** At the beginning, while Dorothy is still on the farm, she walks along the pig-pen fence and then falls in. When Bert Lahr picks her up, her dress is perfectly clean.

When the Lion is singing about being king of the forest, the Tin Man breaks a flowerpot to 'crown' him. Pay close attention, as the break marks on the pot change. In one shot there's a big jagged edge sticking up (obviously longer than the others) and in the next scene most of the edges are even.

X-Men When Wolverine stabs Rogue, her nightgown is conveniently ripped away in the back so we can see the claw punctures, but as she backs away there are no holes in the front.

When Wolverine crashes into the tree knocked over by Sabretooth, notice that the entire front of the truck gets completely folded up and the windshield breaks into a thousand pieces. In the next frame, Wolverine gets thrown through the *unbroken* windshield and the front of the truck is practically undamaged.

Some of these can be basic continuity errors, but on occasion there's a valid cinematographic reason. On occasion, directors/editors need to flip the negative of a film in order to make sure the action is going in the right direction, or that actors are pointing the right way, and this can have the unfortunate side-effect of mirroring some things. Often though, it's just a screw up ...

American History X After the shooting, when Derek (Edward Norton) is being arrested, he is on his knees and the cop behind him helps him to his feet. The cop wraps his right arm across Derek's chest, the camera then cuts to the angle from Danny's view, and it's now the cop's left arm across Derek's chest when he gets to his feet.

American Pie When Finch is moping through the house, depressed, he goes through a door marked KEEP OUT. The door handle is on the left side, meaning that from inside the room the handle must be on the right. However, when he plays with the pool balls, we can see that the door he must just have come through (there's no other door visible) has the handle on the left.

When Finch is at the party after the prom and he goes in the room with the sign on the door where Stifler's mom is, he opens the door out. But at the end of the movie, when Stifler is trying to get in the room, there is a chair in front of the door and it opens the opposite way.

Animal House When Larry meets Karen Allen's character at the frat house, she offers him a beer. When you see the back shot of Larry, he is holding the beer glass in his right hand. When it switches to a frontal view of Larry, he is holding the glass in his left hand.

Armageddon   When Harry goes into AJ's room, he gets mad and sticks the end of the golf club at AJ's throat, with the tip of the club to the right. The next scene, the tip of the club is facing to the left.

Bad Boys   Mike and Marcus go to meet Sanchez and Ruiz on the steps, and Sanchez is sitting down holding a doughnut (or something) in his right hand and a coffee in his left. A few seconds later, when talking about bongos, there's a close-up shot and the items change hands. Back to a wide shot when Mike and Marcus enter, and they switch back.

Beetlejuice   When Barbara shows that they have no reflections by moving the horse in front of the mirror, Adam is seen waving his left hand (in the over-the-shoulder shot) and it cuts to a longer side-shot as he's finishing waving his *right* hand.

Blade Runner   When Deckard shoots the snake-woman in the back and she falls through several layers of glass she lands on her stomach, with her head lying on the left side. In the next scene Deckard is standing beside her, but now she has turned her head, lying on the other cheek.

The Blues Brothers   John Belushi grabs some salad with his left hand, then when the angle changes, it's suddenly in his right hand.

The Bourne Identity   When Jason Bourne and Marie begin to kiss in the hotel room, his wristwatch is on his right wrist; when the camera angle changes and they are still kissing, his wristwatch has mysteriously changed to his left wrist.

Braveheart   At the wedding scene near the beginning of the film, Wallace challenges Hamish to throw a large rock at him. He throws the rock, and it is clearly headed just to one side of Wallace's head. The camera cuts to a different angle, and the rock is seen going past on the opposite side of his head.

The young Murron swaps places with her sister during the funeral. They're to the right of the priest. In a close-up shot Murron (shorter, in the dress) is on the left, with her taller sister in a smock-type thing on the right. It then cuts to a long shot, and suddenly the shorter one (Murron) is on the right.

Broken Arrow In the scene where Christian Slater and the ranger are radioing for help in the ranger's truck, the enemy helicopter comes from behind a ridge and shoots at them. They get out of the way, and the bullet fire continues and hits the truck on the driver-side door, the roof above and then the ground. In the next scene, you can clearly see bullet holes on the hood, going from front to back, but the fire was from right to left.

Cast Away When Tom Hanks is on the plane he sets down the pocket watch in the lower right corner of the groove in the seat; next time they show the watch it is closer to the upper left corner of the groove.

A Clockwork Orange In the scene where Alex and his droogs come in on Billyboy making ready to rape the young girl, the first shot shows the lacing of a shoe or sandal on the girl's left calf, but afterwards it jumps to her right.

Clueless Tai and Cher are hugging when they are watching Travis's skateboarding competition. Cher starts out on the left and Tai on the right. They hug in that position and then mysteriously end their hug on opposite sides.

Coyote Ugly Near the beginning at Violet's going-away party, she and Gloria are up on the stage singing and, from one cut to the other, Violet and Gloria change places.

Dazed and Confused While they're driving round town, talking about college, you see the three guys in the back seat. The camera goes to another angle, then a few seconds later, you see them in the back seat again, but the guys have switched places.

Demolition Man When Simon Phoenix gets out of the sewer system (after gunning it out with the rebels and John Spartan) his left eye has the brown contact and his right eye has the blue one, after going the entire movie with those contacts in the opposite eyes.

Die Hard: With a Vengeance When McClane and Zeus (Samuel L. Jackson) are in the taxi, as they enter the park we see McClane turn the wheel to his left, but the next shot shows the car going in the opposite direction, to his right.

Dogma In the scene where Silent Bob renders the demon disabled by using the anti-odour spray, you see him take the spray out of his coat and spray with his thumb. However, it cuts to a front view, and he is clearly seen using his index finger. It then cuts to Bob's rear, and he is, again, spraying with his thumb.

Dr. No When fighting the bad guy who picks him up from the airport, James Bond (Sean Connery) pulls back with his right arm, but punches with his left after a change of angle.

Dumb and Dumber In the scene when Lloyd asks if the bartender knows Mary, he originally grabs the bartender with the left hand. But in the next shot he lets go of him with his right hand.

In the scene where Jim Carrey and Jeff Daniels are in the restaurant, just before they encounter Seabass and right after they call the waitress 'Flo', Jeff's Coke glass is on his right side. The next shot shows it on his left, then his right, then his left again, without him touching it.

🎥 **Evil Dead 2**   When Ash is crawling through the cellar, he finds some pages, and he holds them in his right hand. Only problem is, he cut off his right hand earlier and attached the chainsaw to it – the film was flipped so he'd appear to be crawling in the right direction.

🎥 **Exit Wounds**   In the scene where Steven Seagal extends his hand out to help the little girl up, he first puts out his left hand, then in the camera view you see his right hand being grabbed by the little girl, then when the view changes again, she is holding his left hand.

🎥 **The Fifth Element**   When Zorg is first seen walking, and the screen only shows his legs, there is an audible clank as he steps with his *right* leg. After that, the clank is heard from his left foot.

After Leeloo fights the Mangalores in the Diva's room but then has to give the stones box to Zorg, she throws it to him with forward rotation, but when the box is flying through the air in slow motion, it's rotating backwards.

🎥 **First Knight**   When Lancelot is fighting with the leader of the bad guys, you can clearly see that Lancelot throws the leader's sword up in the air, but when Lancelot is cutting him, you can see the sword back in his right hand.

🎥 **Full Metal Jacket**   In the opening scene, Gunnery Sgt Hartman is making his speech and passes by Privates Cowboy and Joker on his way to the other side of the barracks. On his way he passes Private Pyle standing a few people to the right of Private Joker. Later in the scene, when he rushes over to confront Private Joker and then moves on to Private Cowboy and then Private Pyle, Private Pyle is a few people to the left of Private Joker.

There's a scene where Sgt Hartman goes to punch Pvt. Joker in the stomach. If you look carefully, he starts to punch with his left, then we instantly see Joker getting punched by his right.

Gangs of New York   Cameron Diaz pokes Leonardo DiCaprio with her knife on the right side of the neck as he is trying to retrieve his medallion from her. Shortly afterwards, while walking back with her, he keeps dabbing the left side of his neck.

Gladiator   During the enactment of the Battle of Zama, Russell Crowe rides his horse round a bend with his sword in his left hand. When we cut to close-up, it's back in his right. Looking at the left-handed shot in freeze-frame, you can see the frame has been flipped, left-to-right (check the armour). This was probably for continuity reasons. Similarly, Maximus jumps on the horse and his shoulder protector is clearly on his injured left shoulder. However, a few frames later, the protector is on his right shoulder, then it moves yet again back to the correct spot, the left shoulder.

GoldenEye   When the GoldenEye satellite is revealed in space, Earth is turning one direction in one cut, and the opposite direction in the next cut. In the first shot, it's moving slowly, but it's clear to see if you look closely.

GoodFellas   When Ray's girlfriend is showing off her apartment to her two girlfriends, they walk down the hall to the bedroom. The camera then changes to them entering the bedroom door and the order of girls has changed.

When Liotta's character is in jail and talking with his wife, the child is playing with a stack of coloured toy blocks. The order the blocks are stacked in changes in different shots.

Grease   In 'We Go Together', they all dance forwards. When the camera changes angle, Frenchy and Doody have switched sides. It's during the 'When we go out at night' line.

Halloween   When Laurie is beating on the door to Tommy's house and telling him to open it, the door knob is on the right side of the door. When it shows Tommy opening it from the inside, the door knob is also on the right side (it should be on the left).

Harry Potter and the Philosopher's Stone   At the start-of-term feast, after Harry is sorted into Gryffindor, he sits down on the right side of the table next to Ron. When the food appears, Harry is on the other side of the table next to Hermione.

Near the start, Percy says, 'Boys upstairs and down on your left, girls the same on your right.' After the three heroes have been to investigate Fluffy and they go back to the dorms, however, when they reach the top of the stairs Hermione goes to the left and the boys head right.

Hollow Man   When the doctor opens the freezer door, she's behind the wires that are connected to it. A second later, without moving, she's suddenly on the other side of them.

When Kevin Bacon's invisible character shoots another character in the chest with a dart, the dart changes position. First it is on the upper left side of the chest, then it is in the exact centre.

Independence Day   When jets are sent in to attack the giant UFOs, a missile is fired at one of them and is shown to turn one way, but when it flips to another angle the jet and missile are shown turning in opposite directions to a few seconds before.

Jaws   In the scene where Chief Brody is sitting on the beach and staring at the water, you can see his watch is on his right hand. In the next scene, the watch is on his left.

Jerry Maguire   When Cuba Gooding Jr is out cold in the end zone, watch the ball. Sometimes it's cradled in his left arm, with the right outstretched, other times it's the other way round.

When they're all in the restaurant together and Marcee's baby starts coming, Rod grabs the two children. There's a quick cut, and suddenly they're the other way around in his arms.

🎥 **Jurassic Park** In the scene at the badlands when Hammond's chopper has landed and Grant goes to the trailer and opens the door, if you watch the hinges of the door, they're on one side then it cuts to the inside of the trailer and they are on the other side.

When Nedry is trying to escape, and his jeep gets stuck on the mud bank, the camera shows the road below him, and there's an arrow pointing straight ahead. A bit later, the camera shows it again, and the arrow's pointing left.

🎥 **Mallrats** Mr Svenning's junior college class ring mysteriously jumps from his left hand to his right hand just in time to get stink-palmed by Brodie.

🎥 **Meet the Parents** After everyone returns from their dinner and a race home, Pam and her father discover that the cat has torn everything apart. When they all get into the house they stay in one room. You can see one of the doctors standing next to a lampshade. It starts leaning one way, then changes direction.

🎥 **Men in Black** At the end, when the bug leaves with his UFO, the two MIB are going to shoot it down. When they fire, Will is on the left side. After the shot he is on the right side.

🎥 **Men in Black II** In the scene where K is flying the car through the subway, K and J switch seats so J can drive. In the next scene when they land on the roof of a building, J comes out of the car on the passenger side.

📽 **Minority Report**   The handle on the door to room 1009 switches sides.

📽 **Miss Congeniality**   When Victor says he is leaving and Gracie is in his room, he gets toilet paper from the bathroom. The toilet paper changes from his hand to underneath his arm.

When Gracie is practising in the blue dress in the middle of the night, while she is removing her weapons etc., her sash falls off both her shoulders and is hanging on her arm, but a second later, it is hanging on one shoulder.

📽 **Mission: Impossible 2**   In the car chase scene with Nyah, after they split and hit again and are spinning, look at Ethan's car. The driver-side in the close-ups was on the American side, then in the spin it is reversed to an English side (it is a negative image – the licence plate is reversed). The next image is back to normal.

📽 **The Mummy**   While Rick, Jonathan and Ardeth are shooting Im-Ho-Tep's priests in the treasure room, Jonathan switches from the left side of Rick to the right side of him.

📽 **A Nightmare on Elm Street**   When Freddy jumps out from behind the tree in Tina's dream, his glove is on his left hand, then it cuts away and back and it's now on his right hand.

📽 **The Patriot**   When Mel Gibson rides over the hill holding the fluttering flag, the flag is in his left hand. They cut to show Chris Cooper and the others, and when they cut back to Mel, the flag is in his right hand.

📽 **The Perfect Storm**   When they pull the hook out of Murph's hand, he puts a spoon in his mouth – it's facing right, but when he's done it's facing left.

🎬 **Pretty Woman** When Vivian is eating dinner and the snail 'flies' away from her, it goes to the far right of the screen, disappearing, and then in the next screen you see the waiter catch it. It flew too far to the right for him to catch it.

At the beginning of the scene, where Edward is picking up Vivian at the hotel for their first dinner out, he walks up to the phone bank and picks up the phone with his left hand and his briefcase is in his right hand (down at his side). He speaks with the manager, then he hangs up the phone, still with his left hand, and then reaches up on the counter with his right hand to get his briefcase (which he never set up there). He keeps his right arm down at his side the whole time.

🎬 **Pulp Fiction** While Mia and Vincent are eating at Jack Rabbit Slim's, Mia's cigarette keeps changing hands.

🎬 **Road Trip** At the end, when Kyle's dad meets up with the guys, E.L. is standing next to Ruben in one shot. Soon afterwards, without anyone moving, he is standing over by Josh.

🎬 **Robin Hood: Prince of Thieves** When Robin reaches the cliffs of Dover after escaping from prison, he jumps out of the boat and starts kissing the ground. He then reaches out with his left hand for help up, but when the camera switches, he's being lifted by his right.

🎬 **The Rocky Horror Picture Show** When Tim Curry is about to pull the switch to send Dr Scott into the room, he starts to lift up his left leg. In the close-up, it's his right.

When Janet is fainting after Frank comes down the elevator, she is lifting up one hand. In the close-up it's the other hand.

While riding his motorcycle round the lab during the 'Hot Patootie' number, notice how Eddie's black eye changes sides.

Scooby-Doo   When Mary Jane grabs Scooby and Shaggy by the neck and holds them off their feet, she grabs Shaggy with her left hand. In the next shot it is her right hand holding Shaggy's neck (without her turquoise bracelet) then back to her left hand.

In the first scene, when Velma is explaining how the Luna Ghost is able to fly, she hits the button that inflates the balloons with her right hand. When the shot changes, she is shown hitting it with her left hand.

Scorpion King   After the fight scene between Mathyus and Balthazar and the tribe celebrating, Jesup arm wrestles with a woman. In the first shot he is wrestling with his left arm and in the next shot he is wrestling with his right arm and loses.

At the end, when The Rock is battling Menon, he is punched and falls off the little ledge they are on. He falls face first but, in the next shot, he lands on his right side, breaking a table.

Scream   When Tatum goes into the garage before she gets killed, she goes to get beer. She then walks over to the garage door opener with the beer in her right hand. Her left hand is reaching up to push the button, but as they show the close-up, it is her right hand pushing the button.

Scream 2   When Sidney and her friend get into the police car to be taken into protection, Sidney sits on the driver's side. When the car crashes, she is on the passenger side.

Se7en   The phone on Detective Mills's desk changes position (parallel to the desk, then angled towards Brad Pitt, then angled away from him) several times when he enters his new office.

The Shawshank Redemption   When Warden Norton points to Red after Andy has escaped (shouting 'Him!') he points with his left hand. In the next shot, he points right handed. You'll need to freeze-frame it because it's a very quick shot of his right hand, but it's definitely valid.

🎥 **The Silence of the Lambs** When searching the basement, the first door that Starling approaches is hinged on the left side, with the door handle on the right. She opens it with us on the other side of the door, and it's suddenly hinged the other way round. They must have made two sets and didn't plan it very well.

🎥 **Sleepy Hollow** Johnny Depp's character repeatedly plays with a picture of a little red bird in a cage during the movie. Towards the end, he is riding in a carriage and playing with it. We see a shot from his point of view and the bird is upright, meaning if we were seeing it from the opposite side it would be upside down. But immediately after that, we see a shot facing Ichabod. The bird is upright, not like it should normally be. We then cut directly to another shot from Ichabod's view, and the bird is upright yet again!

🎥 **Spider-Man** When Peter is drawing up ideas for his costume the hand is that of comic artist Phil Jimenez. Phil Jimenez is right-handed and actor Tobey Maguire is left-handed: in one of the cuts the pen is in Maguire's left hand but it shows him drawing with his right.

At the World Unity Festival, Peter is taking pictures. When he looks up at Harry and MJ on the balcony, the shot is reversed – it's easiest to see this by looking at his camera and his parting.

🎥 **Spy Kids** When Juni handcuffs the metal box to his arm, it is on his right wrist. Later it shows it on his left wrist. When he hits it against the wall it is back on his right.

The Sum of All Fears   In the scene where Jack Ryan uses the radio after the helicopter crash, the film is reversed – the word 'FREQUENCY' appears as a mirror image.

The Terminator   When the Terminator is approaching the tanker's cab, he is limping (why?) on his right leg. But when he loses his skin, he limps on his left leg.

Arnold looks on the left page of the phone book to find Sarah Connor's name, but when Sarah herself looks for her name she finds it on the right page.

Terminator 2: Judgment Day   When John's bike gets run over, it falls facing away from us, but when we see it from another angle, it's facing the other direction.

Titanic   Look closely at the location of Rose's beauty-mark the first time you see her at the dock. It is on the opposite side of her face during the rest of the movie.

Unbreakable   When David Dunn talks his son out of shooting him, the boy leaves the gun on the table. In the next scene, we see a close-up of Dunn's left hand grabbing the gun on the table. Then it cuts to a full-body scene where he is shown picking up the gun with his right hand.

When Harry Met Sally   At the beginning of the film, when they're leaving the diner, Sally pushes the door open with her right hand. When the angle cuts to outside, she's using her left hand.

The Wizard of Oz   At the end, when they all confront the Wizard, keep an eye on the order they're standing in – in different shots the Scarecrow is standing in different places.

The Lollipop Guild teleports all over the scene. As Glinda departs, they are behind Dorothy. As Glinda's bubble rises, several Munchkins run to where she was and wave goodbye, yellow-shirted Lollipop Guilder (Jerry Maren) among them. Cut to Dorothy and Jerry's still behind her.

After the witch has thrown fire at the Scarecrow, the handle of the Tin Man's funnel hat switches from right to left in three shot changes.

🎥 **X-Men**   When young Magneto is struggling with the guards at the concentration camp, the father's star switches from one side of his chest to the other.

At the beginning, when Storm and Cyclops are rescuing Logan and Rogue, Cyclops fires his eyes using his right hand. A moment later the screen shot changes to shooting from behind Cyclops and Storm and it clearly shows Cyclops's left hand being used, with his right hand by his side.

🎥 **You Only Live Twice**   When Aki drives James to see Tiger, and when she collects him from Osato Chemicals, her car changes from left-hand to right-hand drive as the camera follows them along.

Time applies to us all, even film-makers. Of course almost all films need to jump around in time, leaving out periods of inactivity to accelerate the story. However, when clocks start jumping around and night falls in seconds, something's definitely up . . .

Apollo 13   Just after the explosion, there is a shot of *Odyssey's* instrument panel with the mission timer reading 91 hours and 34 minutes. The accident occurred around 56 hours into the flight. The next time the mission timer is seen, it reflects the proper time.

Armageddon   In the sequence where they are disarming the bomb, when the clock gets down to 00:24, the picture is reversed. It's the very short shot when they're pulling the clock out of the bomb. It's upside down, which confuses the issue a bit, but use the 'armed' indicator as a guide. It should be at the top right of the screen, as we see in an earlier shot (when it reads 30 seconds), but if you mentally rotate the display the display is mirrored, with the 'armed' display at the top left, and the display reading seconds, minutes, hours.

Austin Powers: International Man of Mystery   In the scene where Liz Hurley gets drunk and the laptop rings, the first time it shows the laptop, there is an alarm clock behind it. First it reads about 10:30 or so. The second time it is off.

Being John Malkovich   When John Cusack first finds the portal, the clock on the wall says 4:30. Then he looks in the office and that clock says 2:30. When he goes in the portal John Malkovich is eating breakfast and is getting ready to leave in the morning then, when he gets back to the office, Maxine (Catherine Keener) is leaving work at 5:00.

The Breakfast Club In the scene where the five are running through the halls trying to dodge the principal, they run past a window where it is full-on dark. Since the detention took place on a Saturday morning and afternoon, there is no way this could have actually happened.

The time on the clock in the hall, which we see as the troublemaker guy runs by, is way different to the clock in the gym when we see the same guy a second later shooting basketballs.

Broken Arrow In the scene in the copper mine, Christian Slater accidentally arms the bomb. As it counts down it is at 26 minutes. Later it counts down to 22 minutes. When John Travolta finds the bomb and begins stroking it, the timer is back to 26 minutes.

Clerks The funeral and selling of the cigarettes both happen at 4:00.

Daredevil In the scene in the subway a clock is counting down to the next train, at about 01:55. When it cuts to the other end of the station, though (instantly, because Daredevil's still coming down the stairs), the timer reads 01:35.

Evolution In the scene where Dan Aykroyd is discussing the aliens with the military, the digital clock behind him reads different numbers each time they show it.

Fatal Attraction When Glenn Close calls Dan in the middle of the night he even says 'It's two in the morning', but when it pans to Glenn Close talking to him, her apartment is lit up with sunlight and you can see the sun rays through the window.

The Fugitive When Harrison Ford is being chased by Tommy Lee Jones in the St Patrick's Day parade, there are three clock shots, all of which show totally different times.

Halloween   When Michael Myers, as a child, walks through the living room with the knife, the clock on the wall reads 9:40, but just 5–7 seconds later, the clock chimes 10 times.

Home Alone 2: Lost in New York   In the first film, Kevin says that he's 8 years old at the checkout counter in the grocery store. However, in this film, at the hotel counter scene, he says he's 10. When his parents are in the Miami airport security office, they say that he was left alone last Christmas. That would make him 9.

The Hunt for Red October   When the Political Officer reads the orders, they're supposed to test the silent drive and return home 'on or about the sixteenth of this month.' Shortly afterwards, Jack Ryan is briefing Jeffrey Pelt and asks, 'Isn't it the twenty-third?'

Jaws   On the death report of the girl it says that the day of death is July 1st. But later on, the reward paper posted by the little boy's parents says that the date of his death was June 29th. He died after the girl, not before.

The Lost World: Jurassic Park   Near the end of the movie, Peter Ludlow (the snivelling nephew of John Hammond who wants to create Jurassic Park in San Diego) is addressing company stockholders as they wait for the cargo ship to arrive. He says something to the effect of: 'I'd like to thank you all for being intrepid enough to show up in the wee small hours of the morning.' Those last six words and the colour of the sky make it seem like it is four or five in the morning at the latest. For that early, San Diego is a busy town. The buses are running, businessmen are out, video rental stores are open (and with plenty of customers), and generally a lot of people are out to run away from the T-Rex.

Men in Black II   In the scene at the lockers in Grand Central Station, Agent K takes his watch, an illuminated Hamilton digital, back from the little animals living there. In one shot, Agent J puts an illuminated, non-digital watch in the locker as a replacement, but in the next shot it is the same old Hamilton digital owned by Agent K.

🎥 **Minority Report** Tom Cruise's wristwatch is an Omega Speedmaster X-33, but it shows a Bvlgari display when he looks at it for the countdown to the murder he is to commit. When he's not looking at it, though, the watch can be seen with its original Omega face. One example of this is in the tub scene where one of the spiders is peeling off Cruise's eye bandage – the watch shows its Omega display (white hands on an LCD digital background).

Before Tom Cruise goes into the building to meet Leo Crow, he looks at the timer on his watch, which is counting DOWN. The timer goes from 12:42 to 12:43. It should be counting down, but it goes up instead.

🎥 **Monsters, Inc.** After the Scare Floor shuts down at 6:00 and Sulley goes back to do Mike's paperwork, the clock reads 5:48. After he returns again to put Boo back, it still shows 5:48. Finally, after Randall leaves and Sulley sets off from the Scare Floor for the restaurant, the clock reads 6:48.

🎥 **A Nightmare on Elm Street** When Johnny Depp falls asleep on his bed, the television signs off, the announcer saying that its midnight. After he's already dead, and the police are there, Nancy talks on the phone with her dad, who is at the crime scene. She asks him to come over and break the door down in 20 minutes, at 12:15.

🎥 **Pulp Fiction** In the flashback scene with Christopher Walken, we see him hold up the watch, and its hands are clearly pointing in different directions. But when we see a close-up of the watch, it is set to either 12 noon or midnight.

Red Dragon   When Reba first strokes the tiger on the table her watch says 11:15, on the next stroke her watch says 11:20. Then the doctor hands her the stethoscope and her watch says 12:00.

Speed   After the first bus explosion, when Keanu Reeves answers the phone, he looks at his watch, which shows 8:05 a.m. If you look closely, the watch is on alarm, not regular time.

The Sum of All Fears   In the aircraft scenes after the blast in Baltimore, watch the clocks closely. The times go forwards, backwards, and everything in between.

Swingers   During the hysterical Sega hockey scene, watch the score and time remaining in the game as they show the TV. The score goes from 9–5, to 3–1, to 8–5 all in the same continuous game.

Terminator 2: Judgment Day   In the scene where Sarah has just shot Dyson and she is crying against the wall, John comes up to her and starts hugging her. Every time the scene changes back to the hugging, look at John's watch. The time changes every time.

WE'LL WEATHER THE WEATHER

You can't help the weather. If you're forced to use takes from different days, with different light and weather, you've got to take it with a grin, and hope no one notices. But someone always does . . .

Blade II When Blade fights Nomac in the rave for the very first time, it's sunny outside. This is an important point, as Nomac tries to avoid the sunlight and, in fact, runs along the wall in the only shadow. However, at exactly the same time, Blade's assistant is in the van outside trying to fight off some Reapers – in a dark downpour.

The Bourne Identity At the farmhouse when Marie is leaving, the camera switches back and forth between Bourne and Marie. As it switches it is alternately snowing a lot and hardly snowing at all.

Catch Me If You Can In the scene where Carl comes to the engagement party to arrest Frank, it is so windy that, when the window in the bedroom is left open, money is flying around. However, in the shots of the party outside it is shown to be a calm night with no wind at all.

Chicago In the scene after Roxie has been found not guilty, the pressmen run outside to see the woman who shot her lawyer. Roxie looks out of the window, where there are drops of rain running down the pane, but in the shot outside the courthouse it isn't raining.

Die Hard When Takagi explains to the terrorists that he doesn't have 'that code,' the trees outside the window are clearly swaying in the wind. The next shot is a panoramic view of the room, but now the trees outside are still.

Dirty Dancing When Jennifer Grey and Patrick Swayze leave the resort to go to practise balancing over the creek in the forest, it's pouring rain when they're leaving. However, when Johnny realises that his keys are in the car, he goes over to knock the pipe out of the ground with his foot and it's sunny over there, three feet away from the car.

Enemy of the State In the scene where Gene Hackman is talking to Jon Voight there are clear skies and it's sunny. As soon as Gene starts running it's raining.

Independence Day When Will Smith is dragging the unconscious alien across the desert, the sky alternates between overcast and perfectly sunny depending on if it's a close-up or far-off view of Will.

The Sound of Music In the opening scene, when the helicopter camera zooms in on Maria, it's bright and sunny, but when it switches to a regular camera, the sky is suddenly cloudy.

You've Got Mail When Tom Hanks and Meg Ryan are sitting at the outdoor cafe near the end of the movie, in a far away shot it's windy, but up close it's not.

TAKE 23

INDEX

INDEX

INDEX